FASCISM TODAY

WHAT IT IS AND HOW TO END IT

SHANE BURLEY

FOREWORD BY **MATTHEW N. LYONS**

AK PRESS

Praise for *Fascism Today*:

"No better volume exists to understand the nexus of Alt Right bigotry and antifascist resistance in the United States than *Fascism Today*. Burley's work is an essential 'tool for opposition' that brings to bear years of in-depth research and investigation into the resurgence of the far right. To destroy fascism, we must first understand it—that understanding starts here."

—Mark Bray, historian and author of *Antifa: The Anti-Fascist Handbook*

"Burley leaves no stone unturned in this vigorous and indispensable guide to modern fascism and the interlocking movements that oppose it, issuing a clarion call for ethical, intersectional resistance."

—Alexander Reid Ross, author of *Against the Fascist Creep*

"Shane Burley was one of the first people to recognize the influence of the Alt Right and closely track its political development and intellectual approach. I highly recommend *Fascism Today* as both an accessible and comprehensive account of the Alt Right and related white nationalist groups—as well as their antifascist opposition."

—Spencer Sunshine, author of *Up in Arms: A Guide to Oregon's Patriot Movement*

About the authors:

Shane Burley is a writer and filmmaker based in Portland, Oregon. His work has appeared in *Jacobin*, *In These Times*, *Waging Nonviolence*, *ThinkProgress*, *Labor Notes*, *ROAR Magazine*, *Upping the Anti*, and *make/shift*.

Matthew N. Lyons has been writing about right-wing politics for over twenty-five years. He writes regularly for the radical antifascist blog Three Way Fight, and his work has also appeared in the *Guardian*, *New Politics*, *Socialism and Democracy*, *teleSUR*, *Upping the Anti*, and other publications. Lyons is co-author with Chip Berlet of *Right-Wing Populism in America*, author of *Arier, Patriarchen, Übermenschen: die extreme Rechte in den USA* (Aryans, Patriarchs, Supermen: The Far Right in the USA), and contributed the title essay to the book *Ctrl-Alt-Delete: An Antifascist Report on the Alternative Right*. He is author of the forthcoming book, *Insurgent Supremacists: The U.S. Far Right's Challenge to State and Empire*.

Fascism Today: What It Is and How to End It
© 2017 Shane Burley
Foreword © 2017 Matthew N. Lyons
This edition © 2017 AK Press (Chico, Oakland, Edinburgh, Baltimore)

ISBN: 978-1-84935-294-9
E-ISBN: 978-1-84935-295-6
Library of Congress Control Number: 2017936239

AK Press   AK Press
370 Ryan Ave. #100   33 Tower St.
Chico, CA 95973   Edinburgh EH6 7BN
USA   Scotland
www.akpress.org   www.akuk.com
akpress@akpress.org   ak@akedin.demon.co.uk

The above addresses would be delighted to provide you with the latest AK
Press distribution catalog, which features books, pamphlets, zines, and styl-
ish apparel published and/or distributed by AK Press. Alternatively, visit
our websites for the complete catalog, latest news, and secure ordering.

Cover design by Margaret Killjoy, www.birdsbeforethestorm.net.
Printed in the USA on acid-free, recycled paper

CONTENTS

Foreword

Donald Trump's unexpected march to the presidency, coupled with the sudden rise to prominence of Alt Right white nationalists and misogynists, has put the topic of fascism in the U.S. front and center once again. A week after the November 2016 election, Merriam-Webster reported that people were looking up the definition of "fascism" over four times more often than they did in 2015, and the word had zoomed to number four on the list of all-time look-ups. A similar trend was reported for Google searches.

Trump and the Alt Right didn't come out of nowhere. Trump's authoritarian demagoguery and racist, Islamophobic scapegoating are worse than any other U.S. president in generations, but his election would have been impossible without the dramatic rightward shift that's been going on since the 1970s—not just in the Republican Party, but in both major parties. The Alt Right's clever internet memes and online harassment campaigns have brought the dream of a white ethno-state into the twenty-first century, but its rise builds on previous upsurges by other far-right currents in the 1980s, 1990s, and 2000s.

The Alt Right is just one part of a broader array of fascist and quasi-fascist political forces that have both contributed to and been buoyed by Donald Trump's victories. This synergy between the activist far-right and a successful presidential candidate is something dangerously new, and it will have lasting consequences whatever happens to the Alt Right, and whatever happens to Trump. But for all their points of agreement, fascist activists differ radically with Trump in their ideologies, goals, and strategies.

All of this means that the fascist danger today is both more deeply rooted and more complex than many people realize. Yet there's no agreement on what fascism even means or how it applies to our political situation. All through the 2016 presidential race and thereafter, leftists, liberals, and even conservatives debated this question, with no resolution in sight.

Let's not get hung up on trying to find the "true" definition of fascism. As the historian Roger Griffin argued years ago, the way we define or conceptualize fascism isn't objectively true, it's just more or less useful to help us understand political movements and regimes—and, I would add, more or less useful to help us develop antifascist and liberatory strategies. In that spirit, I offer a few suggestions on how to think about fascism today:

> *Fascist politics has a contradictory relationship with the established order.* Contrary to claims that we face a struggle between fascism and "democracy," fascism grows out of and reinforces authoritarian tendencies and systems of oppression that are deeply rooted in our society. Contrary to claims that fascism is a tool of the ruling class, it's about overthrowing existing political elites and destroying the liberal-pluralist political system that has helped keep U.S. capitalism stable for over two centuries. Fascists may collaborate with current-day rulers to a degree, but they are an autonomous force with their own agenda, and their hatred of the status quo is one of the key ways they attract people to join them. For radical antifascists, this means that the fight against fascism and the fight against an oppressive social order are interconnected but distinct—both are needed. It also means that urging the state to crack down on fascists is dangerous, because such repression can easily be redirected against the left.

> *Fascism takes different forms and adapts to meet changing circumstances.* In the 1930s, fascists glorified the large-scale totalitarian state and colonial conquest. Today many fascists repudiate empire-building and advocate decentralist approaches such as "leaderless resistance" and "tribal" enclaves. And current-day fascists disagree about issues ranging from the role of women in the movement to whether they should ally with Putin's Russia. These changes and

disagreements are important, and understanding them can help us combat the far-right more effectively.

Fascism interacts with forces across the political spectrum in complex ways. Fascists often rely on conservative fellow-travelers to help spread their message and enhance their public legitimacy, but they also vilify conservatives as sellouts, opportunists, and cowards. Fascists attack leftists as an evil influence to be destroyed, but they also appropriate elements of leftist politics in distorted form, from environmentalism to anti-capitalism. Even more insidiously, they also work to poison the left with their own ideas—such as antisemitic conspiracy theories—and sometimes seek alliances with leftists against the state.

Fascists endanger us in multiple ways. The most extreme threat is fascists gaining state power and implementing their supremacist—or genocidal—vision. More immediately, fascists foment and carry out physical violence and harassment against oppressed communities and the left. They also create space for mainstream political actors to intensify their own oppressive and repressive policies while looking moderate by comparison. And, as Don Hamerquist warned fifteen years ago in his section of *Confronting Fascism: Discussion Documents for a Militant Movement*, by channeling popular anger at the ruling class into supremacist scapegoating, fascists can "cause massive damage to the potential for a liberatory anti-capitalist insurgency."

We need a range of approaches for combating fascism. The fight against fascism has to be broad and allow space for people to act in different ways and with different politics. As Anti-Racist Action put it in their points of unity almost thirty years ago, we need to practice non-sectarian defense of antifascists—set aside our differences to support those who are serious about opposing our common enemy. Some approaches will involve direct physical confrontations with right-wing forces. Some will involve nonviolent protest, writing and speaking, legal or electoral initiatives, community organizing, or even engaging with people who are attracted to fascism to try to win them away from it. Although people often think of militant and non-militant approaches as mutually exclusive and in conflict, they work best when they complement and reinforce each other.

Shane Burley's book speaks to all of these points. The book includes a wealth of information about today's far-right groups, ideologies, strategies, and subcultures. It offers a nuanced discussion of how fascists interact with other political actors, such as the Alt Right's love-hate relationship with the so-called Alt Light. It is written from a place of opposition to institutionalized systems of power, although that is not its focus. The book also says a lot about the need for a multi-pronged approach to antifascism, and it illustrates this argument with numerous and diverse examples of antifascist activism, past and present. It is the kind of book we need to help us understand—and end—fascism today.

—Matthew N. Lyons
August 2017

Preface: It's Happening Again, It's Happening Still

The old world is dying, and the new world struggles to be born:
now is the time of monsters.

—Antonio Gramsci

Fascism is itself less 'ideological', in so far as it openly proclaims
the principle of domination that is elsewhere concealed.

—Theodor Adorno

In 1965 two scholars, Angelo Del Boca and Mario Giovana, wrote *Fascism Today*, a study of the roots of fascism and a survey from country to country. This volume helped define what fascism meant after the Second World War, arguing that the burgeoning identity-based authoritarian movements were not new inventions, but a continuation of those from decades past. While these new movements, from the skinhead scene to the growing "Fourth Era" KKK, were dramatically different in form and strategy than those that took power in European statehouses in recent past, there was an essential core to their line of thinking that showed a continuity.

It is in that spirit that this book is written, borrowing its title and a part of its mission.

Around 2011, in advance of some counter-organizing around the appearance of notorious Holocaust "revisionist" David Irving, I was researching the movement that would endorse his talk. The trend toward "suit and tie Nazism" had been developing for decades, but a new profile was forming. Websites republishing French fascist philosophers, resurrecting Aryan mystics, and linking up the "Men's Rights" movement with a more advanced form of scientific racism were coming together, creating a language and culture of their own. Around this time I stumbled upon a podcast interviewing Merlin Miller, the presidential candidate for, what was at the time the American Third Position Party. The young guy conducting the interview quickly revealed Miller's incompetence, going way over his head when discussing a white nationalism steeped in the heady world of German Idealism, Traditionalism, French New Right thought, and the varied history of Third Positionist meta-politics. The man on the other line was Richard Spencer, who had months earlier started the infamous yet now defunct website AlternativeRight.com. As he would famously say in 2015 as their movement emerged from the shadows, "something was happening." Spencer's views differed from those of the radical right nationalist movements of the past. This new movement was confident in its fascism, it was discovering an intellectual and ethical underpinning, and it was open about its sanctification of essentialism and inequality. In the years that followed they would expand outward, consolidating their "big tent" into a rabid movement that would take on "capitalism in decay" through their own revolutionary prophecy. They wanted to take the vestiges of the left, crush them, and see through a national rebirth (palingenetics) to build a new world in the minds and hearts of white people, the first stage to making the thought flesh.

Their rise, and the right populism sweeping the world, has led to a shocking jump in racist violence and activism. For years fascism was considered a hyperbolic fear, animated by the occasional fringe terrorist act, but now it could happen here. It is happening again. Fascism reveals what has always been: systemic inequality, white supremacy, patriarchy, and systems of power that remain invisible while infecting all aspects of our lives. A fascist movement makes the implicit explicit and forces us to choose sides. Spencer had certainly chosen his.

The purpose of this book is to survey the world of fascism—and its opponents—in a twenty-first century U.S. context and to frame it categorically so that the book becomes a tool for opposition. Underline passages, scribble in the margins, and return to it as needed. The first half of the book is designed to outline what fascism is, starting with the world today, elucidating the theory, then outlining fascism's different manifestations including the Alt Right, "Race Realism," anti-Semitism, the syncretic Third Positionism, its religious angles, and so on. Going into the second half I shift gears by highlighting movements that take on fascism as it creeps into society. By looking at historical, current, and theoretical strategies, grounded in actual victories and failures, antifascism is elucidated as a multifaceted movement that pulls from a myriad of traditions and intellectual forebears. Together the sections are intended to show how fascism operates today and how antifascism can cut it down before it is fully realized.

The narratives inside are sewn from a patchwork: from journalists and organizers to survivors of hate campaigns and fascist ideologues themselves. Through this confluence a new vantage point should emerge, one that sees how the "new" threat of today defines itself in relation to the failures of modern society, yet maintains the component parts that made interwar fascism the iron brigade that decimated the globe. A monster of this magnitude requires a collective consciousness of refusal, the willingness for the people to strike it in every conceivable way. It requires partisans. That is what is evolving today, and it is a battle I hope to capture if only in some small way. Although it was my hope, not every single movement or project is represented herein. I have to acknowledge that this book is a snapshot due to the evolving situation. Likewise, not all movements I discuss reflect my personal politics, nor do they represent equally effective models. Instead, the point has been to create an accurate picture of what a mass movement to combat fascism looks like, with messy vision, different types of participation, and varied conceptions of what the struggle is. That communities unite in struggle is more important than the specific model of organizing. Together we make history.

Now is the time for monsters, and the fight is all of ours.

Glossary of Key Terms

III% (Three Percenters):
> A decentralized Patriot militia movement that builds on many of the same far-right themes that other groups do, including implicit racism, conspiracy theories, and violent interpretations of ultra-conservative orthodoxy. Their name comes from the unproven believe that only "3%" of American colonists took up arms against the British. They have been tied to increasing acts of violence, both against government officials and against people of color and leftist activists.

4Chan:
> An internet message board where much of the extreme and "anti-PC" rhetoric of the Alt Right and Manosphere was formed. It revels in anonymity, boundary pushing, and explicit white supremacist language, though it is also a place for other types of internet dissidents as well.

9/11 Truth:
> A conspiracy theory about the role of the government(s) and secret agencies involved in executing and/or covering up the truth about the September 11, 2001 attacks on the World Trade Center. This theory has been a crossover point for fascists who use it to employ an anti-Semitic theory about Israeli involvement in the attack and Jewish manipulation of world affairs.

Alt Light:
> The layer of commentators and activists that associate with and are similar in behavior to the Alt Right yet do not have the ideological consisten-

cy and extreme positions of the Alt Right. This would include right-wing provocateurs like Milo Yiannopoulos, Lauren Southern, Gavin McInnes, Ann Coulter, *Breitbart News*, and others.

Alt Right:

Short for Alternative Right. A "big tent" term that links together white nationalists with misogynist movements, racial pagans, "race realists," Traditionalists, and other currents into a contemporary, internet-focused, nationalist movement. This is typified by ideas like ethnic nationalism/conflict, traditional societies and social roles, human inequality, essential identities, and an aggressive "troll culture" of internet dialogue.

Anarchism:

An ideology that opposes to all forms of social hierarchy, and argues for a form of communism that is free of the state and systems of coercive authority. It can be labeled as egalitarian, antiracist, anti-heteronormative, feminist, and against all forms of oppression.

Anarcho-Capitalism:

An extreme form of libertarianism where the state, as a mediator of human rights and social redistribution, is negated in favor of market determination of power and authority.

Antifa:

A direct-action iteration of Anti-Fascist Action developed by autonomist and anarchist blocs in Germany, France, and the U.K. and adopted as a primary antifascist organizing method worldwide. It differentiates itself by direct engagement with fascists in the streets, fighting over "contested spaces," and using a "no platform" strategy.

Anti-Racist Action (ARA):

ARA precedes Antifa in the U.S. and was formed in the early 1980s to confront the growing white supremacist movements in urban and subcultural spaces.

Christian Identity:

A white supremacist version of Christianity that sees white Europeans as the biblical Israelites, while Jews are a demonic race spawned either from an unholy union of Eve and the Serpent or of a mongrel enemy tribe. Non-whites are seen as the "beasts of the field" that lack souls. Christian

Identity people have an explicitly revolutionary and eschatological view. They are extensively tied to white supremacist terrorism as well as having inroads with the militia movement.

Civic Nationalism/Nativism:

A form of nationalism and anti-immigrant sentiment that, though focused on the existing nation-state, does not have a complete ethnic/racial perspective. This often results in a form of "Ultra Patriotism" that seeks America First economic and foreign policies, is critical of immigration, forces assimilation into the dominant culture, and is socially rigid.

Creativity Movement:

A white supremacist "religious" movement that hails the white race as the "Creators" by virtue of their genetic endowments, and constructs a traditional supremacist narrative about the role of other races in relation to whites. It is anti-religion in the traditional sense, openly genocidal, and linked to white supremacist terrorism around the U.S.

Cuckservative:

A meme created by Alt Right figures (and popularized by the *Right Stuff Radio*) that attempts to "call out" traditional Beltway conservatives for working against their own ethnic interests in relation to "mass immigration." It is a racist dog whistle for white men whose wives seek out stronger men (often black men) for sex.

Cultural Marxism:

An anti-Semitic idea built on a conspiracy theory. Owing to the idea that the Frankfurt School of Marxism was a Judaic ploy to undermine the ethnic determinism and Faustian spirit of the West, cultural marxism is believed to be all the ideas of Marxism applied to social life and now reflected in contemporary liberalism.

Elitism:

The anti-egalitarian belief that superior "elites" should rule over the masses, from social control to the functions of the state. This plays into the idea of personal hierarchies, where some people are more fit to rule than others and a benevolent elite needs to control the populace. This elitism is based in the veneration of ideal types, using essentialist metrics for value, such as IQ, body type, and moral character, as well as possibly elite castes and the divine right of kings.

European New Right:

A fascist philosophical tradition started in the late 1960s to build on the cultural shifts around the New Left and attempting to rebrand the ideas of racial supremacy and exclusivity. Using the language of anti-colonialism, it argues for the "right to difference" of groups to remain separate in traditionalist enclaves.

Ethnostate:

A governing state whose criteria for citizenship is determined by the ethnicity/race of the dominant body. An example of this would be a pan-European, white nationalist ethnostate, where the criteria for citizenship would be being a member of the white race.

Feminism:

Ideology that is against the oppression of women and non-masculine/para-masculine people.

Folkish Heathenry:

Nordic paganism that builds on the original archetypal explanation of Carl Jung, which says that the Nordic gods are archetypal metaphors for the minds and spirits of people of Northern European ancestry. This is specifically an "ethnic religion," one that says that heathenry is only for people of that specific sub-ethnic group. There are folkish interpretations of other regional paganisms, such as Celtic, Welsh, Hellenic, or Rodnovery, but folkish Heathenry is the most practiced by Western white nationalists.

Globalism:

A right-wing interpretation of the effects of globalization, usually indicating the negative effects of multiculturalism or cosmopolitanism. For the anti-globalist, this could mean the destruction of ethnic identity, traditional familial or gender roles, the dominance of traditional authority or the church, the destruction of interpersonal relationships, and so on. This is fundamentally different than left-wing anti-globalization since it centers itself on the maintenance of nationalism, essential identity, and traditional hierarchies and authorities rather than looking at the effects of globalization from left-wing value sets, such as the destruction of organized labor and the targeting of marginalized indigenous groups.

Holocaust Denial:

The belief that what is understood to be fact about the Holocaust, like the number of Jews exterminated or the role Hitler played in it, is untrue and instead a lie constructed by those who have something to gain by the falsehood (almost always Jews). This can also include minimizing the importance of the Holocaust in history, and the attempt to diminish recognition of it.

Identitarianism:

A new form of white nationalist branding developed in conjunction with the European New Right and youth-oriented far-right social movements in France. Identitarianism focuses on the importance of *identity*, and their campaigns and rhetoric are structured around the reclamation and restoration of essential identity.

Jewish Question:

Shortened by the Alt Right to the "JQ," this is the question of "Jewish power," or the conspiratorial view that Jews wield disproportionate power on "host nations" through various mechanisms, such as investment finance, foreign policy, or Hollywood. The JQ is used variously to question the role of Jews, or to suggest that anything identified as progressive, modern, or "multicultural" is a part of Jewish subversion.

Kek:

An Alt Right meme that attempts to appropriate the Egyptian God of the same name and assign Pepe (the Frog) to him as his current avatar. This sees the ancient Egyptian religion as Aryan, with Kek's role as a "God of Chaos" representing the Alt Right troll storm that will clear away multiculturalism and allow for a great Aryan ascendancy.

Kinism:

White Kinists see non-white people and Jews as fully human, it believes there must be tribal exclusivity in worship and community. They also see Jews as uniquely deceptive and problematic, and they have made large inroads with the Neo-Confederate and Southern Nationalist movements.

Left-Hand Path (LHP):

A term used to label multiple religious, esoteric, and occult paths that divert from what is labeled as Right-Hand Path religious traditions, which are those based in commonly accepted moral tenets and that hold onto universalized systems of moral responsibility. LHP adherents may propose libertine sexual ideas, believe in retribution rather than blanket forgiveness, support ethical relativism, and seek the empowerment and indulgence of the self as a high moral ideal. These traditions may include LaVeyan and theistic strains of Satanism, Thelema, the Temple of Set, Vamachara Vedic practice, some forms of Tantra, and various forms of post-modern magical practice. Most LHP adherents wholly reject fascist and racialist politics, but there are some that maintain those political connections.

Manosphere:

A loose-knit collection of blogs, podcasts, and message boards united by a male-centric perspective on social issues, one that is deeply mistrustful of women, transgendered people, and liberal society. Made up of different sectors such as Men's Rights Activists (MRA), who argue men are oppressed by "feminist society," or pick-up artists (PUAs), men who share skills in "picking up" women. Many argue that this is the gendered equivalent of white nationalism, and that the movement is largely founded on misogyny.

Meta-Politics:

The ideas, culture, and inclinations that motivate politics down the line. Meta-politics, in the neo-fascist sense, are the cultural projects that attempt to influence ideological positions without engaging strictly in political practice. This includes art, music, and philosophy that suggest fascist ideas in the social sphere without making their political implications explicit. Some of the best known of these are the romanticism, nationalism, and the focus on "identity" present in neofolk.

Misogyny:

The hatred of women, both individually and institutionally.

Modernity:

An amorphous concept used on the far-right to indicate those aspects of the post-industrial world in which traditional authority, gender roles, racial exclusivity, and mystification have been undermined by liberalism, democracy, and often global capitalism.

National Anarchism:

A non-state form of fascism whereby identity exclusive (usually racial) enclaves are formed as tribal communities. This is usually mixed with anti-Semitic, anti-modern, and traditionalist ideas about social organization.

Nationalism:

The focus on a nation or ethnic group as an exclusive system of value, with morality, politics, and identity being held fixed with that group. This can mean strong allegiance to the interests of an ethnic group, race, or sovereign country, yet often denotes a far-right-wing view of this group identity as defining, organic, and superseding other identities.

Neofolk:

A romantic genre of music that venerates the sound and cultural indicators of premodern Europe, including indigenous paganism, imperial governments, chivalry, nature worship, ancestral veneration, and other elements. While the genre is not fascist per se, it was developed by many fascist ideologues as a meta-political project to build cultural affinity with European identity.

Neo-Nazi:

A neo-fascist who attempts to bring the principles and key ideas of Hitlerian National Socialism into modern situations. While all neo-Nazis are fascists, most fascist ideologies are not a perfect fit for the term "neo-Nazi."

Neoreaction:

Philosophy developed by Curtis Yarvin and Nick Land focusing on criticisms of egalitarianism, democracy, and modernity. Focuses heavily on restoring traditional hierarchical systems of power, esoteric ideas on tradition, and restoring a contemporary society based on pre-Enlightenment, pre-Reformation social orders, possibly including theocracy, the monarchy, and elitist rule.

Oath Keepers:

A Patriot militia group made up of former and current first responders, veterans, and law enforcement officers, engaged in "upholding the Constitution." This amounts to a far-right reading of U.S. laws and history, including extreme libertarian economics, anti-Federal-government rhetoric, opposition to liberalism, and conspiracy theories.

Paleoconservative:

A form of conservatism developed in response to the rise of Neoconservatism in the GOP in the 1980s. It stresses America First policies, economic nationalism, extreme social conservatism, reactionary racial policies, and isolationism. Pat Buchanan is the best known figure, and the Rockford Institute, *Chronicles*, and the *American Conservative* are the best known institutions.

Palingenetic Ultranationalism:

A definition of fascism developed by academic Roger Griffin meant to describe a form of nationalism born out of a mythological vision of the past and the desire to return to a lost "golden age."

Populism:

A mass movement linking politics directly into "the people" as a group and often utilizing emotional qualities to motivate political choices.

"Race Realism" and Human Biological Diversity:

These are different names for the same pseudoscientific concept that essential personality characteristics and mental faculties are determined by ethnicity. The most dominant of these is that different races have different innate intelligence, but it can also refer to "characteristics" like criminality, patience, "time preference," sexual restraint, and sociability. These theories have been widely discredited by all mainstream scientific institutions.

Rock Against Communism:

A White Power version of skinhead punk music, built as a reaction to the Rock Against Racism phenomenon. The term has gone on to represent the specific genre of aggressive and violent neo-Nazi Oi! music that has typified many of the more extreme white supremacist subcultures in the West.

Skinhead:

A subcultural fraternal organization of working-class people often centered on music and friendship. In common understanding, skinhead denotes the explicitly neo-Nazi variety that rose in the late 1970s in England and predominated in American cities. There are also explicitly antiracist skinhead groups, such as the Skinheads Against Racial Prejudice (SHARP), as well as non-racist, non-political skinhead groupings known as Trojan Skinheads.

Third Position:

Fascism that borrows elements from the left, or uses left political ideas for far-right values and motivating meta-politics, so as to develop a synthesis that can appeal beyond their base. This includes fascist appropriation of environmentalism, anti-imperialism, post-colonialism, animal rights, and anti-capitalism.

Traditionalism:

Used to signify the spiritual ideas of Julius Evola and others, or to refer to a supposed "traditional way of life." In the Evolian concept, it refers to the underlying "Tradition" that synchronizes up all world religions in different manifestations of a divine hierarchy and "natural law."

Trans-Exclusionary Radical Feminism (TERF):

This is a form of second-wave radical feminism that takes issue with transgender people, specifically transwomen. TERFs suggest that transwomen appropriate women's spaces, mainstream effects of pornography, and they reify gender roles by recognizing their legitimacy. TERF politics have extended beyond their "leftist" origin to have collaborationist elements with the far-right.

Tribalism:

A sense of group identity that is absolved of universal morality toward non-group members. Lines are drawn along identifying factors like essential identity, which may include race but may also include other markers like sexual orientation, gender, and some cultural or religious boundaries. Nationalism is a form of tribalism but is specific to an ethnic nation (however that is defined).

True Right:

How we describe fascism today, the True Right includes those ideas that sanctify *inequality* and make up the true ideological inverse of the left.

White Genocide:

A propaganda meme used by contemporary white nationalists to argue that there is a global conspiracy (either consciously conducted by Jews or unconsciously by the forces of democracy and globalism) to wipe out Caucasian genetic stock. This often references the killing of Boer farmers in South Africa, which has been falsely labeled a genocide. It also references the recessive Caucasian traits, bringing about the "one drop rule" that sanctifies whiteness with a sense of purity that is erased when it comes in contact with non-white phenotypes.

White Nationalism:

A rebranding for white supremacist ideas around the concept of ethnic statehood, the creation of a country or society that is racially or ethnically exclusive.

White Separatism:

A term that rose in popularity after it became passé to openly identify with white supremacy as an ideology. It indicates that the races should be kept separate, and that the primary motivator to racialist politics is white sovereignty as opposed to racial hatred or feelings of supremacy. It is largely considered to be a coded term for traditional white supremacy yet has been replaced by the term "white nationalist."

PART I

What Is Fascism?

Introduction:
Drain the Swamp

Not even the most far-flung psychic prophesying the nature of American politics would have guessed this. No one watching the GOP primary speeches at the time would have anticipated the turn it would take, not least the white nationalists screeching on Twitter. From his first press conference, Donald Trump set up the theatrics that he would use to drive a wedge of fear in the voting public:

> When Mexico sends its people, they're not sending their best.... They're sending people that have lots of problems and they're bringing those problems with us. They're bringing drugs, they're bringing crime. They're rapists.[1]

This wasn't a dog whistle, it was the Southern Strategy made explicit: this was a campaign for white people.[2] Trump picked up on talking points that many white nationalists have used for decades. In 2011, white nationalist organization the National Policy Institute (NPI)—which has since developed into the central institution of the Alt Right movement—put out a paper and held a press

---

1   Donald Trump, "Presidential Campaign Announcement" (speech, New York City, NY, June 16, 2015).
2   Lee Atwater admitted in later interviews that the Southern Strategy was an explicit effort to disenfranchise black voters who were volatile in their political interests. They did this by signaling to racist attitudes rather than stating them explicitly: calling people "welfare queens" rather than racial slurs. The audience understands what you mean, you reinforce racist stereotypes, but you have plausible deniability.

conference in which they argued that the Republican Party should employ the "The Majority Strategy." If, as voting records show, the GOP was essentially the "white people's party," then they should act like it and refuse to target minority voters, the NPI said. If they drop people of color, queers, and those with no historic record of voting for the right, then they can more effectively call their white base.[3] It's a strategy reminiscent of that found in business literature, which declares 80 percent of profits comes from 10 percent of customers, so capitalists must tactfully figure out how to ignore the other 90 percent.

Trump took Lee Atwater's advice in racial scapegoating—to use code words to link economic liberalization with the blaming of minorities—but came closer to calls for racial violence than any major candidate in recent memory, and the growing fascist movement heard this loud and clear. The message sent was not necessarily that one of their own was running, but that a loud politician, backed by unimaginable wealth and iconoclastic prestige, was leaving the door open behind him.

Escape the Ghosts of the Past

Many of those organizing against a far-right groundswell encounter people who believe that fascism is dead and gone. Francis Fukuyama's idea that we are living in the "end of history" has made waves not only in the world of capitalist apologists, but on the left as well.[4] Fascism, as a revolutionary reactionary movement, one that targets both finance and the left, was often viewed as too disruptive to international capital and so could not "break the spell" of increased consumerism, automation, and sweeping development. The cracks evident now could not be seen in a machine built on perpetual economic growth and planted in volatile markets.

Fascism has often been dismissed as "too European," as an antiquated system designed in a culture of European ethnic conflict and Catholic aesthetics. And the racialist organizations that dot the landscape of modern American history—from the Southern White

---

3 Richard Spencer, "The Majority Strategy," *The National Policy Institute*, September 9, 2011, http://www.npiamerica.org/research/category/the-majority-strategy.

4 The "end of history" is a reference to a concept proposed by Francis Fukuyama who suggested that the later stages of international capitalism had ended the battle between nations and ideologies, resulting in the final stage of human history and social evolution.

Knights of the Ku Klux Klan to Volksfront—are too buffoonish and anti-ideological to actually lead a meta-political movement that could change both the values of Americans and the state that oversees them. Instead, it is the systemic violence baked into police departments and current economic conditions that are responsible for the ongoing racial terrorism in Western countries, rather than the reactionary machinations of some white people frightened by their eroding privilege.

This monolithic description of white supremacy was smashed as pollsters, shocked that Trump's comments didn't immediately end his campaign, saw skyrocketing approval ratings. Trump refused to apologize for any of his missteps, rolling the dice that his base would be just as bigoted and angry as he was. He stood up and declared that Senator John McCain, who spent five years in a North Vietnamese prison camp, was not a hero because Trump preferred people who evaded capture. Trump insulted GOP candidates to their face during nationally televised debates, laughing at Jeb Bush, calling him "low energy" and mocking his poll numbers. He baited Ted Cruz's wife, suggesting that she was unattractive.

All of this sped up the Trump Train, made it more efficient, more energetic. It created a feedback loop, where the exhaust from one act of abusive rampaging only fueled the next, and the crowds screamed with approval. This all led to his decisive moment, one where he bet it all on black:

> Donald J. Trump is calling for a total and complete shut down of Muslims entering the United States until our country's representatives can figure out what the hell is going on.[5]

Calling for "a Muslim ban" raised his support to a fever pitch; unleashing the country's Islamophobic Id, which has been stoked by politicians, talk radio jockeys, and evangelical preachers alike.[6] In Trump, the growing Alt Right knew they had an ally that would go after some of their most tarnished villains, and help them to unite with European nationalists over what they saw as a "Muslim invasion."

---

5   Donald Trump, "Total Muslim Ban Speech" (speech, Mt. Pleasant, SC, December 7th, 2015).
6   The Fairness Doctrine, which guaranteed balance in media political representation, was dropped after heavy media lobbying in 1987, unleashing the reactionary sphere of cable news and radio hate speech.

Internet Nationalism

While Trump was stoking racial fears across Middle America, the Alt Right/white nationalists were seeing unprecedented growth. Crossing into mainstream discourse through social media, they resurrected talking points taken from falsified race and crime statistics, discredited scientific and eugenics theories, and declarations of "white interests." Against the backdrop of Trump's calls for tacit white identity, white nationalists found a perfect synergy between the reactionary impulses of America made explicit through a right-wing populism that frames economic and political strife in racial terms. Trump, a fabulously wealthy man maligned for cartoonish behavior, was not their perfect vision, but they saw an advantage as Trump encouraged white voters to see themselves *as white*.

As Trump continued riding the wave of his own talk-radio-inspired one-act play, his connections to white nationalism only solidified.[7] Multiple KKK organizations endorsed his bid, as did David Duke, one of the most notorious white nationalists in the U.S.[8] After the official Duke endorsement came through, Trump was confronted on CNN but refused to disavow him, saying he did not know anything about Duke.[9] This runs counter to a 2000 ABC interview Trump gave when he ran as a presidential candidate with the Reform Party, where he said, "As you know, the Reform Party has got some pretty big problems. Not the least of which is Pat Buchanan, David Duke, Fulani, and it's a problem."[10]

Trump's campaign continued to shrug off public embarrassment as William Johnson, well-known white nationalist, founder of the American Freedom Party, and writer of the nativist "Pace

---

7   His father, Fred Trump, made his fortune in properties around Queens and semi-working-class areas of New York City. In 1927 he was arrested for his participation in a fight that brought in upwards of a thousand people as the Ku Klux Klan rallied to make NYC a place for "Native-born Protestant Americans." Phillip Bump, "In 1927, Donald Trump's Father Was Arrested After a Klan Riot in Queens," *The Washington Post*, February 29, 2016, https://www.washingtonpost.com/news/the-fix/wp/2016/02/28/in-1927-donald-trumps-father-was-arrested-after-a-klan-riot-in-queens/?utm_term=.c3c34c57589d.

8   David Duke was, for years, the best-known white supremacist in the U.S., working as a KKK leader in the 1970s and becoming a Louisiana state legislator in 1989.

9   Melissa Chan, "Donald Trump Refuses to Condemn KKK, Disavow David Duke Endorsement," *Time*, February 28, 2016, http://time.com/4240268/donald-trump-kkk-david-duke/.

10   Donald Trump, Interview by Matt Lauer, "Donald Trump Says He Will Not Run for President in 2000," *NBC Today Show*, NBC Universal, February 14, 2000, https://archives.nbclearn.com/portal/site/k-12/flatview?cuecard=2526.

Amendment" was selected as a Trump delegate for California.[11] The "/r/The_Donald_Trump" subreddit became an Alt Right hive, as did most Trump internet forums, and Trump only encouraged their fandom with Q&As.[12] Donald Trump Jr., who became a popular surrogate for his father, flaunted his white nationalist connections. He retweeted people like Alt Right science fiction author Vox Day and anti-Semitic white nationalist Kevin MacDonald, and even went on the *Political Cesspool* radio show, which has made a name for itself as a meeting point for the radical right.[13]

As his popularity increased, white nationalist groups lined up behind Trump uniformly, including the *Radix Journal*, the white nationalist web journal published by the NPI. They ran a "symposium" of well-known fascists and "race realists" who wrote short pieces explaining their support for Trump. The NPI conference, the most popular "suit-and-tie" fascist gathering of the year, named their 2015 and 2016 conferences after Trump, and the racialist *American Renaissance* also celebrated him at their yearly event. It was Trump's appointment of Steve Bannon, the former CEO of the far-right *Breitbart* news site, which sent the enthusiasm of the growing racialist base into the stratosphere. Bannon's far-right credentials are not the most unique part of his pedigree, though the openness of his flirtation with white nationalism is brazen. It is, as Connor Kilpatrick notes, "how well he understands liberalism's failures and how willing he is to craft a fraudulent and reactionary program for those who've only experienced decline during the Clinton and Obama years."[14] His Third Position is built in the wake of neoliberalism's failure, taking the revolutionary aims of the left and feeding them through a filter of white victimhood narratives.[15] Bannon was known as a bulldog Goldman investor and Hollywood producer, involved

---

11   Josh Harkinson, "White Nationalist Party Claims More of its Members are Delegates," *Mother Jones*, May 19, 2016, http://www.motherjones.com/politics /2016/05/white-nationalists-trump-delegates.

12   Trevor Marin, "Dissecting Trump's Most Rabid Online Following," *FiveThirtyEight*, March 23, 3017, https://fivethirtyeight.com/features/dissecting-trumps -most-rabid-online-following/?ex_cid=SigDig.

13   Heather Digby Parton, "Donald Trump Jr. and the White Nationalist Alt-Right: A Pattern That Goes Way Beyond Coincidence," *Mother Jones*, September 21, 2016, http://www.salon.com/2016/09/21/donald-trump-jr-and-the-white-nationalist -alt-right-a-pattern-that-goes-way-beyond-coincidence/.

14   Connor Kilpatrick, "Steve Bannon's Autobahn," *Jacobin* (February 2017): 12.

15   Third Positionism is a fascist ideological current that describes opposition to both "communism and capitalism," looking for a "third way." This will be outlined in detail in the "A Third Way" chapter below.

with nine films that range in content between tributes to Sarah Palin and attacks on the Occupy movement. All maintain a strong sense of what one writer for *Politico* called the idea that "Western Civilization as we know it is under attack from forces that are demonic or foreign." It was this concept of the invading threat that he injected into the Trump campaign, signaling to the racialist base while also helping to gain a shocking 81 percent of evangelical voters.[16]

White nationalists had cemented their "crossover" to the mainstream with the various pro-Trump provocateurs and internet celebrities that were rising up and willing to flirt with Alt Right ideas. They used *Breitbart* to continue to race-bait and attack feminism, social media and message boards to give them a cultural allure, and the Trump campaign to expand their influence on issues like immigration, the Black Lives Matter movement, and the "refugee crisis." A perfect synthesis was created, where the ideological currents of "Race Realism" and ethnic nationalism, developed over decades, were popularized through an internal jargon, podcasts, and "Alt Right Twitter"—the sphere of commentators that echoes far past its ideological base—and "troll culture," allowing it to develop its own edgy subculture. Inside this perfect storm, fascist ideologues gained legs and set their sights on conservatism, attacking Beltway politicians and journalists and "memeing themselves into reality."[17]

If Trump had not existed, fascists would have invented him. Without a populist crossover, without a translator who speaks to Middle America, they could never rebrand genocidal racialism as red-blooded Americana. White nationalism has been restated and repackaged as the "Alt Right" for a Millennial generation that developed its politics in the back alleys of the internet, fueled on the anger of eroding privilege and opposition to twenty-first century feminism. The organizations that backed this new upsurge were as old as the movement, resurrecting periods when races were believed to have different qualities and evolutionary histories, where some believed we could intervene on that evolution to create a "fitter" human species. The Alt Right hit the scene during a "whitelash" across Middle America, and its hashtags and memes seemed so new that

---

16   Theo Anderson, "The High Priest of the Church of Trump," *In These Times*, December 27, 2016, http://inthesetimes.com/article/19767/the-high -priest-of-the-church-of-trump-stephen-bannon-evangelicals.

17   Richard Spencer, interview by Elle Reeve, "The face of the alt-right," *Vice*, December 10, 2016, https://news.vice.com/story/we-memed-alt-right-into- existence-our-extended-interview-with-richard-spencer-on-white-nationalism.

few could see that its ideological and organizational history traced back to the fires of World War II.

What was different from its historical counterparts was the Alt Right's strategic orientation, how they were going to approach organizing, and what success would look like. Fascist movements have always required a crossover, a stopover point they use to moderate their views and prepare them for new converts. This new culture of white nationalism rejected the failed swastikas and hoods of the past as the losing spirit of a poor reactionary militancy, and instead their middle-class backgrounds and tech orientations gave their "movement" a new lease. These players would seek cultural influence, culture being viewed as a pre-determination of politics, and would develop relationships with challenging figures on the social right rather than cozying up with politicians. They waited for the politicians to come to them.

Tuesday Night Lights

The morning of November 8, 2016—Election Day—the majority of Americans *knew* that Trump would not win. NPR, the *New York Times*, and *FiveThirtyEight* were uniform about the narrow path to victory that Trump had to the White House. The *NPR Politics Podcast* discussed this as a near impossibility—unless he miraculously won states like Ohio, Florida, New Hampshire, and West Virginia.[18] *FiveThirtyEight* set his chances at 28.7 percent, and *The Upshot* set them at only 14 percent.[19]

As the day wore on, social media posts began to increase in speed and anger. Against the odds, Trump took Florida. Then North Carolina. Then Iowa, Indiana, and West Virginia. Next, Michigan and Minnesota went into play, defying not only pundits and pollsters, but also historians and political scientists. Then Pennsylvania went red.

Videos and eyewitness accounts of Trump rallies during the campaign year portrayed a frightening cacophony of reactionary anger, where racial slurs were belted out with salivating venom, and protesters of color feared for their lives. "Build the Wall!" became a

---

18   "Tuesday, November 9" *NPR Politics Podcast*, November 8, 2016, http://www .npr.org/podcasts/510310/npr-politics-podcast.
19   Lucy Westcott, "Presidential Election Polls For November 8, 2016," *Newsweek*, November 8, 2016, http://www.newsweek.com/polls-2016-presidential-election-trump-clinton-518280.

common taunt to provoke immigrants or simply to show that there was a united white front against their personhood. That attitude only amplified once it was validated by Trump's election. In the ten days after the election the Southern Poverty Law Center (SPLC), which tracks hate groups, listed almost nine hundred reported hate crimes, a number so astronomical it had no precedent. Muslim women reported having hijabs pulled off their heads, while Latin American students told stories of being surrounded in lunchrooms as white students hurled racial slurs.[20]

White nationalists have a revolutionary vision, one that opposes the state and dominant white culture as much as it does the left and non-whites. It wants to reimagine this world as one that is exclusively for white interests, where the "strong" rule over the "weak," where women know their place, and gender is firmly enforced. They have reached into the culture and gotten a firm grasp and are going to use this moment in the sun to grow, to expand their influence, to make themselves a militant threat to the values of democracy and equality. The challenge for those on the left, the organized faction interested in greater human equality, is now to understand who the Alt Right are and what they want, and they must look past the contradictory phrasings and confusing tactics to do that. The incidents of reactionary violence, the mobilization that figures like Trump and his racial scapegoating has inspired in working-class people, and the mainstreaming of explicit nationalism has made real the threat that was only in the background of many political battles over the last sixty years. Fascism has never been silenced exclusively by its own ineptitude but instead by the concerted efforts of organizers that risk everything to stop it. Fascism attacks all of our movements: from the labor movement to antiracist struggle, the growth of the LGBT fight to that over ecological liberation. Fascism makes these battles intersectional since it acts as an orchestrated attack on the core constituencies of all of these movements, making real the idea that all oppression has a common center. Fascism is an attempt to answer the unfinished equation of capitalism, and, instead of challenging the inequalities manifested through this economic system, it hardens them. With Donald Trump's election, this "worst case scenario," fascism taking a hold, now seemed possible, which added material

---

20   Cassie Miller and Alexandra Werner-Wilson, "Ten Days After: Harassment and Intimidation in the Aftermath of the Election," *Southern Poverty Law Center*, November 29th, 2016, https://www.splcenter.org/20161129/ten-days-after-harassment-and-intimidation-aftermath-election.

impetus for movements on the left to link up and take charge. This changed everything.

Trump's America

As Trump took the stage to mimic a gracious acceptance for his election win, much of the liberal left stood in horror, mouths agape. For years people of color had, without interruption, sounded the alarm, saying that not only was this Trumpian rhetoric common through the streets of America, but that someone like him would soon come along. Richard Spencer appeared at the Trump victory party in Washington, D.C., taking selfies with *Buzzfeed* reporters and posting videos yelling, "We won!"

It sure seemed that way.

While the logic of "It's the economy, stupid," was being used to explain the Trump phenomenon, the evidence spoke more directly to the lines of contentious identity than economic peril. A University of Massachusetts study conducted in the months after the election concluded that the defining factor was racial attitudes. While Trump's explicit racism and sexism cost him votes substantially with educated white voters, overall it gave him more of a boost than a loss with the white base.[21] This demonstrated a growing American divide and showed a GOP that has been looking for a soul since the final Bush presidency cost them legitimacy with a shifting voting demographic. Forgoing the well-coded Southern Strategy, explicit nationalist populism and racism may be their only path forward. The Alt Right simply updated this logic, using a new language of memes and GIFs expressed in irony, allowing Pepe the Frog to be the "Welfare Queens" for Millenials. This shift in the mainstream right did not occur in a vacuum, as a left opposition was growing in tandem with the Trump Republicans.

The Spoken Majority

Before the results were even final, people flooded the streets in major cities around the country. In Portland, Oregon, hundreds gathered downtown by 1:00 a.m., flowing in on a stream of rage from the

---

21 Brian Schaffner, Matthew MacWilliams, Tatishe Nteta, "Explaining White Polarization in the 2016 Vote for President: The Sobering Role of Racism and Sexism." Available online: http://people.umass.edu/schaffne/schaffner_et_al_IDC_conference.pdf.

vitriol of racist attacks that ended up ushering a right-wing populist into the White House. Wednesday, the day after the election, was something close to an insurgency.

Portland's protests swelled to over two thousand, instigated by high school students walking out of class, politically activated for the first time. Protesters swarmed the busy I-5 freeway near the onramp to the Rose Quarter, where the Oregon Trailblazers reign, halting rush-hour traffic.

"This size of a crowd is going to do what it wants for as long as it wants," Chief of Police Simpson said. "There is no way to remove 2,000 people who don't want to be moved. We're asking for patience from people."[22]

The next day, there were almost four thousand in the streets, in a procession that stretched out for almost a mile. In their wake, insurrectionary contingents did an estimated $1 million worth of damage to trendy commercial areas of the city.

In Seattle, students again led the charge as five thousand middle and high school students left class, a model replicated in city after city. In Minneapolis, five thousand people arrived at a march organized by Socialist Alternative, which headed to the local GOP headquarters before occupying the I-94 freeway.[23] Five thousand overwhelmed the streets of New York City chanting "Not my president," and the Trump International Hotel in Washington, D.C., became a major target for mass action. In the week after the election, hundreds of thousands of people came out in cities from Boston to Los Angeles, disrupting traffic and commerce, screaming about the threat of racist violence that Trump represented.[24] With a promise to deport undocumented immigrants, block Muslims from entering the country, "bomb the hell" out of the Middle East, and lock up just about every opponent, the country was now controlled by a wild card.

That the protests were the last gasp of the Hilary Clinton campaign were untrue, as the vast majority of those mobilizing, even

---

22 Dirk VanderHart, "Cops Helped a Massive Anti-Trump Protest Shut Down I-5 On Wednesday," *Portland Mercury*, November 9, 2016, http://www.portlandmercury.com/blogtown/2016/11/09/18686307/portland-cops-have-let-a-massive-anti-trump-protest-take-i-5.

23 "A First-Hand Account Of The Fuck Trump March In Minneapolis," *Conflict MN*, November 18, 2016, https://conflictmn.blackblogs.org/a-first-hand-account-of-the-fuck-trump-march-in-minneapolis/.

24 Euan McKirdy, "Thousands Take to The Streets to Protest Trump Win," *CNN*, November 10, 2016, http://www.cnn.com/2016/11/09/politics/election-results-reaction-streets/.

for the first time, never supported the Democratic candidate. Clinton's liberal-leaning austerity politics failed to connect with the anti-establishment uprising that was happening, and it especially failed to attract those who supported Bernie Sanders in the primary. Instead, this was the politics of negation, the nihilism of Trump's ascendancy signaling a new stage in American repression, urgently necessitating a new revolutionary paradigm rather than Democratic negotiations and harm reduction.

Regional organizations working to manage fascist threats saw a flood of interest, and new organizations were being formed daily, such as Portland's Resistance, which in a matter of days brought hundreds together to begin organizing actions. Organizations that had identified the threat, including labor unions like the SEIU, pushed for coordination and community partnership, building a block of resistance against the coming Trump administration. One example of this was the Portland Assembly, which was organized on a traditional "spokescouncil" model where groups could come together to discuss different wings of struggle, such as labor, environmentalism, neighborhood organizing, anti-racism, and community defense. If Trump was going to repeal the Affordable Care Act, institute Right to Work on a national scale, and pull out of the recent Paris Climate agreements, then it meant that those confronting the rising fascist tide had allies in the various strands of the left. If those material costs could be connected with his populist racialism on the other hand, then connections could be made between issues that had failed to solidify in decades of coalition work. The possibility of a united opposition was palpable, if only it could be grasped and held onto.

The call to challenge Trump was now coming from all directions. A boycott was announced for all Trump-owned businesses as well as companies that endorsed Trump at any stage of the election, including New Balance, Yuengling, and Hobby Lobby.[25] News outlets like *ThinkProgress* and NGOs like the SPLC set up user-friendly tracking tools to report hate crimes as we saw an increase in street harassment—such as men laughing as they tried to "grab women by the pussy" or angry subway passengers tugging at the hijabs of Muslim women riding home from work. The collective dread grew, creating an underlying anxiety about a world that could

---

25   "Boycott Trump: List of Pro-Trump Businesses," *ArbiterNews*, June 27, 2016, http://www.arbiternews.com/2016/06/27/boycott-trump-list-pro-trump-businesses/.

flip so easily into racialist barbarism. Trump's attacks on the media, and their lack of access to him, made outlets like *Slate*, NPR, *Salon*, and *Mother Jones* wonder if their profession was going to be under threat and if journalists could be targeted for legal revenge, charges of libel, or worse.

The broad-left began uniting under the banner of "The Resistance," with certain large tendencies emerging to influence the direction of this growing well of emotion. Democratic Party staffers formed Indivisible—which enabled people to link up with progressive local organizing—based on a Tea Party model for "practicing locally-focused, [an] almost entirely defensive strategy." The "town hall" phenomenon came to be in early 2017. In these community meetings, conservative politicians were raked over the coals in the style of the Tea Party attacks on the Affordable Care Act as its replacement was debated. #KnockEveryDoor attempted to unite the left-end of the Democrats, trying to build an organized base to shift government institutions back to the left come the 2018 midterm elections. Swing Left took a similar approach, motivating new people to become active in liberal partisan politics. Run for Nothing tried to recruit a slew of new Millennial candidates to challenge the GOP, while Movement 2017 worked toward funding additional electoral campaigns.

These projects and dozens of others were founded at a time when 40 percent of polled Democrats were moving to action, yet much of this effort was to meant to funnel people back into the tepid world of Democratic electoralism, rather than action. What these organizations did do, however, was connect people to the first spark of organizing, and from there, a more radical direction—one that saw the potential of mass movements and direct action, an alternative to the recycled optimism of biennial elections—could be taken. Projects like Movement Match were meant to direct new people to organizations that fit them, but the organizers lacked a deep understanding of the kinds of projects and forms of resistance that were available, so participants were being funneled back into party front-groups rather than into base-building organizations. Even with the obvious failures of many of the dominant organizations of "The Resistance," the amassing of consciousness and the first shift in a mass population provided huge opportunities.[26]

---

26   Joshua Holland, "Your Guide to the Sprawling New Anti-Trump Resistance Movement," *The Nation*. N.p., January 8, 2017, https://www.thenation.com/article/your-guide-to-the-sprawling-new-anti-trump-resistance-movement/.

Many expected a "deer on the headlights" response from the left as Trumpism erupted, and while many labor and political leaders began to compromise with Trump, there was a vocal and visible commitment across the country against the wave of bigotry that this election appeared to unleash. Almost immediately after the election, the "safety pin campaign" came to be. Safety pins were worn to indicate that people were actively opposed to bigotry and stood in solidarity with anyone who was threatened. Though criticized for its lack of tangible effect, the support of the symbol by many thousands showed a certain level of commitment from unorganized sectors to engage in some type of action. At the same time, organizations and businesses en masse identified their premises as safe spaces for those being victimized, such as the popular Powell's Books retail locations in Portland. Across the liberal left, people were becoming passionate about opposing the new administration, even if to some the strategy was lacking in depth, long-term analysis, and the blistering focus necessary to confront the threat of a Trump-occupied federal government and the stormtroopers who were radicalizing online.

Twenty-First Century Anti-Fascism

As left organizations, from every part of the spectrum—liberal to anarchist, newly formed to decades old—were scrambling to address the incoming Trump administration, they were faced with an emboldened neo-fascist contingent. Anti-fascism today is a struggle against neo-fascism, which, almost without exception, is understood as fascist projects without state power. While there have been fascist state apparatus in other countries, it is hyperbolic to refer to administrations over the past seventy years as synonymous with the racialized identitarian power centers that most white nationalists advocate. Instead, even when those movements have state actors and passive support from the instruments of institutional violence—those of the state and its police and military enforcement—they are in opposition to the consciousness of the citizenry. Today that may have shifted, moving to the "second stage" in Robert Paxton's "Five Stages of Fascism," where the fascist movement, which spent years thinking and spreading the reach of its base, has entered the political stage.[27] Because Trump is not fully aligned with white nationalists'

---

27   Robert O. Paxton, "The Five Stages of Fascism," *The Journal of Modern History* 70, No. 1. (March, 1998): 1–23. These stages are broadly outlined on page 46.

defining policy programs, he is more of a window rather than the vessel, but his coming to power presents the fascist right with options and access to power (even if it is only in terms of ideas) that have not been viable previously.

The question for antifascist organizations is then how to address this fascist movement when the government itself could become part of that spectrum?[28] This means expanding the scope of the work while continuing to go after the hard white nationalism that is edging its way into the Overton window, the bounds of thought considered "acceptable" by polite society. The growth of these racist grouplets has been dwarfed by a growing antifascist consciousness, which is developing a mass movement approach that syncs the growing opposition to Trump's civic nationalist government. This growing movement sees the enemy as both those subcultural celebrities carrying the banner of racial nationalism, such as Richard Spencer and Jared Taylor, as well and the macropolitical solutions that Trump has presented to stoke the white base.

The coming together of these ideas is seen in the growing mobilizations and the coordination between groups in opposition to Trump and his policies. Issues like immigration and the environment suddenly become intersectional when years of organizing did not succeed in making them so. From November 9 until Inauguration Day, January 20, the cities were erupting, and a broadly understood "united front" was appearing to the left of the Democratic Party. While inauguration day is just a focal point and celebration for any new administration, radical groups like Crimthinc, Redneck Revolt, and numerous antifascist organizations endorsed the call for a #DisruptJ20 action, a huge public demonstration in Washington, D.C., the day the Trump motorcade brought him up Pennsylvania Avenue. Actions began several days in advance at the Martin Luther Day Action Camp, where participants were given direct action trainings on bystander intervention and engaged in workshops on the core issues of capitalism and white supremacy. With the surge of interest that comes from a catalyzing event, the impetus was to disseminate skills to a large and radicalizing population quickly, to channel anger into effective protest. A mass movement has the challenge of being made up of large numbers of people from varying political tendencies,

---

28   It would be extremely hyperbolic to call the U.S. government fascist, whether or not Trump is in the White House. Instead, when far-right populists are entering the halls of power, it shifts government institutions into the scope of fascist movements, meaning the fascists are becoming relevant.

with different levels of experience and backgrounds. This can be turned into a strength when opportunities for education and preparation are made accessible to them, especially around broad-based actions that can help to increase mobilization and prepare for more prolonged and specific types of organizing later.

The call to disrupt the Inauguration Day festivities, turning Washington, D.C., into something akin to the 1999 social revolt against the World Trade Organization conference in Seattle, was announced by dozens of independent coalitions of organizations, with varying levels of coordination. After a new liberal-leaning project called Refuse Fascism, with a number of mainstream activists like Imam Aiyub Abdul-Baki of the Islamic Leadership Council of New York and actors like former SAG-AFTRA leader Ed Asner, was formed, the Oath Keepers[29] declared that "communists," with funding by George Soros, were intending to overthrow the government on January 20, 2017.[30]

Inauguration Day saw a worldwide wave of protest, with over six hundred regional events being held across the U.S. and around the globe. The capital swelled with 500,000 anti-Trump protesters descending upon the city, while black bloc protesters set cars on fire, blockaded roads, and smashed the windows of the towering corporate buildings that line the streets. As happened at George W. Bush's inauguration, Trump was unable to finish the walk to the White House because of the opposition. About 150,000 people rose up in Chicago, shutting down the city, and Portland had to suspend public transportation as thousands occupied the streets.[31]

Becoming Who They Are

White nationalist Richard Spencer, the Alt Right founder who had become a celebrity in 2016, had spent the previous couple of months being hammered as the media spectacle he had created finally turned on him. After he accosted the press at his 2016 NPI conference, he was filmed leading a crowd in "Seig Heil" salutes, forcing

---

29 The Oath Keepers are a Patriot militia of current and former members of law enforcement, the military, and emergency response organizations.

30 Jack Navy, "Communists Intend to Overthrow the United States Before Inauguration Day (Updated 01/12/2017)," *Oath Keepers*, January 10, 2017, https://www.oathkeepers.org/navyjack-communists-intend-overthrow -united-states-inauguration-day/.

31 "Donald Trump Protests Attract Millions Across US and World," *BBC News*, January 21, 2017, http://www.bbc.com/news/world-us-canada-38705586.

condemnations from crossover supporters and a further split of the Alt Right.[32] As his home of Whitefish, Montana turned on him and his family and the Alt Light condemned him, Spencer was protested and confronted everywhere he went. He continued to make headlines as everything he said and did became news, and he ate it up, knowing that this moment in the sun was his best advertisement. The Alt Right still rode shotgun in Trump's coterie, possessing the ability to influence the direction of the state like a warrior-philosopher throwing ideas out, just as conservative revolutionaries did during fascism's first rise. They wanted to flesh out Trump's right populism, injecting a more deeply understood racial nationalism that would give it a pseudo-intellectual core.

Spencer moved full-time to Arlington, Virginia, and started a new life centered in the Washington, D.C., area without close family ties, which he could no longer maintain as a white nationalist leader. Moving in with Alt Right academic and Arktos Media editor Jason Reza Jorjani, he created AltRight.com as a central hub for all major Alt Right media outlets like *The Right Stuff*, *RightOn*, Counter-Currents, Red Ice Radio, and his own *Radix Journal*. By doing so, he pulled together more European nationalists, and increased the writing of policy recommendations. He rebranded the Radix Podcast feed as "Alt Right Radio" and created an "Alt Right Tonight" talk show format that ties in video as a way of creating a synergistic fascist media empire.[33]

Spencer stepped out into the open to broadcast the inauguration from Periscope, braving the cold breeze in his "Make America Great Again" cap. That afternoon, while he was doing a spontaneous interview where he arrogantly insulted passersby who asked about his nationalist orientation and explained the significance of Pepe the Frog to the Alt Right, a black-clad protester ran up and punched him on the side of the head. As is his habit, Spencer then went back on social media to declare that Antifa had taken a step more toward "European anti-fascism" and is becoming more "violent."

"My only mistake was in giving an interview to someone on a public street while animals tore through D.C.," said Spencer, as he

---

32   "Let's Watch as the Alt Right Implodes," *Anti-Fascist News*, December 4, 2016, https://antifascistnews.net/2016/12/04/lets-watch-as-the-alt-right-implodes/.
33   Daniel Friberg, Jason Jorjani, Henrik Palmgren, Richard Spencer, and Tor Westman, *Alt Right Now-The Beginning*, podcast audio, Alt Right Radio, MP3, 59:26, January 18, 2017, originally posted at https://soundcloud.com/altright/altright-now-1-the-beginning, but has since been removed.

posted rapid-fire on Twitter. "If law enforcement can't protect us from Antifa assaults we will begin protecting ourselves."

Nathan Damigo, the founder of the youth-centered Alt Right group Identity Evropa, live-streaming from Berkeley on the opposite coast, was pepper-sprayed as he publicly celebrated the next step in American white nationalism.[34]

In years past, without the visual cue of a Klan robe or a flag emblazoned with a swastika, it was difficult for the left to mobilize against white nationalists unless they were extensively coordinated. As the profile of people like Damigo and Spencer rose, often through their own efforts, they became obvious targets for the antifascist anger that had permeated a segment of society that watched in horror as explicit white supremacy headed toward the mainstream. While Spencer's assertion that "Antifa" had become more violent may seem like hyperbole, what he was picking up on is that anti-fascism had become more understood, popular, and determined. In response to Spencer's attack, WeSearchr posted a bounty on the masked combatant's head, which, through donations, rose quickly to several thousand dollars.[35] Almost immediately, the internet erupted with support for the person who landed the punch and Philly Antifa started a fundraiser for him.[36] To show solidarity, others posted that they were "the one who punched Richard Spencer," and Spencer's home address and phone number were shared widely. Articles appeared in major publications across the country grappling with what is or is not an acceptable response to a well-dressed man talking about ethnic cleansing on the street corner, and op-eds and articles came out for and against "punching a Nazi."

Opponents to the punch were few and far between, and Spencer could see that this event only further cemented his status as "public

---

34   "It's Not Alt-Right: Richard Spencer Attacked in DC; Nathan Damigo Pepper Sprayed In Berkeley," *It's Going Down*, January 20, 2017, https://itsgoingdown.org/not-alt-right-richard-spencer-attacked-dc-nathan-damigo-pepper-sprayed-berkeley.

35   WeSearchr is a unique phenomenon: an Alt Right friendly website that elevates crowdfunded "bounties" often for information on celebrities. Its founder, Charles Johnson, has ties to the Trump administration through consultations with the transition team, but also has relationships with the explicitly white nationalist wing of the Alt Right and has appeared on podcasts like the white nationalist *Fash the Nation* from *The Right Stuff* podcast network. "Expose the ANTIFA Who Sucker Punched Richard Spencer," *WeSearchr*, January 24, 2017, https://www.wesearchr.com/bounties/expose-the-antifa-who-sucker-punched-richard-spencer.

36   Philly Antifa militant antifascist community organization in Philadelphia.

enemy number one." WeSearchr was pulled from Twitter because of the bounty it was offering. Spencer admitted, in another of his stream of videos, that the antifascist strategy of refusing him a platform was the antifascists' greatest weapon:

> We have to get serious about security protection or we can't have a public movement. And if we can't have a public movement then we can't win. Period…. We could think of this as a Civil War that's raging in this country.[37]

Charles Lyons, the famed Twitter troll and white nationalist known for popularizing anti-Semitic conspiracy theories, wrote in the *Radix Journal* that this was a "new era" for clashes between the right and left:

> Our political opponents are emotionally and spiritually invested in seeing that we are all destroyed. This is the reality of the situation we find ourselves in. It is time to act accordingly.[38]

Mike Enoch of the *Daily Shoah*—the Alt Right podcast popularized through their use of racial slurs and in-jokes—was still reeling from his own recent doxxing.[39] Enoch argued that the growing public face of the Alt Right needs to start coming out against the "Antifas" bent on their destruction, and the culture that supports them.[40]

On the eve of the inauguration, Mike Cernovich, the "MAGA Mind-set" internet celebrity, and Peter Thiel associate Jeff Giesea held the much-publicized Deploraball in Washington, D.C.—an event named as a campy throwback to Hillary Clinton's unfortunate "basket of deplorables" quip about Trump supporters. The event was conceived of as a meeting of the "trolls," a celebration of the culture that "meme'd [Trump] into the White House." The ball lacked strong ideology and instead was a celebration of

37   Richard Spencer, *Attacks on The Alt Right*, YouTube (AltRight.com), January 22, 2017, https://www.youtube.com/watch?v=6_rFe2n8fi0.
38   Charles Johnson, "The Intolerant Politics of Reality," *Radix Journal*, January 21, 2017, http://www.radixjournal.com/blog/2017/1/21/the-intolerant-politics-of-reality.
39   Doxxing is the revelation of personal information of an individual, often so that they can have their actions made public to stakeholders in their life.
40   Sven, Mike, Alex, MeinKraft, *Daily Shoah #124: Sucker Punch*, podcast audio, Right Stuff Radio, MP3, 2:09:37, January 24, 2017, https://radio.therightstuff.biz/2017/01/24/the-daily-shoah-124-sucker-punch/.

Twitter message boards, snarky graphics, and the ability to sway conversations through a mean-spirited, tech-savvy persistence. It was as if someone had taken the culture of the Alt Right and stripped out the hardline white nationalism, leaving only an internet culture of "anti-PC" web-warriors who would rather be right than white. Trolling, the ability to offend, is their politics, and people like Spencer and Damigo only side with that behavior if it can create a space for white identity politics.[41]

Cernovich and Giesea, who had been running the pro-Trump MAGA3X organization, had become leaders in the Alt Light, with Cernovich, known for his right-leaning online self-help books, battling it out with Richard Spencer over who held the rights to the term "Alt Right."[42] The Deploraball was supposed to be a large Alt Light meet-up and did attract people like Neoreaction-friendly tech impresario Peter Thiel, but *Breitbart* antagonist Milo Yiannopoulos and conspiracy hero Alex Jones were notably absent, and Spencer had been banned outright in Cernovich's effort to kick out explicit white nationalists.[43]

Though it attracted a couple of hundred inside, it was the angry waves of antifascist protesters that completely overshadowed the event from the outside. Organized in part by Refuse Fascism, which had been organizing mass counter-actions in response to the Alt Right and the Trump inauguration, protesters dragged trashcans and newspaper dispensers into the street to block off the roads and taunted attendees.[44] James O'Keefe, the *Breitbart*-allied sensationalist who staged videos to disgrace ACORN and Planned Parenthood, released videos of the D.C. Anti-Fascist Coalition who were planning direct actions during the inauguration and at the Deploraball.[45] While the Alt Right and their coterie were in a period of jubilant

---

41 Ira Glass, *The Revolution Starts at Noon*, podcast audio, American Life, MP3, 1:05:51, January 20, 2017, https://www.thisamericanlife.org/radio-archives/episode/608/the-revolution-starts-at-noon.

42 As will be outlined in detail later, the Alt Light is the sphere of commentators and activists that help to mainstream the Alt Right without committing to its more controversial white nationalist ideologies.

43 Park MacDougald, "Why Peter Thiel Wants to Topple Gawker and Elect Donald Trump," *NYMag*, June 14, 2016, http://nymag.com/selectall/2016/06/peter-thiel.html.

44 Gideon Resnik, "Anti-Fascists Crash Alt-Right Deploraball," *The Daily Beast*, January 19, 2017, http://www.thedailybeast.com/articles/2017/01/20/anti-fascists-crash-alt-right-deploraball.html.

45 Madeleine Weast, "'DC Anti-Fascist Coalition' Talked About Ruining Inauguration Event with Butyric Acid," *Washington Free Beacon*, January 16, 2017, http://freebeacon.com/culture/coalition-ruin-event-acid/.

celebration, their step forward was marked less by success and more by a wall of opposition.

Into the Mass Movement

Two years earlier, no one as obscure as Cernovich could assemble hundreds of protesters, and even Richard Spencer was barely known as recently as 2014. But as the Alt Right entered the public arena, more traditional white supremacist organizations got a steroid injection. Trump inflated the racist subconscious of America, and the urgency of the situation fertilized the growing resistance. As Spencer alluded, there is a growing clash between the right and the left, yet those who are building a base against white nationalism are the dominant faction by far. With antifascist organizations reaching numbers not seen in years, the Alt Right became the catalyst for left opposition. This dialectic was a microcosm of the political polarization in the country as a whole. It was no longer the hardcore ideologues of Antifa organizations that were confronting the fascists, but regular people skewing to the left, and the concept of anti-fascism as a political program went from abstract to concrete as the threat of fascism became tangible. While the Alt Right intended to move the conversation to the right, they moved the left further left, and their weight pulled the Overton window back with them, thereby mainstreaming antifascism.

What does it mean when a minority movement, one meant to confront a marginal threat, moves from the edges to the mainstream? What happens when white supremacists shift from a threat of vigilante violence and radical co-optation to national political influence? As the enemy leaves the gate and the left's numbers swell, the answer to confronting rising fascism lies in reframing the proposition of a "diversity of tactics" to see the complex patchwork that makes up mass movements as the coalescence of that diversity. The concept of "mass movement antifascism" implies a strategic choice, one that looks at all available options and finds the best possible route rather than an ideologically favored one.

As Trump entered his first week in office he tried to keep his promises about Muslim immigration, working with reactionary politicians like Rudy Giuliani to pass an executive order halting immigration from seven primarily Muslim countries. This created pandemonium in airports across the country as refugees were turned away, students and professionals were detained without access to attorneys, and LAX and JFK became holding pens for those who suddenly had their visas revoked. This order was met with some of the largest spontaneous protests in recent history, with airports all over the country overflowing with protesters. Public pressure, as well as a court order that overruled Trump's decision, helped push through international travelers, and showed that Trump's attempts to close the border would not only be opposed, but would also be openly defied.

Trump's White House was stacked with all elements of the "respectable" far-right. Steve Bannon's "American Nationalism" was met by controversial figure Steven Miller, who had an organizing relationship with Richard Spencer and anti-immigrant zealot Peter Brimelow in college and now acted as a stalwart against refugee resettlement and non-white immigration programs across the board. Sebastian Gorka rounded out the most controversial slate of appointees in years, eventually being outed for his relationship to an openly fascist and anti-Semitic Hungarian militia, the Hungarian Guard, and the "chivalrous" Order of Vitéz.[46]

After the election, *Vice News* producer Reid Cherlin described a 2014 attempt to write a story about an almost unheard of publication called *Breitbart* and the collection of far-right ideologues that populated their lively townhouse party, including Gorka, Bannon, Jeff Sessions, and Milo Yiannopoulos, as well as head of the nationalist U.K. Independence Party Nigel Farage. "At the time, if you had said this room was full of the most important future policy thinkers in America it would have just been so implausible. Because they were so fringe."[47]

An executive order like the travel ban may not have inspired such quick and decisive action in the pre-Trump era or without the specter of advisors he was amassing, but as the Alt Right grew and America's racism became more explicit, a culture of resistance quickly matured. In Trump's America, there is bigotry and state violence, and there is also a passionate movement to support the most

46   Lili Bayer, "EXCLUSIVE: Controversial Trump Aide Sebastian Gorka Backed Violent Anti-Semitic Militia," *Forward*, April 3, 2017, http://forward .com/news/national/367937/exclusive-controversial-trump-aide-sebastian -gorka-backed-violent-anti-semi/.

47   Reid Cherlin, "The Beginning of Now," *This American Life*, April 28, 2017, https://www.thisamericanlife.org/radio-archives/episode/615/the-beginning -of-now?act=0#play.

marginalized, to live up to the phrase "Never Again." The mass turn toward antifascism comes from a culture ready for resistance, a culture ready to bring protest to a scale necessary when the state is friendly to or occupied by a fascist movement.

The lessons of the past loom heavily on the development of a mass antifascist movement, including the lineage of organizations, both in the United States and internationally, that have been doing this work in various capacities for decades. White anti-fascism has a direct continuity from before the Second World War to the present day, making the streets of London a cauldron of confrontation between the British Union of Fascists and 43 Group, Combat 18 with Anti-Fascist Action. The United States also has a unique history. There is a tendency to delineate between liberal antiracism and antifascism, but we can broadly define movements by highlighting their purpose. The purpose of antifascism is a complete repudiation of fascism and its removal from the culture. The point is not that there is no tactical difference, or even that liberal approaches have often reinforced the state and undermined effective challenges to fascist growth, but that the boundaries that are outlined are fuzzier and more easily redrawn than we have thought. While direct confrontation is never off the table, not all organizers approach every situation in that fashion. Instead a new antifascist ethos may be taking hold, one that sees multiple approaches as valid, as they are all matched by the same motivating impulse: fascism is to be ended, not debated.

What may be different in this shift to a mass movement is the willingness to put a public face to antifascist organizing, to operate in plain sight. Security has always been paramount in many areas of antifascist organizing, which brings benefits as well as challenges for scaling up a movement's size. Achieving mass involvement—with participants of varying commitment levels and skillsets—requires recruitment, public information, and a certain level of openness. How this plays out now will depend on existing organizations, how they relate to each other, and how public they can be given the violent revenge often sought by insurrectionary racists. Coalition efforts have often provided the answer to this. In coalitions, various groups take up different components of a particular project or committees that can determine exactly what degree of public profile are necessary for the job.

A mass movement approach means drawing from a range of social movements—conceivably, all those touched by the reactionary right—each with their own political trajectory and history of gains and losses. The structures of different resistance, from organized labor to the tenants' movement erupting in America's urban core, provide structural lessons for confronting the far-right in the halls of power and the creeping white nationalism all around. The revolutionary white nationalist current, led by the Alt Right, has begun creating strong institutions from media outlets to regional cadre organizations bent on seeing material gains through wedge issues. This shift creates the opportunity to borrow from the strategies that the left has used over a long history of struggle. The current, more public nature of the white nationalist movement means that formalized campaigns against them can grow, and they can have a layer of organizers and an outside ring of supporters who rely on public communication. This allows for a range of tactics including escalation campaigns, boycotts, mass mobilizations, building occupations, and so on. "Community organizing" is stripped down to its bare essentials and reframed to target fascist threats. The tactics of community unionism, hailing from the early syndicates of the shop floor and brought into the neighborhoods through tenant resistance, provides a range of solutions, such as defending both against white supremacist violence as well as protecting undocumented people against the impending ICE raids of Trump's fantasies. The model here is less to replicate the blueprint of successful antifascist movements of the past, than to use the entire toolkit of revolutionary organizing. During the civil rights movement that resisted Jim Crow from the 1950s to the '70s, the battle against both the insurrectionary advances of the Klan and the embedded white supremacy of the apartheid state ran parallel, and the successes depended on the ability to expand involvement while adopting tactics and strategies that worked in each particular venue.

Any successful social movement allows for diversity in roles, matching the different personalities, interests, and skills of the actors, creating a patchwork that reflects the constituents as much as the goals. Movements developing today that seek to stop the growth of the far-right are moving toward an inclusionary framework that makes mass movements work: they have different tasks for different people. How this is structured pragmatically can and should depend on the people involved, how they work best, and what the unique situation is of a given area. For people forming new groups, a broad-based community strategy requires external communication, educational and community-building events, campaign planning, public actions, research and information dissemination, and all the other component parts. Many antifascist organizations previously ran on tight, information-restricted formulas, yet this could limit their ability to expand beyond a close-knit cadre of committed organizers, and would also preclude most people from participating. What movements in this new climate will grapple with is how to best make use of every interested person in relation to the larger organizing goals, which means that a fully realized antifascist movement will have different types of campaigns, multiple approaches, and a complex web of support systems. The challenge will be to make these facets work with one another rather than creating conflicts.

Defining Fascism

For those on the left whose political consciousness developed in response to neoliberalism and the GOP's war on the most marginalized, the term "fascism" has been tainted beyond recognition. Whether it is used to describe the authoritarian personal invasions of Ralph Reed's Moral Majority, the totalitarian state apparatus of the Bush administration, the assault on the labor movement, the deregulation of the financial market, or Reagan's victimization of drug users and the poor, the term "fascist" has incorrectly become synonymous with right-wing political policy. While fascism is certainly an attack on the most marginalized, it is not diffuse and applicable to all forms of reactionary state policy. It has a specific meaning, one that makes it distinct from most forms of conservatism, and needs to be defined according to its unique qualities.

Authoritarianism, in its various forms, is not the central tenet of the fascist project, nor are the creation of a police state, the enhancement of state apparatus into the life of the citizenry, or intervention into foreign states. We must define fascism through its meta-politics and motivating positions, which redefine "in group" and "out group" and shift our values. If we consider political scientist George Hawley's definition of a right-wing political movement as one that puts anything other than equality as its highest social aspiration, then it suggests that authoritarianism can come from the left or the right.[1]

The same difficulty of definition occurs when we consider the difference between a fascist *ideology* and a fascist *movement*. As we have

---

1   George Hawley, *Right-Wing Critics of American Conservatism* (Lawrence: University Press of Kansas, 2016), 11–12.

seen in Trump's proto-fascist campaign, the populist anger that gave Trump his numbers and the white nationalists who used this as an opportunity were not twins. Instead, a fascist *movement* can often slowly adopt ideological fascist positions, even if those ideas were not its motivations in its infancy. Robert O. Paxton, who *Democracy Now!* calls the "father of Fascism Studies," has identified this process in which a fascist movement develops, defining it in his book *Anatomy of Fascism*, in a list of ideological qualities that occur during this process.

> Fascism may be defined as a form of political behavior marked by obsessive preoccupation with community decline, humiliation, or victimhood and by compensatory cults of unity, energy, and purity, in which a mass-based party of committed nationalist militants, working in uneasy but effective collaboration with traditional elites, abandons democratic liberties and pursues with redemptive violence and without ethical or legal restraints goals of internal cleansing and external expansion.[2]

Paxton identifies five particular stages in a movement becoming a fascist state apparatus, describing how ideas amorphous and minor move beyond their own internal logic and take on the qualities we call fascism. The first stage is the "intellectual exploration" and the discovery of national myths, which take root because of the current system's failure. Next, an arrival to power as conservatives align with ideological fascists; the exercise of that power as they take over institutions of the state; and the final radicalization as the state, now taken totally by the project, moves toward militancy.[3] The early stage, where the hardcore fascist ideologues cultivate relationships with conservatives and left dissidents inside of a larger populist movement, is illustrative of the role that the Alt Right has played in the larger Trump surge. That raw ideology could battle for hegemony, relying on elite leadership to unite the factions, but fascists, when they take power, behave differently than their purist ideological propositions. This is how a fascist ideology erupts into a wave, taking state power and becoming capable of enacting a vision of systemic social upheaval. The fascist rise then requires a unity with populism, the anguished masses looking to place blame. Antifascist author Chip Berlet notes that Right-wing populism can act as both a

---

2   Robert Paxton, *The Anatomy of Fascism* (New York: Vintage Books, 2005), 218.
3   Robert Paxton, "The Five Stages of Fascism," 1–23.

precursor and a building block of fascism, "with anti-elitist conspir-acism and ethnocentric scapegoating as shared elements."[4] Fascism needs populism to cross over from ideology to mass behavior. This describes the process of interwar fascism in Europe well and provides deep insights for what process could take place in the contemporary world, as right populism provides an opportunity for the intellectual development and the right-wing coalition necessary for state infiltration. We would have to look further, however, to see the ideological core of fascism. This is more critical today as fascism remains not just a threat in the seizure of state power, but as a *minority* movement that battles the left for hegemony. Fascism today is something that becomes intensely ideological because it is not de-veloped out of the compromises of electoral coalitions, state poli-cy, or active international warfare. Instead, it is an *idea that people choose*, a radicalism that develops out of the crisis of modern tension and strife. Plainly put: fascism challenges the radical left about who owns the right to dissent, to provide a radical analysis, and develop a revolutionary program. Fascism's primary component parts are: the essential identities and inequalities, the violence fascists rest their im-pulses on, the revolution they require, and fascism's ability to adopt new ideas and adapt to changing social environments.

Generics

The search for what is called "generic fascism" has been ongoing since the Second World War. Does the Third Reich serve as a model even though it gave in to suicidal imperialism and a genocidal flurry of ethnic rage? Is the Iron Guard the perfect example even though it suppressed all other points to their prime enemy, "the international Jew?" Does Mussolini define the term since he invented it, though his racial policies were less pronounced than most? Does National Shinto in Japan provide a proper model even though its religious nature and distinct cultural landscape makes it unique?

The journey, instead, has been to find a clean definition that would encompass all historical instances and, by virtue of its de-scriptive qualities, begin to rope in more recent movements, putting small insurrectionary movements on the same ideological footing

---

4   Chip Berlet, "Populism as Core Element of Fascism," Political Research As-sociates, December 21, 2016, http://www.politicalresearch.org/2016/12/21/populism-as-core-element-of-fascism/#sthash.L6ZwkyJK.ews9xw3H.dpbs.

as those that terrorized Europe. Many want to define fascism as a specifically interwar project, describing it in terms of its state policies, aesthetics, and particular aims—a definition that presumably leaves it in the past as no movements of any consequence match the National Socialist German Workers' Party (NSDAP) or Italian Fascist Party directly. For many far-right philosophers, like Alt Right co-founder and former paleoconservative professor Paul Gottfried, fascism was merely a brief political project that attempted to reclaim the "True Right." That right, he asserts, is in opposition to the "false right" that makes up much of American conservatism.[5] Gottfried would agree with Hawley that American conservatism has been made up, primarily, of three elements: hawkish foreign policy, free market economics, and conservative social ideas defined, largely, by Christianity. But how does conservatism relate to human equality?

Roger Griffin presents a concise, intensely ideological term to define fascism: "palingenetic ultranationalism."[6] His definition, which was taken up broadly by what is referred to as the "new consensus," rejected the view popular in academia that fascism is defined by its structural qualities, those unique to World War II, instead of its ideological core. Instead of having a perfect generic example, Griffin identified the ideological types that are shared across cultures and time periods, using the theory of "ideological morphology." Originally proposed by Michael Freeman, ideological morphology looks at what defining features a broad set of specific ideologies needs to be "recognizable." This means the aesthetics, style, and organizational form does not define it, but rather the ideological qualities that can be shared broadly, in entirely different contexts. Fascism then is a form of extreme nationalism, broadly defined, that bases itself on a mythological past that a group intends to return to.[7] This term does not reflect state policies, whether authoritarian or libertarian, because all of those are subservient to its meta-politics. The fascist project is not about achieving totalitarianism, it is about reclaiming

---

5   Richard Spencer and Paul Gottfried, "What Is Fascism?" podcast audio, *Radix Journal*, MP3, 36:15, January 3, 2014, http://www.radixjournal.com/podcast/2014/1/3/what-is-fascism.

6   The more complete description from Griffin of the "ideal type" of fascism actually reads: "Fascism is a political ideology whose mythic core in its various permutations is a palingenetic form of populist ultra-nationalism." Roger Griffin, *The Nature of Fascism* (London: Pinter, 1991), 26.

7   Roger Griffin, "Fascism's New Faces (and New Facelessness) in the 'post-fascist' Epoch," *Our Fascist Century: Essays by Roger Griffin*, ed. Matthew Feldman et al. (New York: Palgrave Macmillan, 2008), 181–88.

the mythological identity and order, and if totalitarian means are the way to get there then so be it. The fascist projects of the past have used authoritarian political parties as their avenue to power as well as command economies to see a vision through, but all of that was due to their situation and political climate. In the modern fascist movement, a whole range of political possibilities are welcome, as long as they share a (somewhat) agreed-upon vision of the essentials.

Fascism Viewed from the Left

I present an alternative to the popular and innacurate view of fascism: Fascism is what many on the right have argued is the "True Right." While many movements on the ostensible right make equality a lower priority, such as the submission of equality to market liberty—whether as plain market fundamentalism or the extremes of "anarcho-capitalism"—they rarely agree that inequality is a sacrament. In contrast, inside of fascism inequality is explicit, as is identity. At the same time, I define fascism not from the center but from the left.[8] A definition of fascism needs to remain vital and evolving and must provide examples and understanding that is useful not only for historical tracking, but counter-organizing and resistance. To do this I develop a definition of fascism that is broader, one that includes the various strands that connect to each other. Proto-fascism, para-fascism, right populism, and others, can be identified as movements that do not meet the definitive rigor of *fascism* but are aptly targeted by antifascists since they are a proven part of the fascist progression. For those who identify as antifascists, these groups can be thought of as concentric circles, movements that are using the same logic as fascism without filling out its entire ideological checklist. While most movements that I discuss do not use the term "fascism" to define themselves, they either fit its definition perfectly (the Alt Right) or flirt with it so openly (the militia movement) that they can be seen as ideological allies.

In keeping with Roger Griffin's project to outline a key rhetorical definition for fascism, I offer one that, though seemingly universal, does have its own problems, as finding the perfect terminology to define all fascist movements may be a quest without end:

---

8   While up to debate and inquiry, I am broadly defining the left as movements toward greater equality. The way that is interpreted and manifested is hugely divergent, yet that attempt at social and economic quality is what defines various left movements from liberal democracy to socialism and anarchism.

"Inequality through mythological and essentialized identity" is an attempt to sum all of these threads up, hitting the various points that fascism uses to define itself.

Inequality

Standing before the London Forum in 2012, Richard Spencer said that the defining characteristic of the Alt Right was inequality. "We hold these truths to be self-evident, that all men were created unequal," he said, making a clear break with the foundational document of American political independence that the conservative movement clings to as their moral authority.[9] For fascists across the board, the defining factor of their ideology is more than the conservative de-emphasis of equality: inequality, for them, is critical, crucial, and correct. They believe that people are of different abilities and skills, qualities and characteristics, and that those differences should be ranked vertically, not horizontally. How this inequality is interpreted often shifts between different schools of thought and political movements, but they often take antiquated notions about race, gender, sexual orientation, national origin, body type, and other qualities to show that groups of people, defined in a myriad of ways, can be ranked as "better or worse." Even between those groups, such as inside of the "white race," people are not seen as fundamentally equal. Equality is a social lie that leads to an unhealthy society where the weak rule over the strong through democracy. In a properly stratified society an elite of some kind would have authority over the unwashed masses, though the way this authority plays out is so radically diffuse in contemporary fascism that there is no universally agreed upon blueprint. While identity is central to this constructed inequality, there is a heavy focus on analyzing and ranking abilities, from the size of biceps to the numbers generated from outdated IQ tests.

Populism

It is impossible to have fascism, either as a semi-coherent ideology or a movement, without some element of right-wing populism. This could take the form of anti-elitism, ranging from opposition to international

---

9 Richard Spencer, "The American Right: Can Americans Be Conservatives?" (Speech, London, U.K., November 8, 2012), Traditional Group Britain, https://www.youtube.com/watch?v=DSSKSK1ZHdI.

banks to perceived tribal elites as is true in anti-Semitic conspiracy theories. This anti-elitism plays into the revolutionary character of fascism, adds to its appeal to the working class, and is an attack on the left and the bourgeoisie. As will be mentioned later, this attack on elites is not an attack on elitism as such, as fascism, in the way we define it here, requires an elite caste of some sort. In the political sense, populism is the force by which hard fascist ideologues gain traction to move their political voice onto the national stage, often riding the same inspiring forces that the left does, such as labor issues, environmental catastrophe, and war. While this may seem a force used opportunistically by the ideological fascist contingent—such as explicit neo-Nazis or the Alt Right—there is an element of this right populism, the "common man against the elites," that is present even in the most reasoned and consistent fascist political thought, from the German Conservative Revolution to the French New Right. Fascism is particularly modern this way, even though it is a repudiation of that modernity, since it requires a mass movement and could not have been possible in an age before mass politics.[10]

Identity

Identity is the second part of our proposed definition, in which I use the amorphous qualifier "essentialized." Identity is a crucial part of the fascist project, but it is primarily not a chosen identity. Instead, they argue, identity is something that moves far beyond nominal politics, social signifiers, and cultural attitudes. Identity can be something that echoes from deep in your past, the "story of your people," a national myth, a tribal uniform. This is why race has been the most common form of identity that fascists consider crucial and also underlines the importance that racism still has in Western society. For identity adherents, race informs their past, who they are related to, who they should have allegiance to, and it drives their personality, intelligence, and vices. Gender, in the same way, should also be seen as essential, and traditional gender roles are not social constructs but universal truths that dictate our path. To reject our racial and gender identities as guiding forces is then to reject nature. While fascism, as an invention of the modern world, has often relied on vulgar scientism to define these racial and gender arguments, there are spiritual and metaphysical ones that run parallel as well.

---

10   Robert Paxton, *The Anatomy of Fascism*, 218.

Inequality has to be pinpointed through identity: who you are, rather than what you do. You are a certain race, gender, and national ethnicity, and so those should define your place in a hierarchy and in the groups with which you have affinity. While race is often a major fault line for the boundaries of this identity, there are broader cultural-linguistic ethnocentrisms that can take hold of this, especially when a multicultural nation lacks any central history of monoracial uniformity.

Revolution

The term "revolution" shares the same troubling confluence of definitions, finding little commonality beyond the fact that it is a great "shuffling off" of the past. This is a good place for us to start and to suggest that we define revolution as any attempt to undermine, destroy, and replace fundamental social institutions. In the traditional Marxist-Leninist understanding this meant the taking over of one class by the other, a forced proletarianization of the ruling classes, and a destruction (to a degree) of state infrastructure so a counter-state can be built and run by—and for—the workers (in theory, at least, to increase equality). As J. Sakai says, the fascist revolutionary project is less about the fundamental change in the functions of society and more about how they can use those functions, or replacements, as a vessel for themselves.

> By "revolutionary" the left has always meant overthrowing capitalism and building a socialist or communal or anarchist society. Fascism is not revolutionary in that sense, although it may use those words. Fascism is revolutionary in a simpler use of the word. It intends to seize State power for itself.[11]

Fascists have less ideological consistency because no fascist thinker has created a grand hegemony in thought that defined the movement henceforth. Instead, we can comfortably say that fascism is a revolutionary project, but how that revolution plays out is fiercely debated. At the bare minimum, it is an undermining of the foundational ideas of Western democracy, rejecting the idea that the

---

11   Don Hamerquist, J Sakai, and Mark Salotte, *Confronting Fascism* (Chicago: Anti-Racist Action Chicago, Arsenal Magazine, and Kersplebedeb Publishing, 2002), 55.

people, generally, can rule themselves. If the fascist project intends to see imperial state power as a mechanism for achieving their ends (inequality through essentialized identity), then it could have more in common with the Marxist-Leninist conception of revolution. In this case, it would be destroying the elements of the liberal state in order to further embody a state created to enforce tribal interests and inequality. For non-state fascists, whom I will get to later, it may mean a revolution to destroy the current order and make space for the creation of ethnocentric tribal communities that can then battle for hegemony (or trade, depending on who is in charge). Whatever the distinct vision, the fascist idea is radical; it wants to see systemic change. It does not just want to reinforce the tacit inequality and structural oppression that exists inside of capitalist states; it wants to build a society where inequality and bigotry are explicitly endorsed. This requires a complete reordering of society, even if it is simply giving in to ideas that have been implicit to Western colonialism and white supremacy for centuries.

Elitism

While the "führer" principle is part and parcel of a fascist movement, it can be leadership outside of state or party functions. This brings us back to the idea of institutionalized hierarchy, with an aristocratic elite forming in a variety of ways. In the work of proto-fascist jurist and Nazi-sympathizer Carl Schmitt, liberal democracy must "suspend democracy" in order to continue the project of democracy. Figures of supreme importance move through liberal modern societies past its laws and regulations so as to prop up the illusion that mass rule is maintained, but if democracy were to remain pure, it would collapse under the weight of its own inherent inequalities. Fascism drops the illusion that extralegal authority needs to be banned and instead concludes that the actions of dominant figures should be done by virtue of their superior spirit rather than the mandate of the common man. The central idea here is that some people are superior and that a ruling caste must be established in all levels of social arrangement.

Cult of Tradition

From the fascist view of history, identities are only forged through the mythological belief that there is a tradition that must be returned to. In author Umberto Eco's quest to find the principles of "Eternal Fascism," he identifies the "Cult of Tradition" as the most essential quality of fascism, where a desire to return to a "tradition," which may or may not be true in the literal sense, is a reaction to modern developments like logic, science, or democracy.[12] As we will see with the esoteric spiritual beliefs that color fascist movements, far-right authors like Julius Evola have outlined the idea that there is an underlying tradition of hierarchy inside all of the world's societies and religions. The belief that there is a tradition that must be reclaimed is essential to the revolutionary rightist mission. Fascism is a particularly modernist concept, one that attempts to take the ideas of industry, technology, and futurism, and apply a reactionary understanding of society to it. Fascists often see themselves as trying to reclaim something that is natural, normal, and ever-present throughout history. This means theorizing how a proper society works after all of the modern "degeneracies" are cast off.

The Colonization of the Left

While this is discussed more thoroughly below, one key element of a fascist project is the adoption of politics associated with the left.[13] From deep ecological mysticism that motivated aspects of German nationalism through the takeover by the NSDAP to the anti-imperialist rhetoric of anti-Semitic conspiracy theorists, fascist ideologues need this left-right crossover in order to develop a "new synthesis" that does not play by the conventionally understood left–right political spectrum. This should more appropriately be seen as a right takeover of the left: the use of leftist political tactics and strategies to push the core right-wing meta-politics of inequality and essential identity. If the left uses "state socialism" to enforce equality, the tools of which are command economics and state intervention, then fascism will use a mirror of those state systems to sanctify inequality and tribal privilege. If the left uses anti-colonial struggle to confront the ongoing attack on indigenous communities, then the right will use parallel ideas like indigenous sovereignty and the reclamation of ethnic identity as an argument for white separatism and racial advocacy. While the left develops tools to meet certain larger

---

12   Umberto Eco, "UR-Fascism," *New York Review of Books* 42, No. 11 (June 22, 1995), http://www.nybooks.com/articles/1995/06/22/ur-fascism/.
13   See "Tribe and Tradition" chapter.

goals, fascism uniformly attempts to capture those methods for far different results.

Violence and Authority

Violence is often cited as a defining feature of fascism, by combining the immediatist nihilism of Mussolini's early movement with the sober revelations of Nazi extermination plans into a coherent understanding. Violence is and remains a significant component of fascism, but much of this derives from the idea that the alienating effects of modernity must be smashed, and that mythic warrior societies show a path forward, especially for the veneration of "masculinity." It is this discontent with the pathological boredom of industrial capitalism that has historically created some of its broadest appeals to the left, as well as some of its most pernicious sacrifices of human life and dignity. At the same time, while political authoritarianism may not be a defining feature of fascism, the appeal to some sort of authority, from aristocratic rule to physical "Übermensch," is essential to guiding the unwashed masses.

* * *

Another defining feature of fascism is that it will constantly redefine itsel. It will not resurrect (successfully) the fascist movements of the past, but it will always appeal to the uniqueness of countries, cultures, and contemporary technological and scientific developments. It adapts to religious perspectives, the drive toward ecological conservation, the fear of imperial domination, the regrets of Western colonialism, and the leftist language of national liberation, cultural appropriation, and anti-racism. Fascism necessitates the adoption of elements of the left, as mentioned, and as its opposition shifts and the colors of art and human expression evolve, it will find new vessels for its mission to reimagine the human experience. Fascism is not about politics, it is about consequences, the results of the choices that people make, whether in the halls of power or in the quiet musings where people determine who they are. Fascism grows in the arts, in poetry, in philosophy, in spirituality, in the formation of community bonds, and the ways we see ourselves. Politics is only the public manifestation of a cosmic shift in attitudes and values. In all the ways that inequality is sanctified, that boundaries are made dividing personhood and the struggle for democracy and equality are undermined, a tradition of the "True Right" is establishing its grip on society.

A Great European Ethnostate

The game of rebranding fascism over multiple generations is a war over words. Though contemporary nationalists try to allege that "white supremacy" was a smear term invented by the left, it was used for years by the racist right to describe their own views. The Ku Klux Klan (KKK) often defined their ideology this way, whether they meant the literal supremacy of their race over others or the need to make their race supreme in "their" country. The KKK's allegiance to racial nationalism and inequality places them in the larger history of American fascist movements, even if they have not fit the label in every incarnation. Today I use the term "white supremacy" as a nomenclature to remind people that no matter how fascists self-define, their ideology is still rooted in feelings of supremacy and the historic legacy of white colonialism.

For years there was an effort to rebrand white fascism as "white separatism," a term that had a short life since it fails to actually explain their strategic endgame. While nationalists want to be separate from other races, they do not just mean this in the strategic segregation that marked the Jim Crow South. Instead they want a country that is wholly for "their people"—white people of European descent. They want to think and feel of themselves *as a nation*.

In the 1990s, the term "white nationalism" became popular, and it has continued to live on as the best descriptor of their ideology. This term was rooted in leftist discourse, at its heart taking from black nationalism and indigenous nationalist movements that sought to reclaim identities that were stolen. White nationalists also believed their identity had been stolen from them, even if it was their system of colonialism that "built" the multiracial, "modern" nation-state they were now at war with. Part of this strategic turn was to develop the concept of "white identity politics," where they intend to shift politics from a tool for social organization to one of ethnic advocacy. The term became ubiquitous, appearing in a range of tendencies, from more moderate-appearing fascist organizations all the way to insurrectionary Nazi militias.

White nationalism centers on the concept of the white Ethnostate: a country that would attempt to define itself in racial terms since, they argue, a nation is a "distinct people." Historically the "nation" has been defined in a whole host of ways, including tribal, religious, customary, and in various combinations and completely arbitrary divisions. They would establish an ethnostate that redefines nationhood as "pan-European," one that sees all European white people as sharing a common ancestry, identity, genetic heritage, and now, destiny. For those in America this means an ethnostate on the North American continent since they believe that the U.S., as well as most of Latin America and Canada, is actually the creation of white people born out of their genetic uniqueness. This biological determinism argues that civilizations are the result of the biological qualities of those who built them. Even if the civilization was built on the backs of First Nations peoples and with the hands of chattel slaves, the oppressed constituencies do not own it in any fundamental way. Since they also believe that this civilization was built on a biologically determined intelligence and social personality, they also believe that people of color would be unable to maintain it without the strong hand of white authority.[1]

White nationalists, despite claims that their politics are singularly about white nationhood, include other elements of fascist politics, such as a focus on innate inequality, the necessity of group identity, the need for a "cult of violence," traditional gender roles, a war on sexual minorities, and a disdain for the cosmopolitan ideas of modernity. What their name instructs, more than anything, is that race remains primary. As long-time white nationalist activist Sam Dickson said at the 2015 *American Renaissance* conference, their ethnostate will make race primary before all the other issues are ironed out:

---

1   A broad history and analysis of American white nationalism is Leonard Zeskind, *Blood and Politics* (New York: Farrar, Straus and Giroux, 2009).

Our ethnostate will not be a meeting of the Tea Party; it's not going to be the Southern Baptist Convention. It's going to be a genuine ethnostate with Christians, Catholics, alcoholics, teetotalers, gay people—it's not going to be a subset of the right.[2]

They argue their perspective is about *identity* before ideology, and that identity is rooted materially and spiritually in race. Today the artificial construct of whiteness overwhelms other forms of ethnic identity as they look for some type of "Pan-European" unity, dissolving the argument that their racial caste system is traditional in any way.

A Different Starting Point

The term "Alt Right" has flooded through the media and into public consciousness with controversies like the "Cuckservative" meme and as a hanger-on to the 2015–2016 Donald Trump Presidential campaign. Ideologically, Alt Right is identical to the ideas expressed earlier as white nationalism, and when pressed to be more specific about what they believe, almost all Alt Right people identify themselves as white nationalists.[3] There is a direct continuity between almost every institution and dominant figure in the Alt Right to the long history of fascist and white nationalist organizing in America. While many would like to believe that this is a new phenomenon, or that it is simply made up of iconoclastic trolls bucking "political correctness," the primary differences between the Alt Right and earlier stages of white supremacist organizing is technology and their generation. This is the Millennial version of white nationalist radicalization occurring on internet message boards like 4Chan and /pol/ and with a first language of hashtags and memes. It must be understood that white nationalism is the ideology, while Alt Right is the brand.

The development of what is called the Alt Right today can be traced back to the paleoconservatism of the 1980s and 1990s.[4] This

---

2   Sam Dickson, "Become Who We Are: The Tragedy of Southern Identity" (speech, Washington D.C., October 31, 2015), The National Policy Institute Conference 2016, https://www.youtube.com/watch?v=hrrvJg06xgA.

3   While Alt Right leaders like Richard Spencer don't prefer "white nationalism" because it is too tainted and associated with the more working-class white nationalist organizations of the 1990s, other leaders like Greg Johnson, Jazzhands McFeels, and Matthew Heimbach almost prefer it when the title of Alt Right is under threat.

4   Paleoconservatism, as will be outlined in more detail later, is an approach to conservatism that stressed American Nationalism, isolationism, economic

movement inside of political conservatism originated as a reaction to the post-Reagan era of GOP politics that was shifting toward foreign intervention through Neoconservatism.[5] Paleoconservatism, which was closely allied with the libertarian movement of people like Murray Rothbard, wanted to "reclaim" a mythic conservatism of the American past, associated with the pre-World War II "Old Right." Isolationist in foreign policy, it took an "America First" approach of economic nationalism, and was versed in social inequality and dog-whistle racial divisions. Pat Buchanan was the figure most associated with the movement, and others drifted further toward white nationalism when paleoconservatism faded from conservative discourse. Today we still have many publications that came out of this movement, such as *Chronicles* and Buchanan's *American Conservative*.[6]

It was at *American Conservative* that one ambitious young writer got his start, coming on as an assistant arts editor to replace someone who left because of one contributor, Steve Sailer, and his racist ideas about racial differences in intelligence. Richard Spencer was a PhD student at Duke University before publisher Scott McConnell plucked him to go work at the *American Conservative*. Spencer came from a well-to-do Republican family in Dallas, Texas, and went on to study classics and edgy right-wing philosophy during a University of Chicago master's program. He used an essay on the Nazi-sympathetic jurist philosopher Carl Schmitt to get into Duke, where he intended to focus on Western philosophic history, particularly people like Friedrich Nietzsche and movements like the German Conservative Revolution that built on twentieth-century German nationalism.[7] As he slowly drifted to the right, including on race and the "Jewish Question," Spencer did a presentation on the Duke lacrosse case where he argued that the university's faculty was willing to "turn on the white students" who were accused of sexually assaulting a black sex worker.[8]

---

protectionism, extreme social conservatism, agrarianism, and reactionary racial politics. It grew in the 1980s in a response to the growing hegemony of Neoconservatism in the GOP.

5   Sam Francis, "The Paleo Persuasion" *The American Conservative*, December 16, 2002, http://www.theamericanconservative.com/articles/the-paleo-persuasion/.

6   Hawley, *Right-Wing Critics of American Conservatism*, 179–81, 186, 190–93.

7   Richard Spencer, interview with author, September 14, 2016.

8   Richard Spencer, Roman Bernard, Colin Liddell, and Andy Nowicki, *Become Who You Are*, podcast audio, *The Radix Journal*, MP3, 2:05:00,

It was this presentation that got him the job at the *American Conservative*, but after he was further radicalized, he became the editor of the controversial paleoconservative publication *Taki's Magazine*. There, Spencer started to edge into his racial views and to create a safe space for the fringes of acceptable conservatism, publishing racial dissidents like *VDare* founder Peter Brimelow and "race realist" Jared Taylor and co-hosting a podcast with the "Southern Avenger" Jack Hunter. Along with Paul Gottfried, he became involved with the proto-white nationalist H.L. Mencken Club, which hosted speeches on "aristocratic elites," revisiting the history of the Second World War and the reclaiming of white identity.

In this new community, Spencer began seeing a diverse constellation of dissident right-wing views, including radical traditionalist Catholics, Southern nationalists, white nationalists, ethnic pagans, "natural order" conservatives, National Anarchists, and others. Though there were differences in these right-wing ideologies, they represented a different starting point from the rest of American conservatism. That starting point was the innate belief that human beings were different and unequal.

Spencer started *Alternative Right* as a webzine in 2010, and hosted a lot of the same people from *Taki's Magazine* as well as people associated with the European New Right and others in the pseudo-intellectual consortium of fascist movements that intersected with the Alternative Right. This included blogs from Tomislav Sunic, author of *Against Democracy and Equality*, articles on race differences in intelligence and the question of "Jewish power," and a podcast that acted as a central hub for interviews and conversation on the movement.

Spencer took over the NPI, a non-profit that was formed around the ideas of Sam Francis, a former paleoconservative writer for the *Washington Post* who drifted into explicit white nationalism and was fired from the *Post* for speaking at a 1994 *American Renaissance* conference.[9] He became incredibly influential, given his Republican pedigree and crossover cultural status, influencing everyone from hardcore neo-Nazis to Republican pundits like Ann Coulter.[10] Francis

---

April 29, 2013, http://www.radixjournal.com/podcast/podcast/2013/4/29/become-who-you-are.

9   Howard Kurtz, "Washington Times Clips Its Right Wing," *The Washington Post*, October 19, 1995.

10   Hatewatch Staff, "Ann Coulter – A White Nationalist in the Mainstream?" *The Southern Poverty Law Center*, May 27, 2015, https://www.splcenter.org/hatewatch/2015/05/28/ann-coulter-%E2%80%93-white-nationalist-mainstream.

died in 2005, leaving the organization without leadership until Spencer took it over in an effort to create a central hub for these New Right politics. He took over Washington Summit Publishers, the publishing wing of the operation, and started pumping out books on racial science and fascist political theory. Spencer eventually left *Alternative Right* to form the *Radix Journal* under the NPI umbrella, creating a webzine that has become a central aesthetic and ideological force for the growing Alt Right. He has continued to remain a key voice within the movement, hosting the *Radix Journal Podcast* with the same style of banter that made *Alternative Right* so popular.

NPI conferences have become hip suit-and-tie gatherings for the more "middle class" Alt Right movement. They now host hundreds of attendees twice a year, with speeches from movement celebrities, gourmet meals, and entertainment from neofolk bands. Spencer has led the movement's development, becoming well known in the media in tandem with the term "Alt Right." With a well-cropped "fashy" haircut and high-priced suits, both funded by his inherited cotton plantations and by William Regnery of the Regnery Publishing family, Spencer has set out to make fascism attractive and to articulate his views against a twenty-four-hour cycle of media scrutiny.[11]

Today the term "Alt Right" has that "big tent" meaning that Spencer had hoped for, and it includes the tentacles of various forms of white nationalism and fascist politics that feed from a global network of far-right movements. Because it has continued to rope in various segments of the nationalist movement, it has developed its own jargon and priorities—both online and in actual social communities—which almost always center on the idea that "race is real" and the foundation of identity.

#AltRight

What's different between the Alt Right's early years and its popularity today is not ideological, but instead its heavy focus on internet-savvy behavior. A young, white male army of keyboard warriors take the words of the ideological academics, shorten them, make them snarky, and turn them into memes. The results are appealing to the tech community and are posted and shared on internal message boards. Today

---

11   Josh Harkinson, "Meet the Dapper White Nationalist Who Wins Even if Trump Loses," *Mother Jones*, October 27, 2016, http://www.motherjones.com/politics/2016/10/richard-spencer-trump-alt-right-white-nationalist.

the culture of the Alt Right, which often tries to boil down talking points and troll opponents into submission, is the modernization of the ideas that were developed starting in 2010. The most concerted of this cultural shift is the "memedom" of the new Alt Right, where their ideas have been digitized in an ironic social media echo chamber. Internal jargon, cartoon characters, and 80s-style synth-pop aesthetics make their message of racial nationalism and state terror more appealing and easier to transmit.

A few publications and organizations have risen to the top of this new Alt Right world. The *Radix Journal* and NPI remain leaders but the *Daily Shoah* is the largest game-changer for the Alt Right as it helped developed their style and language. Working a Holocaust joke right into their title, they set out to be an "Opie and Anthony" style "shock jock" show for white nationalists. They mix in audio skits, parody songs, and interviews with fast-paced, jokey conversations laden with racial slurs and anti-Semitism. They developed their own list of terms, often appropriated from the left, and they invented memes like "Cuckservative" and the (((Echo))) signifier to try to identify Jewish-sounding last names in their opponents. Their popularity has led to dozens of similar podcasts, including in their own network, and has defined some of the largest growth for the Alt Right. Their message boards became the "who's who" of the movement and they have moved on to having regional meetings and groups centered around their constituents, which is made up primarily of libertarians who went fascist after the failure of Ron Paul in 2012.

VDare, known previously for being a right-wing anti-immigration publication that had a range of voices, has taken on a special importance in this new Alt Right world. Started by former *Forbes* contributor Peter Brimelow, *VDare* came to fruition after Brimelow turned his anger away from the American Federation of Teachers and toward the immigration system. In 1995, he authored *Alien Nation*, which effectively cemented him in the immigration-restrictionist subculture, and he went on to name his new website after Virginia Dare, the first English child granted "Birthright Citizenship" after she was born. *VDare* has given voice to the Alt Right's prime political focus—halting non-white immigration—and has given open white nationalists a place to mingle with the harder edge of conventional conservatism.

For those who found the aggressive racism of the *Daily Shoah* too light, *The Daily Stormer* linked up the "1488 crowd"—the more traditional neo-Nazis—with the newest generation of the Alt Right. *The Daily Stormer* and its founder Andrew Anglin set out to have a snarky and angry tone on the website's rapid-fire blogging. They combined the Alt Right's style with explicit neo-Nazism, bringing the more working-class white nationalists together with the upper-middle-class Alt Right. The website described itself as "pro-genocide," as it dissents from much of the separatism of the Alt Right, and is generally in support of open race war, as well as possibly reclaiming historical colonial empires in the Global South.[12] Anglin's constant blogging made him one of the loudest voices on the Alt Right, even if the more moderate personalities prefer he wasn't. His alliance with the notorious hacker and troll Weev (Andrew Auernheimer) has afforded them a certain amount of celebrity for their stunts, such as hacking the printers at hundreds of colleges and printing out flyers advertising *The Daily Stormer* and mentioning the pernicious Jewish threat.[13]

The Dark Enlightenment

If the Alt Right were Protestant Christianity, then Neoreaction would be Mormonism. Developed by tech impresario Curtis Yarvin under the pseudonym Mencius Moldbug, Neoreaction takes a more academic tone and discusses the world as a disease lacking in order due to its egalitarianism, democracy, and lack of technocratic hierarchies. Also called the Dark Enlightenment, Neoreaction rose to popularity in Silicon Valley with Moldbug leading the charge and far-right philosopher Nick Land expanding its theory. The movement rejects the Enlightenment values that shifted in society with the French Revolution and often leans toward traditional monarchism or various forms of elitist rule. Usually passivist when it comes to political matters, they align with much of the perennial Traditionalist philosophy.[14] Neoreaction labels dominant intellectual institutions,

12   "Meet the Exterminationist Wing of the Alt Right Who Is Open About Wanting to Kill Jews and Non-Whites," *Anti-Fascist News*, April 3, 3027, https://antifascistnews.net/2017/04/03/meet-the-exterminationist-wing-of-the-alt-right-who-is-open-about-wanting-to-kill-jews-and-non-whites/.

13   Alexandra Markovich, "Hacker Says He Printed Anti-Semitic and Racist Fliers at Colleges Across U.S," *New York Times*, March 28, 2016, http://www.nytimes.com/2016/03/29/nyregion/hacker-weev-says-he-printed-anti-semitic-and-racist-fliers-at-colleges-across-us.html?_r=0.

14   Traditionalism in this definition is a set of ideas about the universal transcendent nature of the world's religious traditions, which come from a single "divine

such as elite universities, as "The Cathedral," the institutions that define the moral perspective of a given society. They share the Alt Right's "Race Realism" and intensive belief in social hierarchy, but their focus on Calvinism, their religious and socio-economic jargon, and tech-utopianism often creates its own subculture that usually camps outside the "big tent" of the Alt Right.[15] That being said, the crossovers are consistent, and publications like *The Right Stuff* went through a Neoreaction period. Prominent Neoreaction podcasts like *Ascending the Tower* will often have Alt Right guests, though their focus is usually on arcane topics like the role of Kabbalah in modern Judaism or the traditionalist aspects of Catholicism.

Pro-White

Throughout the Alt Right's literature is an obsession with what they call a cultural system of "anti-whiteness," where white guilt has replaced white identity. The intellectual core of the Alt Right is the logical evolution of white nationalism, taking its queues from European and Russian nationalist intellectuals, and then popularizing them as best they can. Journals like the *Occidental Quarterly,* an academic-presenting white nationalist journal, set the standard for this before the Alt Right caught on, yet their republishing of European New Right (ENR) figures and articles on "white guilt" and Jewish influence hold a standard ideological line across all the disparate factions. The ENR, including its prime philosopher Alain de Benoist, a nationalist academic who developed a canon of fascist aesthetics and ideas, was the main thrust for the ideological core of the Alt Right. While avoiding much of the vulgar racialism and militarism of traditional fascism, the ENR created a fascist cultural theory that saw the need for racial separatism and "traditional" social order, and was influenced by a range of far-rightist and esoteric philosophers who run completely opposed to the free market Christianity of American conservatism. Though heady in its infancy, the Alt Right quickly found that by boiling down the ENR's key points to their essence, stripping them of academic language, and slapping on the irony and vulgar racism of the American male, they could popularize their ideas.

---

source." This includes the hierarchies, authorities, and chains of initiation.

15   Alexander Scott, "Reactionary Philosophy In An Enormous, Planet-Sized Nutshell," *Slate Star Codex*, March 3, 2013, https://slatestarcodex.com/2013/03/03/reactionary-philosophy-in-an-enormous-planet-sized-nutshell/.

Ironic Pepe the Frog memes replaced the swastikas, and their conversation points often sound more like tech-class debater-speak than someone likely to lace up the jackboots. Many on the left, used to looking for conventional fascist iconography, were confused. This looked more like the culture of teen angst and irony than what they had associated with neo-fascist terrorism, but the content was the same. Their use of social media, which allows them mass outreach equal to that of major political figures, enabled their #Cuckservative hashtag—meant to signify conservatives who worked "against their own interests" on immigration—to go global.[16]

The Alt Right's growth from 2015 forward came from a hijacking of internet troll and message board cultures, harnessing the anger of the Manosphere, and racializing it. The Twitter trolling and meme wars were given depth by the Alternative Right, and together they created an operation whose effect was to make white nationalism so ever-present that it was normalized as a part of the political spectrum. They shifted the Overton window and the "shock and awe" of these racialist ideas has faded, handing them part of their strategic victory.

A study during the growth of the Twitter "shitlords," showed a 600 percent increase, over four years, in white nationalist accounts. In an analysis of 10,000 Trump supporters, one-third also followed these figures. While the Alt Right's foot soldiers were developing their own social culture on message boards, it was Trump's tweet-mania that hand delivered them to an audience less equipped to decode their jargon. By taking the antagonistic tone that was popularized at sites like 4Chan, as well as exploiting misinformation on "black crime" and immigration, Trump used his incredible access to mass opinion to echo the points of identity and inequality that the Alt Right had crafted over years.[17]

16   Bob Steinberg, "Cuckservatives, Trump, and the Future of the West," *The Right Stuff*, July 23, 2015, http://therightstuff.biz/2015/07/23/cuckservatives -trump-and-the-future-of-the-west/.
17   Josh Harkinson, "Make America Hate Again" *Mother Jones* (February 2017): 25–26.

"Race Realism" and the Jewish Question

The modern fascist project has always been centered on race, even if it is intersectional and attempts to tie multiple threads of identity into a coherent worldview. Deepening the role of race in history, science, and culture is critical for white nationalists since it reframes the narrative about the progression of world civilization and the relationship between cause and effect, colonizer and colonized. In a certain sense, fascists attempt to mirror a Marxist materialist analysis of the development of history by replacing class relations with ethnicity and ethnic conflict. In this understanding, all of history and the uniqueness of societies and cultures are the genetic result of the people who they believe built them.[1] In this way, Europe, with its imposing cathedrals and Faustian drive to conquer nations, is distinctly the result of the genetic composition of Europeans, the historically white indigenous people. Sub-Saharan Black Africans, who have one of the longest histories of European colonialism and brutal chattel enslavement, are also canonized in this narrative: their biology makes them less intelligent, more prone to "uncivilized" behavior, and gives them little restraint over their baser sexual urges. The white nationalist narrative about race is always changing and rarely consistent, but it does attempt to explain a whole host of human distinctions and historical events, from the horror of tribal cruelties to the calligraphic pen stroke of languages.

---

1   These claims are usually ahistorical and whitewash the actual complex histories of national development.

Ethnic conflict, then, tells the story of nations, which fascists say are a distinct people and therefore the seed that developed premodern nation-states. Slavery, with its central role in the development of Western capitalism, was just the inevitable result of the conflict between races that arises when they battle for access to resources. This narrative, while re-crafted in recent years, was developed in the earliest parts of the twentieth century as Social Darwinists attempted to hammer together a crude reading of evolution that would extend the "survival of the fittest" notion to racial groups. During this period "racial scientists" attempted to develop a Nordic model that created a racial hierarchy even within European racial groups, placing Northern Europeans above Southern and Central Europeans, and culminating in racial hygiene laws, eugenics research, and strategic ethnic cleansing.[2]

The discourse that comes out of contemporary white nationalism attempts to sanitize the historic role of "race science," stripping away much of the value-laden language and tries to make it sound like legitimate science that is no longer discussed widely because of "political correctness."[3] The heart of this is race and IQ arguments, the belief that IQ, to a large part, is fixed in the genetic structure of an individual and is hereditary.[4] While white Europeans have traditionally been placed at the top of this invented racial ladder, modern discourse has shifted this a bit. Now, East Asians are often placed above whites, then going down through Latin- and African-descended peoples and, at the bottom of the ladder, Australian Aborigines. Ashkenazi Jews sit at the top of the ladder, lending to the idea that their tribal intelligence is leading whites toward enslavement. Whites are then framed as "just right," with Asian high intelligence sometimes eroding other qualities, and African low intelligence leading to violence, promiscuity, and an inability to manage "civilization." IQ differences have been easily explained through

---

2   Chip Berlet and Matthew N. Lyons, *Right-Wing Populism in America: Too Close for Comfort* (New York, London: The Guilford Press, 2000), 91–95.

3   Using one or two particular examples of this reasoning strips it of its meaning as this is the fundamental logic that publications like *American Renaissance* used starting in 1990 into the 2000s. The idea that "legitimate science" has been suppressed because of "political correctness" has been a foundational idea of "Race Realism" and "Human Biological Diversity." This is expounded heavily in the *American Renaissance* newsletter of the 1990s, blogs like *HBD Chick*, or the work of racialist paleoconservative author Steve Sailer.

4   Race realists would dispute this characterization as a simplification. Instead, they would simply say that the "nature/nurture" argument lies far more in the direction of nature than nurture, especially when compared to mainstream science.

environmental factors, including diet, social class, historic oppression, and different types of cultural intelligence, all of which proves how a social construct like race informs reality through its social systems rather than biology.[5]

Rejecting a hundred years of social science, they argue that black people, for example, have high testosterone and low IQ, which leads to a higher propensity for aggression and, therefore, criminality. This ignores studies that prove that, holding for economics and conditions, there is no distinct propensity for crime in black populations. Instead, their thinking plays on long-held stereotypes of the black predator, especially the "sexual nature" of black men. It suggests the frightened role attributed to white women—who they believe are always at risk of being devoured by monstrous black sexuality—in this racial order. This worldview also helps them to strip complex narratives away from discussions about crime, returning it to the racial determinism at the heart of white nationalism.

Studies in "Racial Science"

While much of this sounds easily refutable, these ideas have had success in crossing over into mainstream discourse. Fringe academics made their careers on pushing this discredited racist science in the academy and it has made its way into scientific journals and stuffy conferences, confusing the public about the scientific consensus on this issue. In 1994, a flurry of controversy erupted as Charles Murray and Richard Herrnstein released *The Bell Curve*, a book that argued that IQ often determined class and wealth. This Intelligence Quotient, they believed, was more fixed than previously realized, and within that framework some racial groups were not believed to have as statistically high intelligence. Much of the research, such as twin-studies from the 1970s, was funded by white nationalist foundations such as the Pioneer Fund and researched by discredited academics. Nonetheless, many in the psychology world got behind the book, even if they did not agree with its more controversial claims, and Murray went on to be one of the most-read conservatives in academia.[6]

---

5   Richard Nisbett, Joshua Aronson, Clancy Bair, William Dickens, James Flynn, Diane F. Halpern, and Eric Turkheimber, "Group Differences in I.Q. Are Best Understood as Environmental in Origin," *American Psychologist* (September 2012): 503–4.

6   Linda Gottfredson, "Mainstream Science on Intelligence: An Editorial with 52 Signatories, History, and Bibliography," *Intelligence* 24, No. 1 (1997): 13–23.

More recently, former *New York Times* science journalist Nicholas Wade published *A Troublesome Inheritance*, a popular book on evolutionary biology that topped non-fiction bestseller lists. The book outlined the "recent evolution" of distinct "sub-populations," ascribing many qualities of culture to the biology of the containing nationalities. While it avoided some of the intelligence claims found in *The Bell Curve*, it did ascribe attributes like sociability and family structure to this ethnic determinism. The white nationalist community roundly hailed the book, with NPI doing a special podcast episode about it.[7] Wade went on to be interviewed in race realist publication *American Renaissance,* where the interviewer, Jared Taylor, is well known for his vulgar ideas about race and IQ.[8]

Though racial science was standard throughout the physical sciences since the early days of the colonial U.S., it was challenged after the horrors of World War II became known, and modern scientific studies discredited the claims about racial differences. But that does not mean some academics looked past the mountains of data to find "proof" to aid their own racial ideas.

One of the best known of these is Arthur Jensen, an educational psychologist who focused on the "genetic factor of intelligence" in young school children. He believed that intelligence was largely inherited and that the IQ gap between white students and students of color may be from a lower genetic predilection toward intelligence. When he published his paper, "How Much Can We Boost IQ and Scholastic Achievement?" in 1969, students and faculty protested and demanded the paper never be republished (though it is still republished by racialist activists).[9] The paper itself went on to become one of the most cited in psychological academia, and the genetic essentialism that it lent to questions of intelligence was often referred to as "Jensenism." As Dr. Richard Nisbett has observed in his refutations of Jensen and other racialist scientists' work on the subject, the studies cited use only indirect correlations between heredity and intelligence; there is no correlation between European admixture and

---

7   Richard Spencer, John Derbyshire, and Paul Gottfried, *Human Nature Denial*, The National Report, MP3, 29:27, May 20, 2013, https://player.fm/series/the-national-report-the-national-policy-institute.

8   Jared Taylor and Nicholas Wade, *A Troublesome Inheritance: A Conversation With Nicholas Wade*, American Renaissance, MP3, 45:59, October 31, 2014, https://www.amren.com/news/2014/10/a-troublesome-inheritance-a-conversation-with-nicholas-wade/.

9   Arthur Jensen, "How Much Can We Boost IQ and Scholastic Achievement?" *Harvard Education Review* 39, No. 1 (1969): 1–123.

increased intelligence in biracial people socialized as "black," and the adoption studies used to show intelligence performance gaps in similar socialization situations have been discredited by later studies using a more rigorous set of analytics. IQ itself is malleable, which is demonstrated most clearly by the "Flynn Effect," which shows that IQs have risen over the last hundred years as access to education and technology increased.[10] Over its life the Pioneer Fund's primary purpose was not the funding of Jensen's work itself, but rather the creation of materials explicating the work and the distribution of those to other academics and the general public. Jensen's work was never really about scientific inquiry, nor was he known for his academic rigor, but instead he used the most basic amount of data to create a propaganda model meant to recruit to openly racialist political aims like maintaining segregation, fighting against school busing, and destroying affirmative action.[11]

Richard Lynn made these ideas more central to his work and argued that the world itself could be measured by IQ differences. He suggested that nations could be scored by average IQs, which would reflect their measure of success.[12] Lynn has attempted to ride his work into the public consciousness by connecting it with contemporary controversies, like by naming his book *The Global Bell Curve*. His work builds on the same arguments as Murray and Jensen, and argues that technological discovery, national development, and wealth can be broken down internationally to the intelligence of those in the countries themselves. Africa, which has some of the poorest and most "undeveloped" nations, is so because of their low innate IQ, while East Asians have the cities with the highest IQ populations. Lynn still edits *Mankind Quarterly*, the journal of the neo-Nazi-leaning Pioneer Fund, who has been funding research to prove racial differences for the past eighty years. While his ideas were used heavily in books like *The Bell Curve*, his inclusion into any scientific publication is enough to measure the text unusable considering how he has manipulated data and results. While he may not be popular among career academics, his work has become

---

10   Richard Nisbett, "Heredity, Environment, and Race Differences in IQ: A Commentary on Rushton and Jensen (2005)," *Psychology, Public Policy, and Law* 11, No. 2 (2005): 302–10.

11   Robert Sussman, *The Myth of Race: The Troubling Persistence of an Unscientific Idea* (Cambridge, Massachusetts: Harvard University Press, 2016), 235–42.

12   Edward Dutton, "Review: Race Differences in Intelligence: An Evolutionary Analysis, 2nd Revised Edition (Lynn, R.)" *Mankind Quarterly* 56, No. 3 (2016): 615–18.

foundational to the Alt Right, and Richard Spencer has used it to outline a worldview where non-whites will destroy technological society if left to their own devices.[13]

While there have been many contributors, no one has been more central to the creation of modern racialist science than British import to French Canada, J. Philippe Rushton. Rushton has been so pervasive because of the singular obsession that drove his many studies, such as testing the IQ similarities between twins raised in different home environments in an attempt to prove the hereditarian nature of intelligence and its resulting effects on racial differences in cognition. His entire career was centered on this pursuit, intermixing Pioneer Fund research to prove that intelligence is largely genetic, and, within that, its evolution was both recent and regional.[14] Rushton theorizes that Northern Europeans gain their "high intelligence" from the difficult terrain, where they were forced to endure tough conditions that forced them to develop a high IQ. The Kung! Bushmen and Australian Aborigines were thought to then have a dramatically low innate IQ because they had a forgiving environment. (This is patently untrue to anyone who knows about the geographic area they inhabit.[15]) At the same time, Rushton proposed the idea that "kinship," or supposed genetic similarity, is a driving factor in human development, a notion that white nationalists now use to justify tribalism as a primary factor in "genetic survival," or the impulse to prioritize those thought to have similar genetics to them.[16] Though the hardline racial theorists in this school of thought rarely discuss the role of Jews, many white nationalists allege that Rushton was open with them personally about the "role of Jews in the anti-white political system." Rushton was rejected by academia, dramatically so in the case where geneticist David Suzuki famously dismantled every one of his major theories in a public debate. Mountains of peer-reviewed work has dissolved his thesis, and many of his ideas

---

13   Richard Spencer, "Towards a New Nationalism," National Policy Institute, September 10, 2011, https://www.youtube.com/watch?v=ALvH_jsTlx0.

14   Philippe Rushton and Arthur Jensen, "Thirty Years of Research on Race Differences in Cognitive Ability" *Psychology, Public Policy, and Law* 11, No. 2 (2005): 235–94.

15   Joseph Graves, "The Misuse of Life History Theory: J. P. Rushton and the Pseudoscience of Racial Hierarchy," in *Race and Intelligence: Separating Science From Myth*, ed. Jefferson M. Fish Jr. (Mahwah, NJ: Lawrence Erlbaum Associates Inc., 2017), 68–69.

16   Philippe Rushton, *Race, Evolution, and Behavior: A Life History Perspective* (New Brunswick: Transaction Publishers, 1997).

did not go much beyond the conversational, intended as they were not to make cogent scientific arguments but instead to sway a non-academic audience with their intellectual veneer.[17]

Conservative political commentator Steve Sailer made a major development in this "race realist" perspective by popularizing the term "human biological diversity" (HBD). What HBD says is that human beings are dramatically different, from their varying vulnerability to disease to the allegation that people from Kenya have a superior running ability. Sailer resurrects old racial science arguments to suggest that recent evolution presents dramatic human differences, like arguing that people of African descent have different brain structures that make them unable to survive well in European cultures.[18] HBD has existed in the void created by the absence of a general discussion of eugenic and scientific racist ideas in education, as well as in the discussions that border this in the mapping of the human genome, the popularity of national origin tests by places like 23 and Me, and the use of ethnic origin in determining health risks. Since most people have little education in how racial differences actually play out, the outrageous HBD claims have allowed the more bizarre race realist assertions to gain traction in the imaginations of online audiences. Sailer's work, while influential in this sphere, has seen no scientific backing (he himself is not a career scientist), and instead he has been removed from almost all organs of mainstream commentary.

Jared Taylor is the ringleader of this contemporary movement of scientific racism because he created a central hub for this tract of thought, packaging it for the Alt Right generation. Taylor began his career as a racialist by writing a book on the failure of race relations in the 1980s before forming, in 1990, *American Renaissance* (*AmRen*), a newsletter that publishes articles on race and IQ, arguments

---

17   Rushton has produced papers with people like Donald Templar, a man whose racist speeches are so offensive that they would make KKK members blush (they are available on YouTube). There he would argue that since some species with dark fur have a propensity for aggression, perhaps black skin in humans is likewise a signal of a genetic propensity for aggression. While this was published in an academic journal, there is no research correlation made, just wild conjecture. Yet, the goal was to reach a non-scientific audience and to capture those already with a racialist mind-set, and so papers like these continue to serve their purpose.

18   HBD is a term that has been popularized in the pseudoscience blogosphere and has not gained traction in actual academic circles. The "HBD sphere" generally encompasses perceived psychological differences between men and women, differences between races and between ethnicities within races, eugenics, and racial history, none of which is validated by mainstream academics.

against immigration, and positions in favor of homogeneous white societies. He held the first *AmRen* conference in 1994, and today it remains one of the largest white nationalist gatherings in the U.S., bringing together speakers that (they feel) have a shred of respectability, like Rushton, Sam Francis, and European nationalist politicians. Unlike many of these conferences and publications, Taylor has, until recently, not professed any anti-Semitism, and often likes to say, "[Jews] look white to me!" He has included in his conferences Jewish academics and religious extremists, like race and IQ advocate and CUNY professor Michael Levin and the ethno-nationalist Rabbi Mayer Schiller.[19] While Taylor may be the most crude of this contingent of academic racists, he is the most honest. The logical conclusions of the ideas represented by the lot—that white people are genetically superior—is up front in *AmRen*, and its contributors grab at any shred of "evidence" they have available to create an academic-sounding narrative about racial determinism.

The Tribe

While racial science itself has been central to the growth of white nationalism, giving it the appearance of respectability and academic legitimacy, anti-Semitism has also seen a revival, despite its long history of genocide and embarrassing conspiracy theory. For years anti-Semites have focused on "edge" issues like using Holocaust Denial inside of conspiracy circles or playing on the anger against Israeli atrocities on Palestinians to stoke anti-Jewish hatred. The Alt Right has attempted to revive arguments deep from the past using new language: Jews are tribal, have a secret agenda, control institutions, and have a high intelligence that they use to act as parasites on host populations.[20]

The central figure in the creation of a unified theory of anti-Semitism is former University of California at Long Beach evolutionary psychology professor Kevin MacDonald. After making a name for himself in the fields of psychological development in wolf populations and childhood development, he published a three-volume "Culture of Critique" series that outlined a theory of Jewish

---

19   Leonard Zeskind, *Blood and Politics*, 367–75.
20   Shane Burley, "Anti-Semitism in the White House: Stephen Bannon, Donald Trump, and the Alt Right," *Truthout*, November 20, 2016, http://www.truth-out .org/news/item/38412-anti-semitism-in-the-white-house-stephen-bannon-donald-trump-and-the-alt-right.

development, naming Judaism as a "group evolutionary strategy."[21] He argued that Jews developed a high "verbal IQ" through endogamy and tribal cohesion and created an internal ideology to protect their in-group at the cost of the Gentiles.[22] Jews then entered host countries and infected them with their false ideologies, which are designed to dismantle the "healthy racial consciousness" of those nations while keeping Jews intact.[23] One reason for this is the historic role of anti-Semitism, which they attempt to counter by siding with "mass immigration" and cultural forms of "degeneracy" such as sexual promiscuity, pornography, and homosexuality. MacDonald traces back the role of Jews in the civil rights movement and immigration reform, as well as their role in the development of early capitalism, socialism, Boasian anthropology, Freudian psychoanalysis, Frankfurt School Marxism, and feminism, arguing that these are Jewish concepts that undermine Western nations.

Within this discourse, the term "cultural marxism" has gained the most steam. This is the idea that the Frankfurt School theorists have completely reshaped the values of our current society. Though their ideas may not have made a conscious impact, the theory goes that they infested academia with Critical Theory and applied Marxist ideas of equality to cultural issues. This is cited as a "Jewish" way of thinking, to rip apart the foundational ideas of Western identity and to fill whites with the false consciousness of turmoil.[24] It is alleged that the concept of class struggle, of the proletariat against the bourgeois owners of capital, was reframed as the "oppressed" against the "oppressor" after Jews failed to have the successes they wanted through orthodox Marxism. MacDonald, and most white nationalists and Alt Righters, suggests that this was an "anti-white" concept to undermine whiteness, ascribing all socially progressive ideas to a kind of intellectual Jewish Bolshevism. This plays on every one of

---

21 MacDonald's trilogy is the "*Das Kapital* of anti-Semitism" in the modern racialist movement, becoming increasingly radical as the volumes have progressed. These include Kevin MacDonald, *A People That Shall Dwell Alone* (San Jose: Writers Club Press, 2002); Kevin MacDonald, *Separation and Its Discontents* (Westport, Conn.: Praeger, 1998); Kevin MacDonald, *The Culture Of Critique* (Bloomington, IN: 1stBooks, 2002).

22 MacDonald, *A People That Shall Dwell Alone*, 253–340.

23 MacDonald, *The Culture of Critique*, 304–30.

24 Bill Berkowitz, "Reframing the Enemy: 'Cultural Marxism,' a conspiracy theory with an anti-Semitic twist, is being pushed by much of the American Right," Southern Poverty Law Center, February 7, 2004, http://web.archive.org/web/20040207095318/http://www.splcenter.org/intel/intelreport/article.jsp?aid=53.

the anti-Semitic theories of the past hundred years, as all forms of Marxism have been labeled a Jewish conspiracy since the Russian Revolution of 1917.

The specter of the Holocaust returns again and again for anti-Semites, especially when it is alleged that Jews have inordinate power in the world. In the decades since the Second World War, white nationalists have attempted to shuffle off the burden of the Holocaust in the public imagination by constructing elaborate claims about its purported hoax.[25] Through the 1990s, organizations like the Institute for Historical Review, the Barnes Review, and the Committee for Open Debate on the Holocaust attempted to win by casting doubt on well-known facts about the Holocaust of European Jewry. This failed to win them the gains that they had hoped, and since 2000 there has been a dramatic decline in these institutions, with major Holocaust revisionists coming out and saying the debate has been lost.[26]

A new discourse has begun to be propounded, one that reframes the discussion about the Holocaust. Instead of trying to prove the absence of gas chambers or debating the number murdered, it is largely about ethnic determinism. White nationalists, including Kevin MacDonald, argue that something like the Holocaust is just the result of racial conflict, which is inevitable when you have a hostile population like Jews stoking animosity inside of white nations. A form of "soft denial" happens in that they deny the historical importance of the Holocaust, instead suggesting that Jews have consciously reframed a normal act of war so that their suffering could take on the appearance of disproportionate suffering and therefore offer them a cultural and material benefit. This idea has even seeped into left-wing discourse, where some inside of Palestinian solidarity movements attempt to challenge the narrative of Jewish suffering as a proxy for going after the legitimacy of the Israeli state.[27]

The "Jewish Question" is central to the Alt Right, with Jews taking on a particularly vicious role in their ideological hatred. The Alt Right internet culture has taken to trying to identify Jewish commentators, and relate all non-favorable political development to the

---

25   The most definitive book on the development of Holocaust Denial up to the 1990s is Deborah Lipstadt, *Denying the Holocaust* (New York: Free Press, 1993).

26   Mark Weber, "How Relevant Is Holocaust Revisionism?" Institute for Historical Review, January 7, 2009, http://www.ihr.org/weber_revisionism_jan09.html.

27   "Holocaust Denial and Distortion," *Palestinian Media Watch*, http://www.palwatch.org/main.aspx?fi=650.

influence of Jews, adding a sense of insult and comedy to their racial victimization. The *Daily Shoah* helped to develop the (((echo))) meme, where they use echoes on Jewish sounding last names or cultural developments they think are rooted in Jewish influence. In text, they put parenthesis around Jewish names, and an associate even released a Google Chrome plug-in that automatically puts those "echoes" on Jewish last names.[28]

Holocaust Denial began to make huge gains as a large portion of Holocaust survivors were passing away, stripping their narratives from a living story. What deniers hoped to do was attack people with twisted evidence and fabricated data, with the understanding that most people do not have the historical evidence handy to shut down these claims empirically. When you mix this confusing rhetoric with a culture of mistrust for the media and educational institutions, you get conspiracy theories, and it is in this ecosystem that a pernicious doubt can be sowed about the history of Jewish suffering.

---

28   Cooper Flieshman and Anthony Smith, "Neo-Nazis Are Targeting Victims Online with This Secret Symbol Hidden in Plain Sight," Tech.*Mic*, June 1, 2016, https://mic.com/articles/144228/echoes-exposed-the-secret-symbol-neo-nazis -use-to-target-jews-online#.Qy16i3W7z.

Misogyny

Milo's act had been so disseminated into the culture that everyone knew what to expect when he burst onto the stage. Milo Yiannopoulos had become a fast celebrity after his reactionary rants at *Breitbart* and social media trolling made him an icon in an angry male counterculture. As he stepped to the podium against a wall of music and cheers, donned with pearls and bright designer clothing, he did not look like a figure that could send a crowd of twentysomething men roaring. You'd wonder if his mildly effeminate style, flamboyant personality, and open references to queer sexuality might put off a crowd of Alt Right ideologues, but he had two things going for him: he was a man, and he was gunning for women. As Milo says,

> No matter how you look at it, Feminism is Cancer. Some of you might call me radiation therapy. But the analogy is bad. Radiation therapy damages normal tissue in a desperate attempt to kill cancer.[1]

While his act was meant to take aim at the "pop feminism" of liberal social media, he grounded shock-jock jokes about modern women into a politic older than his audience. His jabs directed at women were not meant for casual laughter, but instead to ease the audience into open misogyny. This wasn't about hating feminists it was about hating women.

---

1   Milo Yiannopoulos, "Full Text: Milo on How Feminism Hurts Men and Women," *Breitbart*, October 7, 2016, http://www.breitbart.com/milo/2016/10/07/full-text-milo-feminism-auburn/.

Over time, as Milo Yiannopoulos was pressed in interviews, the jokes were dropped and replaced by talking points intended to go after the issues of inequality popularized by the women's movement since the 1960s:

> Moral panic about "rape culture" has led to gross violations of due process against male students on campus, who can now be hauled before campus kangaroo courts to answer charges of sexual assault with no adequate legal representation and very low burdens of proof. This isn't about protecting women. It's about man-hating.[2]

As campus movements against rape grow, and the culture of violent patriarchy is targeted, the backlash from male privilege mimics white rage. Milo's shtick is new only in that it takes on the syncretic and frenetic style of the internet culture wars: he was both gay-identified and anti-woman, a combination the media took years to comprehend. While Milo is not a full-fledged member of the Alt Right (instead he is more correctly labeled "Alt Light," a term I will get into later), he takes on some of the most vicious elements of misogyny from fascists, spouting it with a wink on college campuses that have cradled him with fawning applause. The same cauldron that created the Alt Right's newly branded white nationalism created an even more broad institution before it, the various strands that are called the "Manosphere," or simply the rediscovery of violent femme-hatred that defines the far-right.

And a Future for White Children

White nationalism has always been an intensely patriarchal institution because its approach to social relationships is about the resurrection of authoritarian control and mythic traditions. The enforced roles of female subjugation are part and parcel of the project, whereby women in modern society are seen to have been robbed of their "essence" and role in the natural order of gender relations. The atomic family is central to white nationalism in that reproduction—the increase of white populations—is the means by which they gain demographic dominance. As fascists like Richard Spencer

---

2   Milo Yiannopoulos, "Feminists and Progressives Attack College Football with More False Rape Statistics," January 6, 2016, http://www.breitbart.com/ sports/2016/01/06/feminists-and-progressives-attack-college-football-with-more-dodgy-rape-statistics/.

often point out, even if all non-white immigration were blocked, the white population would still lose hegemony in the U.S. through an imbalance in birth rates.[3] In European nations, when Middle Eastern immigrant neighborhoods outpace Caucasian reproduction, it signals to them that an invading nation is occupying and remolding their society. This obsession with non-white reproduction, fueled by their belief that non-white people are subhuman and controlled by baser sexual urges, is then cast onto white women because they have rejected their "proper" role as wife and mother due to degenerate liberalism, multiculturalism, and feminism. Roles and identities are essential; it is believed that they are fixed in biology and spirit. A woman's role is then for reproduction and the management of family and children, while a man's proper role is that of the warrior, conqueror, and the entrepreneur.

While the language is couched in traditionalism (the romanticism for their image of a traditional past) the idealism goes far beyond simply pining for classic gender roles. It is founded in the modern condition, in the belief that women have walked away from their identities and have staged rebellion on the proper social order.

Fascism in America has always found a role for white women, but it has always been one that was tangential to their male counterparts and decenters them from agency. The KKK of the 1920s, which became a massive political force around the country, created a Women's Auxiliary that focused heavily on the needs of maintaining the family and supporting their white husbands. Even in an institution like the Klan, there was a certain amount of contradiction as they even hosted speakers like Planned Parenthood founder Margaret Sanger, who spoke to them about birth control, which they allowed because they could present it from an anti-black eugenic perspective.[4]

The Alt Right has continued this patriarchal thinking as an essential part of their vision of human relations and the role of women in their movement. Part of this is due to the marginalized science of "Race Realism," extending their logic to gendered differences. Like African- and Latinx-descended people in relationship to white and Southeast Asian people, the Alt Right generally believes in a functional difference in brain capacity between men and women.

---

3   Richard Spencer, "Facing the Future as a Minority," Speech, *American Renaissance Conference*, March 2013, Montgomery Bell State Park, Tenessee, https://www.youtube.com/watch?v=FVgXJZ1ZXrI.

4   Kim LaCapria, "Klanned Parenthood," Snopes, September 30, 2015, http://www.snopes.com/margaret-sanger-kkk/.

Through "IQ realism," women are understood to have a lower capacity for intelligence than men, to be less capable of abstract and scientific thinking, and to not be well suited for professions like engineering, computer science, or research.[5] Beyond unproven scientism, this ranking stems from the pseudo-philosophical ideal of the gendered self: Women are thought to be incapable of revolutionary thinking; only men have the "Faustian spirit" to make revolutions, and women, because of their roles as nurturers, are more likely to side with existing power relationships instead of upturning the world. Richard Spencer uses this logic to justify the almost solely male character of the Alt Right, and the same logic defines the ideology of people like male-tribalist Jack Donovan. While the Alt Right was once self-conscious about its missing female contingent, it has recently increased its misogynist discourse as it recruits from online, male-centric communities.

> As the Alternative Right has grown, it has abandoned this kind of self-criticism and debate about gender politics. Going beyond traditionalist claims about the sanctity of the family and natural gender roles, Alt Rightists have embraced an intensely misogynistic ideology, portraying women as irrational, vindictive creatures who need and want men to rule over them and who should be stripped of any political role.[6]

This is a return to the deep anti-feminism that defines the right, the idea that women's liberation movements have been a war on the natural order of the world. This perception has marked the right for decades, yet the Alt Right and other fascist movements make it a defining feature. Anti-feminism has currency in hard-right circles

---

5   Historically, this has been a stop-over point for many on their way to "Race Realism." People like Jared Taylor and Richard Spencer never avoid this IQ realism, though they don't focus on it quite as much since race is their primary political target. Steve Sailer is more explicit about this since he focuses on the pseudo-psychology of "group differences." Since race and IQ arguments are still profoundly unpopular, many people walking that line between paleoconservatism and the Alt Light and explicit white nationalism have used this line of argumentation openly, such as *The Bell Curve* author Charles Murray or Proud Boys founder Gavin McInnis. Charles Murray, "Where are the Female Einsteins," *National Post* (Republished at the American Enterprise Institute), November 22, 2005, http://www.aei.org/publication/where-are-the-female-einsteins/.

6   Matthew N. Lyons, "Ctrl-Alt-Delete: An Anti-Fascist Report on the Alt Right," Political Research Associates, http://www.politicalresearch.org/2017/01/20/ctrl-alt-delete-report-on-the-alternative-right/.

near to the Alt Right because of the intense war on the women's movement since the 1970s, and so it easily acts as a point of community consensus and recruitment. People like Jack Donovan see feminism as a biological outgrowth of the female brain, a nesting instinct that has now manifested into the macro culture of corporate identity politics, therapeutic culture, and rigid social rules that constrict men who fear for loss of social status when behaving outside the bounds of "political correctness."

As Angela Nagle pointed out in her book *Kill All Normies*, the culture that constructed the Alt Right came from online message boards like 4Chan. An identity built on transgression has emerged, going to war with moral constraints, both of the historically rigid right and the increasingly difficult liberal identity politics of college campuses and social media platforms like Tumblr. The techno-utopia of the left, which came out of the use of social media during the Arab Spring and the hopeful possibilities of platforms like alternative currency and file sharing, led to an internal culture of anonymity and tech-extremism that was not really possible in radical circles until the technology was present. This culture ended up shifting dramatically to the far-right, beyond most people's expectations. On 4Chan, /Pol/, and other message boards, acts of transgression were sanctified, from the most offensive brands of pornography to racist and misogynist "jokes" that were taken to the extreme. This culture of nihilism was essentially apolitical; it was simply an act of tearing down the reproductive and establishment systems of power by which they felt constrained, a rebellion against the most trusted moral institutions of both the left and the right.[7]

Trolling was then an act of performance art, a sort of culture jamming, which went after figures of establishment power. Reactionaries filled this cultural vacuum, and anonymity and self-righteous anger was fueled by the growing inability to discern facts in the lightning-fast message board culture. The "ability of people in modern society to construct their entire social lives online" led to the development of a strange kind of person, the alienated white male who felt free to descend into blame.[8] The right then captured this apolitical rebellion, first by anti-feminist movements and then by the explicit racialism of the Alt Right.[9]

7   Angela Nagle, *Kill All Normies: Online Culture Wars From 4Chan and Tumblr to Trump and the Alt-Right* (Winchester, U.K.: Zero Books, 2017), 29–37.
8   David Neiwert, "Birth of the Alt Right," *The Public Eye* (Winter 2017): 5.
9   Ibid, 4–5.

Just as Spencer and the Alt Right believe, the Chan culture of internet rebellion sees women as silencers of this transgressive spirit. Women are agents of conformity as they depend on institutions of power, and they should not be allowed into these revolutionary circles, as they will undermine men's truly transgressive power. Women's role in consumerism is stereotyped and used as a way to show that they lack the independence to confront the system itself. The hatred of women is then couched in the spirit of anti-modernism, where women are seen as the vanguards of liberal capitalism, necessitating men to take the reigns of the iconoclastic movement.[10]

The New Misogyny
In the Alt Right, the real shift to open misogyny came from its relationship with the Manosphere, which was one of the mingling points that allowed it to appropriate and influence the radical online culture of 4Chan and the trollosphere. This broad collection of people, which the anti-Manosphere blog *We Hunted the Mammoth* refers to as the "New Misogyny," is a "big tent" group of blogs, commentators, and talking points that reclaims traditional patriarchy, is distrustful of women, and argues that men are persecuted by modern liberalism.[11] Since fascism is intersectional, it believes in recentering authority, privilege, and hierarchy in all the ways that people experience oppression; gender is one of those components. The Manosphere simply centers gender and is the gendered version of white supremacy, a male-supremacist movement aimed at subjugating women.

This movement is called Men's Rights Activism (MRA), and seeks to undo the "systemic inequality" toward men in society. They use manipulated statistics and news reports to argue that men are unfairly targeted by "systemic" false rape accusations, the out-of-balance legal system, and women's advantages in family court. They claim feminism and the pernicious work of women are the agents of some catastrophe rather than the impositions of capitalism and expectations of patriarchy. MRAs hope to undo the gains of the women's movement, especially the reforms made in the last few decades around divorce, rape reporting, and affirmative action.[12]

10   Angela Nagle, *Kill All Normies*, 114.
11   "FAQ," We Hunted the Mammoth, http://www.wehuntedthemammoth.com/faq/.
12   Mariah Blake, "Mad Men: Inside the Men's Rights Movement – and the Army of Misogynists and Trolls It Spawned," *Mother Jones*, January/February 2015,

Pick-up artists (PUA) have a somewhat different approach, built on similarly misread studies in evolutionary psychology, to present a picture of gender in which men must use their warrior instinct to essentially capture women for sex. Books like *The Game* and figures like Mystery, who gave workshops to socially inept men trying to learn how to talk women into sex, popularized these antics years earlier.[13] While those earlier incarnations were often more innocent, today's versions of the PUAs are openly hostile to women, treating them as subjects in a war of sexuality whereby men must conquer them in a sexual tryst. The PUA approach is somewhat different than the traditional view of women in the center of a monogamous family unit. They believe men are limited in the traditional nuclear family because of their allegiance to women. The value set of the PUA remains the same, a similar essentialist view of women, but their answer is for men to free themselves from the bonds of modern monogamy and to pursue their hedonistic desires against the wishes of the women who desperately hope to pin them down. Men Going Their Own Way (MGTOW) is a more extreme version of this logic. Their hatred of women has led them to voluntarily become celibate male-separatists. They create lives away from women since they believe women, as a group, are dedicated to the manipulation, exploitation, and forced servitude of men.[14] Within this trend there is a large collection of what is often referred to colloquially as "beta males," men that lack the "alpha" qualities of self-assuredness and outgoing personalities, and they hide in internet subcultures. They blame women collectively for their lot—angry that they refuse them sex, that they don't refuse them sex, or that they simply exist.[15]

---

http://www.motherjones.com/politics/2015/01/warren-farrell-mens-rights-movement-feminism-misogyny-trolls/.

13   Neil Strauss, *The Game: Penetrating the Secret Society of Pick-Up Artists* (New York: Harper Collins, 2005). Note: I will not extend the Manosphere to Strauss himself. *The Game* is more a story of his exploration through the subculture, and while many parts are problematic, he stands outside of that sphere as an author and speaker.
      Mystery was the flamboyant pick-up artist who came to fame in the early 2000s, known for many popular concepts in the dating world like "peacocking," the conscious dressing in notable clothing to signal to people in a social space that they are both open to engagement and are interesting. His methodology was designed on giving men tools for how to engage women, but would be considered incredibly tame by PUA's standards today.

14   Mack Lamoureux, "This Group of Straight Men Is Swearing Off Women," *Vice*, September 24, 2015, https://www.vice.com/en_us/article/inside-the-global-collective-of-straight-male-separatists.

15   Robyn Pennacchia, "'Beta Males' Want to Kill Women Because They Can't Get

Hiding Online

The culmination of this online hate had its debut in a controversy known as "Gamergate," in which feminist videogame commentator Anita Sarkeesian was attacked online for criticizing misogyny in the videogame world. Female gamers and journalists were trolled and threatened with some of the most shocking instances of cruelty, while the online Manosphere argued that, by taking part, they were simply upholding ethics in videogame journalism. The careers of Alt Light commentators like Milo, Mike Cernovich, and Vox Day were created during this period, and it crystalized this toxic online misogyny that saw women as the source of all social ills, most centrally the loss of male community and identity. What has developed here is not just a political distrust of women, but a violent misogyny centered in a spirit of vengeance, where maleness has been destroyed by the presence and agency of women, and only acts of violence can return things to normal.

The most common example of this is the trolling culture that victimizes female reporters and figures across the internet, often using threats of sexualized violence. The process of this is twofold, first, maintaining plausible deniability present in the transgressive nature of internet harassment, and second, reinforcing the traditional status of a woman by offering gendered retribution for her invasion into male spaces or roles. The subReddit, "The Philosophy of Rape," which took the Manosphere's rape culture to its logical extreme, was the center of this and, in part, caused people to think of sexual assault as an acceptable act; rape is both belittled and suggested as punishment in the Manosphere. Reddit, as the sort of "Wild West" of the mainstream internet, has been home to some of the most active Manosphere posting forums, including "The Red Pill," a term taken from *The Matrix* and used across the Manosphere and the Alt Right to indicate the process by which a "Normie" becomes conscious to the real anti-male, anti-white bias in modernity.[16] "The Philosophy of Rape" took this a step further by openly advocating for sexual assault on the grounds that it was biologically natural behavior for the Alpha Male, that women secretly enjoy it, and that sexually permissive or modern

---

Laid," *Bust*, February/March 2016, http://bust.com/feminism/15551-mo-beta
-blues.html.

16   Reddit has also become central to white nationalists and the Alt Rights with
     subReddit "communities" like "Coon Town," which hosted a couple dozen
     forums dedicated to "topics" like videos of black people being murdered.

women need to be re-educated through sexual violence.[17] The threats and culture of the Manosphere and Alt Right violence against women has had a chilling effect among feminist blogs and female presenters, and women like feminist author Jennifer McCreight have stopped writing altogether. (McCreight notes she wakes up everyday to "abusive comments, tweets, and emails about how I'm a slut, prude, ugly, fat, feminazi, retard, bitch, and cunt (just to name a few)... I just can't take it anymore."[18])

While some like to dismiss this behavior as the virtual fantasies of disaffected men, those fantasies have stepped offline. When Elliot Rodger entered the Isla Vista campus of the University of California at Santa Barbara, he was looking to take revenge on the women who rejected him. He took the time to write a 137-page manifesto and shoot a video of himself from his cellphone, propped up on the hood of his car, and uploaded it to YouTube under the name "Elliot Rodger's Retribution."

> You girls have never been attracted to me. I don't know why you girls aren't attracted to me but I will punish you all for it. It's an injustice, a crime because I don't know what you don't see in me, I'm the perfect guy and yet you throw yourselves at all these obnoxious men instead of me, the supreme gentleman. I will punish all of you for it. On the day of retribution, I am going to enter the hottest sorority house at UCSB and I will slaughter every single spoiled, stuck-up, blond slut I see inside there.[19]

Rodger had been a frequent contributor to Manosphere forums, identifying as an "InCel," or Involuntarily Celibate. Some of Rodger's inspiration likely came from another MRA killer, George Sodini, who murdered three women in an aerobics class and who has been hailed a hero by many Manosphere trolls online.[20] The *Return of the Kings*, a PUA and general MRA site known for its virulent misogyny, ran a story immediately after the incident arguing that no one would have died if Rodger had just learned how to pick up women for quick sex.

17   Mark Potok, "The 'Philosophy' of Rape," *The Intelligence Report* (Spring 2015).
18   Quoted by Nagle in *Kill All Normies*, 141.
19   Megan Garvey, "Transcript of the disturbing video 'Elliot Rodger Retribution,'" *LA Times*, May 24, 2014, http://www.latimes.com/local/lanow/la-me-ln-transcript-ucsb-shootings-video-20140524-story.html.
20   Susan Candioni, "Police: Gym shooter "had a lot of hatred for women, society," CNN, http://www.cnn.com/2009/CRIME/08/05/pennsylvania.gym.shooting/.

Until you give men like Rodger a way to have sex, either by encouraging them to learn game, seek out a Thai wife, or engage in legalized prostitution—three things that the American media and cultural elite venomously attack, it's inevitable for another massacre to occur.[21]

The article was penned by Roosh V, one of the leaders of this wing of the Manosphere, a man who has made his career by arguing that women need to simultaneously follow their traditional feminine roles and be sex objects for men to manipulate. In February of 2016, Roosh tried to set up a nationwide meet-up for *Return of the Kings* readers, the same sort of "IRL" (in real life) gathering that Alt Right followers of blogs like *The Right Stuff* have moved toward. In his article "How to Stop Rape," Roosh argued in favor of legalizing rape on private property, engendering protests at every meet-up location nation wide, forcing Roosh to indefinitely cancel the project.[22]

The white nationalist/Alt Right's relationship with the Manosphere has been tenuous, but they agree on the maintenance of patriarchy. The gendered dynamics proposed by the Manosphere play into their stratified, hierarchical social arrangements, as well as the establishment of essentialist gender qualities. The Manosphere's focus on rape, devaluing its reality culturally and making it a problem of "women" rather than male violence, has had mixed crossover. Many on the PUA side are rightly identified with sexual assault, and the Alt Right regularly rejects the members associated with miscegenation. When Matt Forney—a Manosphere blogger who shifted into writing for Alt Right outlets like Red Ice Radio—appeared in an interview with members of the white nationalist Traditionalist Worker Party (TWP), he was chastised for his work with Roosh V and *Return of the Kings*, with TWP member Matt Parrot saying that Roosh's treatment of women qualifies as rape. The core of the Alt Right often denigrates Roosh since he is Middle Eastern in ethnicity and regularly has sex with white women. Since the image of the "Muslim rape gang" is a common Alt Right meme—using misleading stories about sexual assault by refugee migrants in Northern European countries—they

21   Roosh Valizadeh, "No One Would Have Died if PUAHate Killer Elliot Rodger Learned Game," *Return of the Kings*, May 25, 2014, http://www.returnofkings.com/36135/no-one-would-have-died-if-pua-hate-killer-elliot-rodger-learned-game.

22   Adam Sherwin, "Roosh V: Protesters call for pro-rape 'pick-up artist' to be banned from UK," *The Independent*, February 2, 2016, http://www.independent.co.uk/news/people/roosh-v-protesters-call-for-pro-rape-pick-up-artist-to-be-banned-from-uk-a6849351.html.

use a reasonably feminist interpretation of sexual consent to establish Roosh as a conventional "Muslim rapist."

At the same time, the Alt Right largely reject the modern conception of what constitutes sexual assault as a "feminist legalism." Richard Spencer spoke about this at length after former Missouri Congressman Todd Akin said on television, as part of his anti-choice agenda, that a survivor's body would simply stop a pregnancy if they suffered a "legitimate rape." Spencer came to Akin's defense, arguing that there is a difference between forcible rape and the sexual assault that is commonly discussed on college campuses, saying these cases were actually situations of "morning after" regret and can only be seen as rape when put through a radical feminist lens about the myth of male violence.[23] This kind of rhetoric is shared across the Alt Right spectrum, with people like Mike Enoch, F. Roger Devlin, and Jack Donovan regularly discussing the fact that normal male sexuality is now framed as sexual victimization because of the distorting effects of cultural marxism.

Donovan argues that rape culture is actually the reframing of men's nature, and women use the weapon of their chastity to control male behavior, just as they did through chivalric codes. Claims of rape, then, are a power battle between the genders, one that women will win by contextualizing natural masculinity as socially taboo and framing it as sexual assault.[24]

Men Against the Ruins

While much of the Manosphere is homophobic and, particularly, transphobic, they and the Alt Right have made alliances with certain queer figures who revel in their own toxic masculinity. Jack Donovan's work is primarily about men rediscovering their "innate" tribal masculinity, including some who will live as warriors outside of the moderating effects of women. This queer misogyny tracks almost all negative effects of modernity back to feminine influences in the same way the transgressive core of the Chan sexism does, where men could follow the "way of the gang" most effectively if returned to the Kali Yuga by femininity.[25]

---

23   Richard Spencer and Andy Nowicki, "The Rape of Todd Akin," Vanguard Radio, August 23, 2012, http://www.radixjournal.com/podcast/podcast/210.

24   Jack Donovan, "Rape Culture Isn't About Sex, It's About Power," *Radix Journal*, May 25, 2014, http://www.radixjournal.com/journal/2014/5/25/rape-culture-isnt-about-sex-its-about-power.

25   As is discussed later, the Kali Yuga is the fourth, and last, cycle in the Vedic

Donovan's vision of tribalism is one of exclusivity that acts as a miniature form of nationalism, in which a type of *essential* affinity is the starting point for strict social boundaries. It is based on the perceived male capacity for caring and friendship, which he believes is limited to a small cadre.[26] Violence is sanctified here as it is what gives men their defining identity.

> Violence doesn't come from movies or video games or music. Violence comes from people. It's about time people woke up from their 1960s haze and started being honest about violence again. People are violent, and that's OK. You can't legislate it away or talk your way around it. Based on the available evidence, there's no reason to believe that world peace will ever be achieved, or that violence can ever be "stopped."[27]

This sacred violence draws from many areas of fascist thought, from the romantic nationalism of Yukio Mishima to the fields of dead soldiers in Ernst Junger novels. For Donovan and his ilk it is the commitment to real moments of violence, ones that tap into man's savage nature and define his personhood, allegiances, and value. What is colloquially called "toxic masculinity" today is preferred, a natural role that men need to rediscover or become subject to another man's authority—or worse, a woman's.

Donovan seeks a warrior cult whereby men have "hierarchy through meritocracy," and warriors govern society in the absence of troublesome woman. The ideas he outlined in *The Way of Men* were largely theoretical until he met his comrade Paul Waggener and joined the Wolves of Vinland, and now their fantasies of tribal in-group dynamics and "loyalty oaths" are being played out in chapters across the country.[28]

Cycle of ages. When used by fascist Traditionalists and philosophers, it uses this to describe the current age of decadence and decline where by humanity's natural hierarchies and authorities have been eroded by agents of modernity, such as feminism and egalitarianism.

26　Jack Donovan, "I Don't Care," *Radix Journal*, October 31, 2014, http://www.radixjournal.com/journal/2014/10/31/i-dont-care.

27　Jack Donovan, "Violence is Golden," Jack Donovan: Masculinity and Tribalism, March 15, 2011, http://www.jack-donovan.com/axis/2011/03/violence-is-golden/.

28　Jack Donovan, *The Way of Men* (Milwaukie, OR: Dissonant Hum, 2012). Matthew N. Lyons, "Cntrl-Alt-Delete: An Anti-Fascist Report on the Alt Right."

Gender Trouble

Whether in the annals of "Mars/Mars" tribes (warrior males who enjoy sexual companionship) or the back channels of the internet, special revulsion is held for transgender people. The Alt Right and MRAs think transwomen have a unique role in misogyny; they are seen as men who reject their natural roles and privileges and "voluntarily" become the hated "other." Trans people, in general, are discussed as the product of a decadent and diseased society—only a culture of consumer capitalism could create this type of individual. Donovan takes the notion that women are uniquely agents of consumerism further as he extends his theories to trans people, presenting them as creations of modernity that lose their gendered essence and act more as mechanical constructs than human beings. This methodology is repeated across the Alt Right, which wavers between portraying trans people as mentally ill or as pure ideology representing the ideas of modernity rather than the pure nature of "man" or "woman."[29]

Bohemians vs. White Knights

The order of masculinity in this New Right complex is divided between the chivalrous—which many MRA types call "white knighting" as an insult—and the more aggressive hatred and rejection of women. This disagreement is not just a confusion of perspective, but it is a frenetic contradiction. While women are seen as critically important for the social order and the proliferation of the race, they are also viewed as agents destroying civilization, identity, and the Faustian spirit to move to the stars (instead of to the Human Resources department).[30] This duality is not new for the right; acting in celebration of women while denying them equality, autonomy, and agency. The dramatic brazenness of the misogyny in the Manosphere and Alt Right also signal an additional break in beltway conservatism,

---

29   Jack Donovan, "That's Ms. Potato Head to You: Transexuality, Transhumanism, Transcendence, and Ecstatic Rights of Highly Conspicuous Consumerism," *Radix Journal*, September 26, 2014, http://www.radixjournal.com/journal/2014/9/26/thats-ms-potato-head-to-you.

30   This obsession with Faustian analogies has lead to a strange obsession with space exploration, especially the colonization of near planets. This romanticism extends distinctly to the early days of the American space program, highlighted most clearly in *Whitey on the Moon*, authored by Paul Kersey, the pseudo-anonymous author of a slew of white nationalist books and the blog *Stuff Black People Don't Like*.

which is still driven by its evangelical base and publicly denounces the sexual exploitation of women.[31]

One of the most vocal women on the Alt Right is Lana Lokteff, who is the wife of Henrik Palmgren and his co-host at Red Ice Creations. Her show, *Radio 3Fourteen*, is one of the most popular on the Alt Right circuit, and she is known for her blunt style and fervent racial nationalism, anti–political correctness, and opposition to feminism. In the same "Gramscian" mold of the Alt/European New Right, she sees a meta-political culture war against Marxism where, by asserting traditional gender roles, she premeditates the political institutions. Feminism drives the selfishness of capitalism since it disconnects women from their proper role in the family. As Sam Miller elucidates in *Jacobin*, this is a part of the re-centering of the natural order, which they believe is biological, a theory that has been destroyed by modern liberal democracies:

> This kind of family structure entails a natural hierarchy: though, as Lokteff admits, women ultimately decide if the race will continue, they are in fact auxiliary and must accept their inferiority to men. Once you believe that men are born as the dominant sex, then patriarchy becomes natural, normalized, even necessary: inferior women should be "taken care of" by men—a euphemism for subordination.[32]

The traditional order of things must be restored, and "white genocide" through immigration requires a full-community response to stop it.

Ayla, who is "Wife With a Purpose" on YouTube and maintains her Nordic Sunrise blog, goes further with her traditionalist model. A pagan for years—even writing a regular column in the liberal "Goddess worship" magazine *Sage Woman*—as time went on, Ayla moved further in the direction of folkish traditionalism. Drawing from Evola's concept that a true spiritual tradition is one that maintains a "Chain of Initiation," she turned to Mormonism, which she saw as the best maintenance of her race's customs and authority. She openly says that her primary racial duty is having children and supporting her husband, but, with people like Lotkeff, she has created a small cadre

---

31 The private behavior of conventional conservatives do differ, however, which can be see in how they deal with women's health, abortion access, the treatment of sex crimes, and the culture of sex shaming and coercion of women.

32 Sam Miller, "Lipstick Fascism," *Jacobin*, April 4, 2017, https://www.jacobinmag .com/2017/04/alt-right-lana-lokteff-racism-misogyny-women-feminism/.

of Alt Right women who are using internet outlets to focus their energy primarily on dismantling feminism and using the edge arguments about non-white sexual assault to recruit others.

Alt Right women often harness the internet culture of celebrity that the Alt Right despises in order to fulfill their agenda. There are strong contradictions about the role of women versus the benefit the Alt Right gets from women walking out of their strict gender role in order to recruit. Tila Tequila is the best example of this contradiction, not the least of which because she is non-white. After her shift into nationalist politics and internet trolling, she was brought on to podcasts like *Fash the Nation*, and invited to speak at the 2016 NPI conference, cementing the image that the Alt Right is actually about "nationalism for all peoples."[33] Tequila's celebrity draws from reality programming and, after she recently declared that the Earth is flat, she presents a problem for Alt Right institutions that see themselves as part of an elitist right-wing culture rather than the "click-bait" her appearance presents. Richard Spencer actually addressed this conflict head on, arguing that he was a realist who sees the value in capitulating with some aspects of modernity, and considered "what would Donald Trump do?" when booking her.[34]

Nasty Women

It surprises no one that the Alt Right and white nationalists as a whole denigrate anyone but a narrow type of "man" institutionally, but that is not something that is totally at odds with its more standard conservative counterparts. The "War on Women" has been a constant feature of conservatism since the creation of the *National Review*, in which policies and cultural practices that may benefit women are always presented as suspect, though discussed through political proxies. Trump's election was simply the most public validation of this perspective in years, and his history of alleged sexual improprieties, including allegations of forcible child sexual assault, were completely ignored by most of the voting public.[35] This extreme

---

33   "Reality Star Tila Tequila on Fash the Nation, Blames Jews, Immigrants, and 'Blacks,'" *Anti-Fascist News*, June 5, 2016, https://antifascistnews. net/2016/06/05/reality-star-tila-tequila-appears-on-fash-the-nation-blames-jews-immigrants-and-blacks/.

34   Richard Spencer, interview with author, September 14, 2016.

35   David Mikkelson, "Lawsuit Charges Donald Trump with Raping a 13-Year-Old Girl," Snopes, November 4, 2017, http://www.snopes.com/2016/06/23/ donald-trump-rape-lawsuit/.

type of 4Chan misogyny has gained acceptance, largely through their war of meta-politics, where the sillier aspects of liberalism are used to discredit the more revolutionary work of radical feminism and anti-oppression organizing. The increase in violent misogyny has had a material effect, as demonstrated by the targeting of women after the election results came in. Reports of men confronting women in the streets and "grabbing them by the pussy" were so numerous that they faded from news reports, and the threats and violence were exponentially increased if the subjects of this hatred were women of color. There were dozens of murderous threats, where black women were approached in public and told that all black people were to be killed now that Trump had "legalized" it.[36]

While the Alt Right's white supremacy was heavily reported on, its misogyny was absent from almost all reportage, and Manosphere figures were often treated with a "boys will be boys" attitude rather than correctly identifying them as male supremacists. Their violent misogyny went under the radar as it often does, because the white evangelical base that finally elected Trump had been floating on an almost open hatred of women since the earliest culture wars fought by the anti-feminists that built the Moral Majority after the *Roe v. Wade* decision. The disposability of women's healthcare, the strict policing of abortion and birth control access, and the unwillingness to acknowledge the pervasiveness of sexual assault is the institutionalization of this anti-women belief in practice, and it has only allowed an aggressive misogynist vanguard to use the language of the left to give the "war on women" a sharp edge. As Alex DiBraco notes, though "Trump's rhetoric reflects MRA vitriol, it is the long fight against feminism by groups embraced in the mainstream, like equity feminists and Republican women, that legitimized the candidacy—and election—of an overt misogynist who has bragged about sexual assault."[37]

This type of rhetoric seems like a screenshot from these internet message boards, but now the anonymity has been dropped and the most public politician in history has validated their violent rage. Trump has a reciprocal relationship with the Alt Right; their rise mirrored his, so they play off each other in the creation of a patriarchal

---

36   "Ten Days After: Harassment and Intimidation in the Aftermath of the Election," Southern Poverty Law Center, November 29, 2016, https://www.splcenter.org/20161129/ten-days-after-harassment-and-intimidation-aftermath-election#antiwoman.

37   Alex DiBraco, "Mobilizing Misogyny," *The Public Eye* (Winter 2017): 11–16.

meta-politic that places blame for eroding privilege on women. The answer to this, much like the response I will discuss for all avenues of fascist entry, is the development of a revolutionary feminist movement that takes on this gendered victimization and works in concert to confront the ways that fascism goes after the different dynamics of class composition.

Tribe and Tradition

Much of what drives white nationalism, from neo-Nazis to the Alt Right, is a belief in some form of "tradition" that emanates from the past. This concept is based on a false read of history, a mythology that nationalists tell themselves about heroism that exists only in stories meant to venerate their ancestry. Racially homogeneous communities are thought to be the way "traditional societies"—ones that center social organization on the family led by the husband and father—existed.

The term "traditionalism" is thrown around by fascists, but it comes from a marginal twentieth-century far-right mystic who became one of the most important figures in the world of white racialism. Julius Evola was an Italian perenialist philosopher whose writings on the various religious traditions, their hierarchies and institutions, outline what many think is the underlying "natural order," though many stray from Evola's worldview.[1] Coming out of Tantra, occultism, Vedic Hinduism, and intersecting esoteric orders, Evola believed that all religions came from a "single divine source," and what ran underneath religious systems was a basic "tradition." Hierarchy was viewed as sacrosanct, and he used the Vedic Cycle of Yugas to explain how society has degenerated from the Golden Age to the Kali Yuga, or Dark Age. In this current order, the "modern world," we have given over to our baser instincts, the common man rules instead of an aristocratic elite, and "lower races" are coming to dominate glorious white nations.[2]

---

1   "Perenialism" is a school of religious philosophy that sees all religions as having some transcendent truth.
2   Nicholas Goodrick-Clarke, *Black Sun: Aryan Cults, Esoteric Nazism and the Politics of Identity* (New York: New York University Press, 2002).

For many, Evola's worldview presents even a secular analysis for
the traditional society we should return to. The "radical traditionalist" journal *TYR* outlines its philosophy and hopes for society with
a few key points of "tradition,"

> Resacralization of the world versus materialism; folk/traditional
> culture versus mass culture; natural social order versus an artifi-
> cial hierarchy based on wealth; the tribal community versus the
> nation-state; stewardship of the earth versus the "maximization of
> the resources"; a harmonious relationship between men and wom-
> en versus the "war between the sexes"; handicrafts and artisanship
> versus industrial mass-production.[3]

A critical point of this traditionalism, whether Evolian or more
broadly understood, is the return to traditional gender roles. This
means that men and women have distinct qualities baked into their
biology and spirit: women are nurturing while men are warriors, and
while some fascists still argue some role for women in civic society, it
is usually proposed that it is a *unique* role centered on motherhood,
domesticity, and the nurturing instinct. Feminism is problematic, as it
displaces women, and men, from their natural roles in the traditional
hierarchy, and takes them away from the intended dictums of nature.[4]

Within the traditionalist understanding of the world there are
essential boundaries for identity within nature. People are happiest,
and society functions best, when all components are set within this
natural order, which exists throughout time and is encoded in our
genes and the physical laws of the earth.

Along with traditional gender roles, sexuality is viewed with an
ultra-conservative lens, and queerness is derided. As fascist philosophy moves further away from traditional Christianity (more on this
later), they are less interested in extremely restrictive sexualities, and
even though queer men have made strides within far-right circles,
they are still viewed as suspect.

---

3   Collin Cleary and Joshua Buckley, "TYR: Myth Culture: Editorial Preface,"
     TYR: Myth-Culture-Tradition 1, No. 1 (2017): 9.
4   Fascist "European New Right" philosopher Alain de Benoist notes that when it
     comes to feminism, he supports a version that he sees as identitarian rather than
     anti-patriarchy. He then lists Simone de Beauvoir as this type of feminist since,
     in his estimation, she acknowledges the "fundamental" differences between the
     sexes and then advocates for women based on this essential identity. Sylvain
     Bryan, interview by Alain de Benoist in *North American New Right*, 1, no.1
     (2012): 84–86.

Male tribalist Jack Donovan, who first made a name for himself with his book *Androphilia*, where he identified himself as a "man attracted to men" rather than a "gay man," has exemplified this. He calls it a "Mars/Mars" form of attraction, where men inhabiting their warrior roles can find sexual companionship in each other. These men are outsiders committed to a tribal ethic and male gender roles even though they have chosen to leave behind the strictures of the atomic family. Donovan has been well received inside Alt Right circles because of his extreme anti-feminism and defense of male violence. His presence helps to round out the Alt Right's ideas about gender, introduces the Men's Rights community to their work, and he has pushed the reclaiming of Nordic racial spirituality and close-knit tribal structures that are ethnically defined.

Homosexuality itself remains one of the more hotly-debated topics inside the far-right, with many in the older fascist organizations still refusing to grant gays entry. Matthew Heimbach of the Traditionalist Youth Network (TradYouth) was banned from NPI after agreeing with "biblical" policies of executing homosexuals, and Michael Hill of the southern nationalist League of the South (LOS) refused to share the NPI stage with Donovan because of his sexual orientation.[5]

Looking for Identity

While Alt Right claims about the traditional world are often presented as fact, they are actually ideological claims meant to back up an ephemeral concept of "identity." The notion underlying much of this discourse is that people of European descent have an identity they must reclaim. Their identity echoes from the past and cannot be "chosen." This identity is *essential*, fixed, and not superficial or nominal. This identity is racial, and more specifically ethnic and national. This identity is one that they often claim has a spiritual drive inside a person, a claim that is derived from "blood and soil," a logic that was implicit to romantic German nationalism that presented a spiritual connection between perceived ethnicity and to the physical land that those distinct "peoples" inhabited.

---

5   Richard Spencer, "The Rainbow Coalition," *Radix Journal*, November 4, 2015, http://www.radixjournal.com/blog/2015/11/4/the-rainbow-coalition.
       Musonius Rufus and Richard Spencer, *Rebel Yell 134: Richard Spencer*, podcast audio, Right Stuff, MP3, 02:10:03, September 5, 2016, https://radio.therightstuff.biz/2016/09/07/rebel-yell-134-radix-richard-spencer/.

Fascists have appropriated a caricature of leftist "identity pol-itics," which frames all political issues, conflict, and advocacy as a matter of identity.[6] These ideologues want to "advocate for the in-terests of white people" as they claim black, Latin, and Asian orga-nizations do for their own constituents. They cite campus groups for different racial and sexual minorities, presenting whites as "just another interest group" that deserves representation. They ignore the fact that these groups were formed less as "ethnic advocacy" and more as a way of undercutting white hegemony. They are supportive of these identity politics since they want people to think of them-selves *as* these identities rather than simply of the ways that these identities exist in a matrix of experienced oppression. They want people of African descent to "realize their African history," to think of themselves as black people and to return to the African continent to live in racially homogeneous communities defined by ethnocen-tric cultural standards. This achieves the return of Africans to Africa, which would cleanse their territory of "undesirables," and would also help white people to think of themselves *as a distinct people*. They believe that identity will transform whites, changing their pri-orities and culture to one of ethnic warriorhood that could fight for racial independence.

Since fascists believe that culture is biologically determined by ethnicity, they argue that the uniqueness of American society, from its national myths to its codes of conduct, is alien to non-whites. By shifting language from an open advocacy of white supremacy (although the superiority of whites remains implicit in their dis-course) to "Ethno-differentialism," they make the case that differ-ent ethnicities need a national culture of their own. Through an appropriation of leftist ideas around decolonization—that America seeks to subsume non-white culture—fascists make a case for eth-nic separatism. They agree that colonization has been a disaster for colonized people, and then argue for strong ethnic barriers to pre-vent that kind of interaction. This comes largely from the French New Right, which tried to avoid the broader right coalitions that traditionally formed fascist movements and instead focused on a tribalist philosophy that was critical of Christianity, capitalism, and multicultural modernity. The argument is that people must

---

6   The National Policy Institute's March 2016 conference was named "Identity Politics," attempting to draw the line that the Trump phenomenon was the re-claiming of "white identity politics."

instead be distinct with their own traditions and spiritual paths in a future with ethnic tribal states that have boundaries and reclaim "traditional life." The rhetoric used by European fascist academics like Alain de Benoist and Guillaume Faye, the people who created the ideas popularized by the Alt Right, is a sanitized racialism that focuses on pseudo-spiritual notions of European identity and avoids vulgar white supremacist jargon. Instead, seeing a need for transnational New Right ideas for a post-1968 world, de Benoist pushed for a politic that could claim opposition to fascism and nationalism while keeping its philosophical core intact. It was this philosophy that gave the Alt Right its ideological thrust, though the Americans were more willing to create a broader ideological coalition than the French. As Tamir Bar-On has expounded, this framing creates one of the critical junctures for the French New Right, mainly that they see themselves as the transmutation of the barrier between the political right and left.[7]

Richard Spencer and others often attempt to reframe non-white opponents and allies also as "identitarians," the descriptor he enjoys using besides "Alt Right." "Identitarian" is a term used by young European nationalist movements, like Generation Identity in France, that want to move beyond the meta-politics of the French New Right and into street activism. These groups reject the "party politics" found in places like the National Front and instead build a grassroots racialist movement where they claim their whole "ideology" is "European identity." In a conversation between Spencer and Latino journalist Jorge Ramos set up by HBO, Spencer argued that Ramos was an Identitarian advocating for "his people."[8] They present organizations like La Raza, which translates as "The Race," as Latin Identitarian organizations meant to help Latinx people reclaim their identity and history and advocate for their interests.[9] Spencer and others want to find "allies of color" that

---

7   Tamir Bar-On, *Rethinking the French New Right: Alternatives to Modernity* (New York: Routledge, 2013), 12–24.

8   Richard Spencer, interview by Robert Stark About the RNC Convention. *The Stark Truth with Robert Stark*, July 23, 2016, http://www.starktruthradio.com /?p=2432.

9   La Raza is a particularly popular example used by white nationalists, especially Matthew Heimbach and the Traditionalist Youth Network/Traditionalist Worker Party. They use this to "prove" that these antiracist organizations are actually about "ethnic advocacy" rather than simply advocating against institutionalized structures of white supremacy. If Latinx people can advocate for themselves openly through La Raza, then white people are simply not looking out for their own interests.

are also identitarians who can respect their right to a white identity.[10] This has been a common tactic among white nationalists for decades, for example, when American Nazi Party founder George Lincoln Rockwell spoke at Nation of Islam Gatherings or the Southern Knights of the KKK invited Muhammad Ali to speak on segregation.[11] More recently, Matthew Heimbach and TradYouth have attempted to make inroads with black nationalist organizations by hosting conversations with leaders on their podcast.[12]

White nationalism in America has historically not been rooted in high culture, instead coming out of the rural and blue-collar communities. Building on their sense of elitism, the identitarian trend in their movement is attempting to buck the stereotype of the "uneducated redneck" by building a far-right art movement. While this may seem tangential to their political project, it is central to their conception of themselves. The fascist project since the Second World War has attempted to not just win the battle in the world of political effects but also in the underlying thoughts and values of the culture. Many in the Western world implicitly embrace Universalism, humanism, equality, and democracy, even if those values are rarely recognized by contemporary states. Fascist ideologues disagree with these values on a fundamental level, especially as it inspires modernity, multiculturalism, and the "rule by the masses."[13]

Meta

To counter this cultural attitude, many fascist ideologues have been working to build a meta-politic, a structure of ideas that would develop political ideas down the line. In this way they hope to reclaim white identity as a driving cultural force as they will not be able

---

10   Richard Spencer and Nathan Damigo, "Allies of Color," podcast audio, *The Radix Journal*, MP3, 46:59, December 8, 2015, http://www.radixjournal.com/podcast/2015/12/8/allies-of-color.

11   Sam McPheeters, "When Malcolm X Met The Nazis," *Vice*, April 15, 2015, https://www.vice.com/en_us/article/when-malcolm-x-met-the-nazis-0000620-v22n4.
      Jim White, "Muhammad Ali's meetings with Ku Klux Klan leaders revealed by documentary," The *Telegraph,* November 10, 2008, http://www.telegraph.co.uk/sport/othersports/boxing/3419060/Muhammad-Alis-meetings-with-Ku-Klux-Klan-leaders-revealed-by-documentary-Boxing-and-MMA.html.

12   There are several episodes on their earlier podcast, *The Traditionalist Youth Hour.*

13   Many in the French New Right referred to themselves as "Gramscians of the Right," referencing the Marxist meta-political philosopher Antonio Gramsci. The notion here is that they need to influence the culture if they are to then have a base on which to build their political projects.

to unseat the political ideas that dominate Western countries unless they first change how white people think of themselves. They want to reclaim a culture of the arts to reframe the ethics and values of the people in the nation, to recenter heroism in the public imagination and to place its value back on romantic nationalism. This means resurrecting artistic currents of the past, from European romanticism to images of strength and valor from antiquity.

While Counter-Currents Publishing has made an effort to publish white nationalist fiction, and *Radix* has focused on film commentary, the primary area where the Alt Right have made strides has been in music. For decades, "white noise" was the dominant form of white nationalist music entry, taking the skinhead Oi! punk of the 1970s–80s and creating a violent racialized version. Often associated with the Rock Against Communism scene and Resistance Records label, this music popularized bands like Skrewdriver, RaHoWa, and Jew Slaughter, all of which focused on vulgar racialism. Instead of building consciousness, these bands and record labels became more a way to fund insurrectionary racist movements and to foster international networking. As Kirsten Dyck points out, the unremitting violence in the lyrics and subcultural spaces it inspires can "Voice the movement's fantasies, and facilitate group bonding rituals."[14] This was critical to the tribal violence of skinhead warfare but did not develop an elitist fascist culture that many in the New Right/Alt Right find necessary for changing politics and race relations over time. It was that failure that helped to create an entirely new thread in white nationalist music, one that appeared different even if the roots were the same.

Neofolk is a post-punk genre developed out of a revival of traditionalist folk music intermixed with electronic/industrial, metal, and rock, all of which play well in the goth and punk subcultures. While it is not monolithically fascist in orientation, the most well-known bands developed the genre around a romantic nationalism, as a way of celebrating pre-Christian European religions, customs, and identities, as well as poring over the work of people like Julius Evola and nationalist philosopher Oswald Spengler. This is what Anton Shekhovtsov calls an "apoliteic music," artistic strands that claim to be non-political while building the underlying fascist worldview and cultural space. In his study of neofolk and its subgenre Martial Industrial, Shekhovtsov looks at the Evolian concept of becoming

---

14 Kirsten Dyck, *Reichsrock: The International Web of White-Power and Neo-Nazi Hate Music* (New Brunswick, NJ: Rutgers University Press, 2017), 4.

an "aristocrat of the soul," creating a purist right-wing culture in the shell of the now-decaying modern world. Neofolk and Martial Industrial then posit the idea that Europe has been lost and that it must be reclaimed, a driving philosophic distinction inherent in the meta-politics of contemporary fascist ideologies. They rely on a mythic understanding of Europe's past and the call for "spiritual rebirth," all precursor antagonisms that lead to "palingenetic ultra-nationalism," the answer to the problem of modernity. Instead of resorting to politics, this meta-political vision rejects the "vulgarity" of fascist politics of the past in favor of "spiritual warfare," which leads to the creation of a countercultural space. Often citing the same alienation felt by left-wing dropouts, they craft a semi-common experience that they can use to recruit from subcultures usually allied with left ideas, like punk music.[15]

Neofolk is best known through the controversial band Death in June (DiJ) and its frontman Douglas Pearce. Though his earlier projects included the antifascist punk band, Crisis, Pearce became interested in far-right esoterics and the anti-capitalist wing of the Nazi Party. He formed DiJ as an experimental vehicle for these ideas, often collaborating with other art music acts and homing in on Odinism, numerology, and intersections with nationalism.[16] Pearce has publicly ranted about the "threat" to Europe presented by non-white immigration and that whites are facing demographic decline because those "who shouldn't be able to are breeding with such frequency."[17] He has claimed a great degree of admiration for "Euro-colonialism" and the emerging nationalist movements across Europe. This is hardly surprising given his financial contributions to the Croatian nationalist movement, known for their violent genocidal politics during the early 1990s crisis between Serbia and Bosnia-Herzegovina. After a brutal act of racist violence by British Nationalist Party member David Copeland in 1999, Pearce dedicated a song to the "White Wolves," a faux-organization that claimed responsibility for the attack that killed three and injured 140.[18]

---

15   Anton Shekhovtsov, "Apoliteic music: Neo-Folk, Martial Industrial and 'Meta-Political Fascism,'" *Patterns of Prejudice* 43, No. 5 (December 2009): 431–57.
16   Alexander Ross, *Against the Fascist Creep.* (Chico, CA: AK Press, 2017), 135–36.
17   Pearce quoted in "Queers to Shut Down Death in June In San Francisco On September 13th / DIJ Exposed by Queer Anti-Fascist," *Who Makes The Nazis,* September 13, 2013, http://www.whomakesthenazis.com/2013/09/queers-to-shut-down-death-in-june-in.html.
18   Ibid.

Made up of members from the previously National Front-associated band Above the Ruins, Sol Invictus has been at the center of the growing neofolk scene.[19] Though founding member Tony Wakeford said his association with the NF "was probably the worst decision of my life" and one he regrets, his connections run deep and his collaborations make up a "who's who" of the fascist music scene.[20] Their seminal record *Against the Modern World* is named after the most famous work by Julius Evola, and their lyrics draw from Evola's perennialism and celebrate the warrior ethic and hierarchical societies they venerate in their image of "traditional Europe."

With dozens of bands defining these genres and crossover to subcultural spiritual and social spaces, there is an avenue of growth here completely disconnected from American conservatism and owing more to countercultural influences commonly associated with the left. Neofolk and interacting genres have failed to crossover into the mainstream, largely because of their uncompromising, controversial vision, but to do so has never been the point. Instead, their purpose is to add depth to a countercultural fascist meta-politic, and to create committed "thought criminals," rather than to become populist propaganda. This cements a critical stage in building a radicalized core, one that is influenced by emotional romanticism rather than political or pseudo-scientific arguments.

There has been resistance to these ideas inside of neofolk, with bands like Rome speaking out against the racialist trend. The problem is that the aesthetics and underlying philosophy was built with a racialist impulse, so bands drawing on their artistic inspiration are forced to walk a difficult line. More recently, Alt Right techno music labeled "fashwave" has been flooding white nationalist blogs, with acts like Cybernazi and Xurious echoing the neo-Nazi entryism that appeared in European electronic music circles in the 1990s.[21]

---

19   "Rock Against Communism: The Roots of Sol Invictus," Who Makes the Nazis, October 3, 2010, http://www.whomakesthenazis.com/2010/10/rock-against-communism-roots-of-sol.html.

20   "DANGER! NEO-FOLK 'MUSICIAN' TONY WAKEFORD OF SOL INVICTUS IS STILL A FASCIST CREEP!" *Stewart Home Society*, https://www.stewarthomesociety.org/wakeford.html.

21   Reggie Ugwu, "How Electronic Music Made by Neo-Nazis Soundtracks the Alt-Right," *BuzzFeed*. December 13, 2016, https://www.buzzfeed.com/reggieugwu/fashwave.

A Third Way

Over the last two decades, the contemporary left has often confused the definition of fascism, especially in discussions about the increasingly authoritarian nature of institutions propping up neoliberal capitalism. While it would be wrong to say that fascism, as a general rule, is purely anti-capitalist, it does implicitly critique capitalism as a free-market system. Capitalism may rely on the latent bigotry and social inequality in a society, but it also disrespects national boundaries, tribal allegiances, and non-economic hierarchies. What this means is that, while the left critiques capitalism for its inability to deliver broad equality, the far-right critiques it for not being explicitly racialized and *unequal enough*. Capitalism benefits merchants who broaden their customer base rather than privileging a specific group, and increasingly globalized trade breaks down national boundaries and benefits an international ruling class. Neoliberalism steamrolls regional diversity and cultural differences in the same way that it destroys individuality and personal expression, as a monster that goes after what makes us human.[1]

A strong anti-capitalist thread in fascism has permeated for decades, coming out of the early National Socialist critiques of capitalism and coming to dominate nationalist circles by the early 1980s. While many on the left would argue that far-right critiques of capitalism, which mimic parts of the "left analysis," are purely rhetorical, anti-capitalism is the dominant fascist perspective today.[2]

---

1   Walter Benn Michaels, "Let Them Eat Diversity," *Jacobin*, January 1, 2011, http://www.jacobinmag.com/2011/01/let-them-eat-diversity/.

2   Don Hamerquist, J Sakai, and Mark Salotte, *Confronting Fascism*, 28–29.

The right would then want to create a counter-economics based on formal hierarchy that privileges certain groups. This has been implicit to fascist political movements since the 1920s, with National Socialism taking on that label since it used "socialist" command-economic methods to formalize social stratification. In Mussolini's Fascist Party, the concept of "class collaboration" comes from this, whereby socialized economic inequalities were meant to reinforce a class structure by eliminating any possible class mobility.[3] The upper classes, the aristocrats, stayed at the top by virtue of their superiority, and working-class and poor populations stayed at the bottom due to an innate lesser nature. When society operates within a hierarchy that essentializes behavior and nature, the economic structures cement that inequality and reward those identities considered to be a part of the nation. The term "right-wing socialism" indicates the use of socialist-styled mechanisms, whether in state or non-state forms, to enforce inequality rather than equality.[4]

While this critique of capitalism went far back into Hitler's intervention in the NSDAP, it was the "Strasserite" wing that proposed a more radically anti-capitalist vision for National Socialism. Coming from brothers Otto and Gregor Strasser, their critique had a populist anti-capitalist perspective and declared Jews as central power players in the growing world of international finance. This narrative has seeped into radical discourse globally, from the more countercultural fascist currents like National Anarchism, a non-state form of fascism, and National Bolshevism, a movement that mixes fascism and Marxist anti-capitalism, to the growth of the militia movement out of the 1980s farm crisis in the U.S.

The influence of early-twentieth-century fascist Francis Parker Yockey's stream-of-consciousness-style ranting was crucial to this development. Yockey's "unity of the left and the right" saw socialism as a tool for national ends, an ensuring of the economic and material means for the maintenance of ruling castes and biologically and spiritually distinct peoples. Rather than equalizing economic liberalization, he believed in the need to formally stratify social roles

---

3   Benito Mussolini, "Mussolini - The Doctrine of Fascism" *World Future Fund*, 1932, http://www.worldfuturefund.org/wffmaster/Reading/Germany/mussolini .htm.

4   Sternhill, Ze'ev. "Fascism," in Roger Griffin, ed., *International Fascism: Theories, Causes, and the New Consensus* (London & New York: Arnold Publishers, 1998). (Note: While Sternhill does not use the term, he does describe this break in the motivating factors of command economics.)

and access to resources, to control the economy so that certain outcomes were guaranteed, but not the ones the Marxists and anarchists proposed. To maintain the metaphysical distinctiveness of the European people he called for some type of international coordination of nationalists, which would make use of meta-politics rather than the failures of militarized fascist parties. When the shift from the language of supremacy to the rhetoric of separatism occurred, Yockey's call of Ethnopluralism against the great Western empire of decadent capitalism was given legs. Yockey had a close relationship with Willis Carto, which helped Carto become one of the most influential nationalists in American history. He is best known for founding the ultra-right Liberty Lobby organization, which worked to mainstream white nationalist ideas into Washington policy for years, as well as to prop up Holocaust Denial through the Institute for Historical Review and to connect far-right ideas with the conspiracy community via the *American Free Press*. While Yockey connected to the more "Americanist" wing of the American fascist movement through Carto, the counter-cultural fascist projects were most influenced by Yockey's magnum opus *Imperium*. Carto's notions of white identity and Western decline are echoed heavily by the Alt Right today, as well as in more sanitized ways throughout the paleoconservative fetish for historical memory.[5]

While this anti-capitalist fascist current has been prevalent since the earliest days of the Russian Revolution, this version of nationalism came to dominate with the British National Front in the 1970s. The principle was to oppose both capitalism and communism, which they saw as being both developed by Jews and being held in captive power by an elite dedicated toward "globalism" instead of the more "natural" nationalism. This was not purely anti-capitalist in the left's terms, as it wanted to break up what it saw as "finance capitalism" and to keep capital in the hands of regional elites and those with an aristocratic stake in the community.

While Third Positionist economic ideas may seem like the marginal concepts on the edges of an already fringe political movement, it has come to dominate in these circles not in spite of its ideological commitments, but *because* of them. Fascism has always required a certain "left-right crossover." In the 1970s, with the Red Army Faction, Marxist urban revolutionary Horst Mahler went to war with

5   George Michael, *Willis Carto and the American Far-Right* (Gainesville: University Press of Florida, 2008), 77–84.

the German government, and was sent to prison for bank robberies and for orchestrating an elaborate escape of incarcerated comrades. He went on a political journey himself, moving toward a Maoist guerilla analysis and then becoming an avowed neo-Nazi and Holocaust denier, eventually joining the neo-fascist National Democratic Party of Germany. From this kind of political development, Jean-Pierre Faye developed "Horseshoe Theory," the idea that sometimes the far left can reach out and touch the far-right ideologically.[6]

The same concept has been used more recently to describe the political development of North Korea, where Kim Il Sung's originally Maoist-inspired revolution developed slowly into a society focused on class collaboration and a "paranoid race-based nationalism," rather than the "Stalinist" state it is often accused of being. Brian Myers has argued that Korea was heavily influenced by Imperial Japanese fascism, which created a mythologized history of rulership and power, which it then used when developing a national identity for itself. Through its revolutionary process Korea eventually rejected the central tenets it had begun with—namely the internationalist and egalitarian endgame of Maoist revolution—and instead saw its own ethnic group as decidedly distinct and spiritually superior. This is to suggest that a "left" analysis shifted to the far-right through a certain flaw that allowed for entry of a fascist politic. In the case of North Korea, it would be the exploitation of ongoing Korean racism, the influence of Imperial State Shinto, and the use of authoritarian leadership, all of which were used to capture the state even though the stated purpose was originally Marxist.[7]

While Horseshoe Theory is an inadequate exposition on the development of political ideas, it shows how a radical analysis, one that breaks apart moral norms, can often leave itself open to ideological entryism from some of the most shocking places. As Alexander Reid Ross points out in *Against the Fascist Creep*, fascism creeps into the public in two distinct ways.

(1) It draws left-wing notions of solidarity and liberation into ultranationalist, right-wing ideology; and (2) at least in its early stages, fascists often utilize "broad front" strategies, proposing a

---

6   "The Horseshoe Theory Says Right and Left Wing Are More Similar," *Curiosity.com*, https://m.curiosity.com/topics/the-horseshoe-theory-says-right-and-left-wing-are-more-similar-than-you-think-curiosity/.

7   Brian Myers, *The Cleanest Race* (Brooklyn, N.Y.: Melville House, 2010).

mass-based, nationalist platform to gain access to mainstream political audiences and key administrative positions.[8]

In the development of fascism, right-wing ideas take on a left-
wing character, often using left-wing political projects for right-wing
meta-politics. When environmental movements shift to a "natural law"
conversation that fetishizes ethnically exclusive micro-communities,
or when anti-colonial movements utilize a form of racial romanticism
to fuel the revolutionary spirit, they begin with a left-oriented prem-
ise and then drift into a far-right methodology and vision. Many of
the movements and writings under the "eco-extremist" umbrella have
been described in this way, starting with the anti-alienation motivations of anarcho-primitivists like John Zerzan and the now-defunct
Green Anarchy magazine, but they leave those values behind for completely new motivations. Drawing heavily on the ideas outlined by
Theodore Kaczynski in his manifesto "Industrial Society and Its Future," and then later in "Anti-Tech Revolution," projects like Individualists Tending Toward the Wild (ITS) have walked an ideological line
that moved into reactionary social politics, equating drug use, egalitarianism, and social movements with the degenerating effects of civilization.[9] As manifestos from the "eco-extremist" journal *Atassa* show,
they quickly moved from the factors that pull some into post-left revolutionary politics (mainly the failure of the organized left to achieve
its aims) and into the veneration of ethnic tribalism, frenetic violence,
and the rejection of all moral or political value.[10] This does not make
anti-civilizationist nihilism suspect on its own, but in the case of ITS's
development their values changed to ones that celebrated inequality,
in-group and out-group tribalism, and the victimization of marginalized people through sacrilized violent acts—including the claimed
murder of two hikers in Oaxaca and indiscriminate attacks that they
say are necessary for anti-civilizational pessimism.[11] The values that

---

8   Ross, *Against the Fascist Creep*, 3.
9   It would be wrong to assess ITS as a fully-formed fascist movement. It is instead
      proto-fascist and further heading in that direction as it breaks away the shackles
      of the left.
10   Abe Cabrera, "The Flower Growing Out of the Underworld: An Introduction
      to Eco-extremism," *Atassa: Readings in Eco-Extremism*, Atassa #1.
11   "Twenty-Ninth Communique of Individualists Tending Toward the Wild/ In-
      discriminate Group Tending Toward the Wild," *Atassa: Readings in Eco-Ex-
      tremism*, May 6, 2017, https://atassa.wordpress.com/2017/05/06/twenty-ninth
      -communique-of-the-individualists-tending-toward-the-wild-indiscriminate
      -group-tending-toward-the-wild/.

underlie the politics are now rooted in the violent inequality of the right, even if they attempt to use socialist economic principles, concern for the natural world, and an opposition to "imperialism" to get there, and even if they started on the left.

As Third Positionism became popular inside fascist circles, it began to share certain critiques of international capitalism with segments of the left. For example, it opposed the "dehumanizing" effects of consumer capitalism, yet its alternative was the proper order of traditional family, community, and church. Catholic Distributism, National Socialism, and other models are often proposed from the right as alternatives to international capitalism. Often these critiques mirrored left-wing discourse so closely that movements like Occupy Wall Street saw entryism through far-right critiques of finance.[12] Attempts to claim that it was "crony capitalism" or the fault of the Bilderberg Group or "Rothschilds" echoes this Third Positionist sentiment, which, rather than critiquing the natural inequality of capitalism, attempt to place the blame on a subversive "hidden elite." This phrase often stands as a proxy for Jews, but even without this explicitly anti-Semitic insinuation it holds to a similar logic that sees a caricature of "traditional life" as the alternative to the destructive effects of finance capital.[13]

Three-Way Fight

The left finds itself in a difficult strategic position when confronting fascism as it has become harder to determine exactly who are the actors in the drama of racial revenge. The blog Three Way Fight was titled as such because, while the left may represent the collective strength of the working-class, "there are more than two poles of political struggle." The establishment class is not synonymous with the fascists, which draws from a variety of competing interests, and may even be at odds with the interests of the rich at times.[14] The term "Three-Way Fight" came in the wake of the

---

12 Spencer Sunshine, "The Right Hand of Occupy Wallstreet: From Libertarians to Nazis, Fact and Fiction of Right-Wing Involvement," Political Research Associates, February 23, 2014, http://www.politicalresearch.org/2014/02/23/the-right-hand-of-occupy-wall-street-from-libertarians-to-nazis-the-fact-and-fiction-of-right-wing-involvement/#sthash.fqRPKzNv.dpbs.

13 The same logic is often at play when "indigeneity," completely undefined, is presented as the alternative to modern capitalism in crisis.

14 Matthew N. Lyons, "Matthew Lyons on the Insurgent Far-Right, Trump, And #DisruptJ20," IGDCast, January 17, 2017, https://itsgoingdown.org/

anti-globalization movement where "divisions in global capital" created complex and contradictory narratives about what side to support in international conflicts, anti-imperialism, and national liberation movements. The "Us vs. Them" narrative required that capital have homogeneous and consistent interests, and the left needed a new way to understand movements like Hezbollah, which was an insurgent force against Western globalization, on the one hand, yet advocated a repressive theocratic nationalism on the other. Michael Staudenmaier describes the forces competing for hegemony as "us, *them* and them":

> At its core, the three way fight is a critique of authoritarianism as much as it is a response to fascism. It is also a way to understand various social movements through a sort of schematic categorization. The two sets of "them" that I mention here can roughly be taken to represent the capitalists and the fascists, and the "us" can be thought of as the anti-authoritarian revolutionary left. But the three way fight is not dogma; it requires that anyone who adopts it as a framework take the time to think through a range of questions and come to their own conclusions, whether individually or collectively. One key question is: is a given group, organization, or movement revolutionary or reformist? If they are revolutionary, we can then ask: are they aiming for an authoritarian revolution or an anti-authoritarian revolution?[15]

This provides potential solutions to the problem of Third Positionist entryism into left movements, especially when it comes to the question of imperialism. Not all movements, ideas, or figures that share enemies with the left are inherently allies. Instead, a revolutionary movement has to share certain components, without which it can easily offer a reactionary vision whose insurgent desires are based on collaboration between the organs of the left and the values of the right.

"Fascism is a revolutionary movement of the right against both the bourgeoisie and the left, of middle class and declassed men, that arises in zones of protracted crisis," says Hamerquist.[16]

---

igdcast-matthew-lyons-insurgent-far-right-trump-disruptj20/. Find more at Three Way Fight: http://threewayfight.blogspot.com/.

15   Michael Staudenmaier, "Anti-Semitism, Islamophobia, and the Three Way Fight," *Upping the Anti* 5, (2007): 117.

16   Hamerquist, et al., *Confronting Fascism*, 88–89.

If the left wants to effectively oppose fascism it needs to view it as generally separate from the state and capital.

Green Nationalism

The Third Position integrates itself into movements associated with the left. Animal rights and radical environmentalism were some of the first left movements fascists attempted to align themselves with, and have been a right priority since the earliest days of the NSDAP. The Third Reich developed a cult of nature that mixed "teutonic mythology, pseudo-scientific ecology, irrationalist anti-humanism, and a mythology of racial salvation through a return to the land."[17] From the earliest days of the volkish movements that evolved in Germany in response to increased industrialism, the concept that an "essential truth" was found in a sensual connection with the natural world was crucial to the ideology that fascism espoused. Though the left also often re-sacralizes the natural world in ecological conversations, the fascist type of re-mystification was built on a nationalism that privileged Germans as inheritors of the earth, and reconstructed an imagined hierarchy implicit in the events of the "unmediated" world.[18]

As Greg Johnson has often pointed out about "ecofascism," the fascist project prioritizes the inviolability of nature, and their intent is to protect the "natural order." Figures like Finish eco-nationalist Pentti Linkola intermixed many "esoteric Aryan" ideas with environmentalism in an effort to create a synthesis that could be portrayed as almost apolitical and centered itself on the rules set forth by the natural world. The modern world is often seen as profane and excessively materialist, a consequence, they say, of the Abrahamic (Jewish) monotheism, but a proper pagan worldview would recenter the spirituality in nature and therefore create an unalienated relationship to the earth.[19] Many of these ideas are reflected in the thought of philosophers who are venerated on the right, like Martin Heidegger, and can be seen in the way that leaders, such as Adolf Hitler, attempted to promote a type of "nature worship." Hitler

---

17   Janet Biehl and Peter Staudenmaier, *Ecofascism* (Oakland, CA: AK Press, 1995), 14.

18   Ibid.

19   Greg Johnson and Robert Stark. "On Eco-Fascism," audio podcast, *Reason Radio Network*, MP3, 56:00, April 2, 2012, http://reasonradionetwork.com /20120402/the-stark-truth-greg-johnson-on-eco-fascism.

built the Autobahn to revolutionize the growing automobile culture of Germany, but he built it in a way that would juxtapose it with the German countryside and force appreciation of its natural beauty.[20] Jonathan Bowden, the enigmatic speaker made famous in the British National Party, often spoke about the left adopting environmentalism, "though it had always been a right wing concept."[21]

The inherent cruelty and determinism of nature is something that has permeated the extreme edges of the environmental movement for years. Biocentrism has been a key point on the environmental right, which has allowed crossover to movements like bioregionalism, Earth First! (EF!), and the animal liberation movement. Elements from these movements have occasionally allied with forces attempting to restrict immigration on the basis of population growth anxiety, which can been seen in early EF! cofounder Dave Foreman and EF! supporter Ed Abbey and appears as well in academic journals like *Population and Environment*, which was edited by white nationalists through the 1990s.[22]

Globalization

As the 1990s came to a close, the decentralized anti-globalization movement exploded into the public imagination with the broken windows of the Seattle Central Business District and massive show of support from organized labor during the "Battle of Seattle." Progressing within capitalism during the 1970s, neoliberalism sought to undo any Keynesian social democratic gains won in recent decades, such as the capitulation with labor, and sought to diminish the regulatory framework that held back the more vicious processes of capitalism. This unleashed the mass privatization, globalization, and liberalization of markets the world over, fomenting an attack on working people internationally and a massive transfer of wealth to the ruling class. Colonialism continued apace in the Global South with resource extraction, the "global land grab," and an intensification of

---

20   Spencer, "What Is Fascism?" *Radix Journal Podcast.*
21   Jonathan Bowden, "The E Word: Eugenics & Environmentalism, Madison Grant & Lothrop Stoddard," Counter-Currents Publishing, April 2016, http://www.counter-currents.com/2016/04/the-e-word/.
22   The formative editorship of *Population and Environment* was done by white separatist and former vice presidential candidate from the American Freedom Party (then known as the American Third Position Party) Virginia Abernathy and then handed over to Kevin MacDonald. As it stands today, the journal seems to have no connection to the racialist academics of the past.

free market solutions and debt. The anti-globalization movement, which challenged neoliberalism around the globe, helped reduce debt carried by the Third World, and the fascist right tried to reinvent itself by developing an entire language of anti-globalization and anti-capitalism. The right saw an opportunity and promoted "localism" as an alternative to globalization. Localism drew on the regionalist right notions that were implicit in thinkers like the Southern Agrarians, a group of Southern poets and authors who romanticized the agrarian society of the antebellum South. As localism became an approach to farming and community planning, it always maintained a right-wing perspective of latent tribalism, which held isolationist positions implicitly if not explicitly.[23]

Many anti-globalization activists began using terms like "para-globalization" to reflect an internationalist anti-capitalist politic, but the boundaries between the left and right in these circles was muddied. Publications like *Adbusters*, while undeniably left-wing, have often put forth points that could find allies on the right and communicated more recent examples of right populism in a suspicion of "globalism."[24] While sites like *CounterPunch* have run questionable articles supporting "critiques of globalism," the Alt Right, InfoWars, and even Donald Trump have positioned themselves as opponents to the pernicious agents of globalism, echoing conspiratorial attacks on finance capitalism but replacing anti-capitalist analysis with anti-Semitism and rabbit-hole theories.[25]

Fascists use the term "globalism" and present nationalism as its alternative—a politicized localism that is rooted in traditional hierarchies like the family and church instead of left-wing values. After the large-scale mobilization against the World Trade Organization summit in Seattle in November 1999, Matt Hale, the violently eccentric Pontifex Maximus of what was then the World Church of the Creator, praised the direct action taken by protesters and declared that it was from this leftist milieu that they must recruit, rather than from the stodgy failures of conservatism.[26]

23   Hawley, *Right-Wing Critics of American Conservatism*, 75–84.
24   "Fascist Entryism: Adbusters and the Problem of Hazy Politics," *Anti-Fascist News*, March 4, 2016, https://antifascistnews.net/2016/03/04/fascist -entryism-adbusters-and-the-problem-of-hazy-politics/.
25   The critique of *CounterPunch* heads back years as they have hosted authors from white nationalist sites, utilize right populist themes, flirt with Holocaust deniers, and have been the center of what some have identified as a modern "Red-Brown Alliance."
26   Hamerquist, et al., *Confronting Fascism*, 36–37.

No War

The anti-war movement has been consistently branded as "left" since the revolt against the Vietnam War by the New Left, but while a left orientation is historically dominant, it is not uniform. The 2003 invasion of Iraq by the George W. Bush administration and his hawkish Neoconservative security establishment saw some of the largest protests since the 1960s. The anti-war movement grew, targeting campus military recruiting through organizations like the Campus Anti-War Network, and Bush was one of the most rightly vilified characters in modern politics. But the left did not own this anti-war movement, as sites like AntiWar.com brought together anti-war voices from the libertarian and paleoconservative right, especially Lew Rockwell who had previously penned the racist *Rothbard-Rockwell Report* with anarcho-capitalist Murray Rothbard. Pat Buchanan's the *American Conservative* magazine also took an anti-war stance.

Their perspective was isolationist. They believed that an "America First" ethic should reign and that the U.S. should be kept out of foreign wars, and they created a model that aided the rise of Ron Paul and paleoconservatism. While the anti-war left often asserts itself on the principle that warfare unfairly targets the oppressed classes of all nations, often comparing the fate of poor American service volunteers and those they end up bombing, the right often takes a nationalist tone. Their opposition, though it sometimes shares the general horror about warfare, differentiates itself with the assertion that war may not perfectly support nationalist aims. Infringement on "human rights" is a historically liberal justification for going to war, and many on the fascist right would object to this, refusing to sympathize unless those being impacted in the region belonged to their own tribal group. While the radical left will almost always reject military intervention, it still often shares a certain disdain for despots and acknowledges that dominant capitalist states will only further punish those under siege. White nationalist publications like *Spotlight* and its *American Free Press* did the same, echoing the strong nationalism at the heart of many anti-interventionist rightists. Beginning with the bombing of Syrian airfields after Donald Trump saw videos of children allegedly gassed by the forces of Bashar Al-Assad, many in the Alt Right broke ranks and openly protested Trump's intervention. Richard Spencer rejected this entirely, saying that Assad was a "moderate" voice in the region and someone that Trump should make alliances with, again distancing himself from the idea that cruelty in war is categorically problematic.

Nationalists Against Imperialism

White nationalists' change in branding has created a space for them to make alliances with the anti-imperialist movement supporting decolonization movements across the Global South and with First Nations peoples. Ethno-pluralism argues for "nationalism for all people," and they simply promote white nationalism because it is their own race. The European New Right labeled this as "equality of difference," conceptualizing a construct whereby racial groups are kept separate and, through this segregation, their uniqueness is celebrated.[27] This logic has lent itself to the development of nationalism from the 1960s onward, which sought to build on the anti-colonial struggles happening across the Third World, where national identity was at play in revolutionary struggle. Ethnic nationalists in the heart of Europe wanted to manipulate this sentiment, arguing that their struggle for "racial sovereignty" shared the same roots and that there should be alliances between the fascist vision of a renewed European society and the freedom sought by indigenous peoples who had been historically victimized by Euro-colonialism. This logic attempts to claim Black Nationalism, First Nations liberation, and other movements as simply different sides of the same coin, the non-white counterparts to white nationalism. This narrative erases the history of oppression that gave rise to these movements, attempting to make the purpose of each identity movement singular, and it also exploits a flaw in identity politics. If race and nation are essentialized, made an end in their own right, and if those movements resort to class collaboration, it is not entryism that allows for white nationalists to break through, it is an open invitation since it has made ideological bedfellows with racial nationalism. Identities discussed in anti-oppression movements, both liberal and revolutionary, exist subjectively because of their imposition on the people experiencing them, not necessarily because of their value in and of themselves. Racial categories exist not because they are biologically or spiritually *true*, but because colonialism made them true through the subjugation of

---

27   Tamir Bar-On, *Where Have All the Fascists Gone?* (New York: Routledge, 2007), 5–6.

certain classes of people. If this distinction is lost, as it often is when politics are taken out of a revolutionary struggle, then it can often appear as simply the battle between identity interest groups, which is to say tribalism rather than egalitarianism.[28]

Within this far-right rhetoric, Palestinian solidarity has taken a role of special importance because it can be shifted to anti-Jewish aims. Drawing on the anti-Semitic currents in Palestinian nationalism, specifically from Hamas and Hezbollah, many have taken on the "struggle against Zionism" as a key point of their revolutionary nationalist politics. Since Zionism is rarely defined in clear political terms, the vagueness has often allowed far-right voices to infect otherwise leftist, anti-Israel projects with anti-Semitic conspiracies, caricatures of Jews, and the idea that it is not Israeli state policy that creates colonialist oppression in the Gaza Strip but Israel's uniquely Jewish character. By making "Zionist" synonymous with "Jewish," it attempts to deflect energy from the Palestinian liberation movement into one that is critical of "World Jewry" and builds a theory of "Jewish power."

The far-right approaches anti-imperialist politics by opposing traditional Western imperialism under an ethno-nationalist framework, absolving itself of colonialism, chattel slavery, and indigenous genocide. Instead, it prefers an "Africa for the Africans, Asia for the Asians" mentality and therefore finds common ground with various movements broadly understood as anti-imperialist. Inside of the left, there is already a problematic alliance between anti-imperialist forces and international movements that could already be described as despotic, nationalist, or both. Marxist organizations like the Spartacist League have turned heads in their support for both North Korea and ISIS, believing they hold merit because they attack perceived Western imperial hegemony, despite both having been identified as fascist.[29] Support for Syria, Muammar Gaddafi, and even Russia are troubling alliances for leftist movements that would normally critique state power, racialist ideas, and the genocidal policies of authoritarian persecution. Left publications including *CounterPunch* have carried writers associated with the far-right under "anti-imperialism,

---

28   I want to acknowledge the complexity of this, as well as to say that the fascist right does not own identity, tradition, and group histories. It is only the distinct boundaries between them that act tribal rather than celebrated differences that do not disallow interconnectiveness and blending.

29   "Syria/Iraq: Kurdish Nationalists Serve U.S. Imperialism," International Communist League (Fourth Internationalist), November 14, 2014, http://www.icl-fi .org/english/wv/1056/kurds.html.

anti-war" headings, even sharing writers with white nationalist publications such as *VDare*, like Paul Craig Roberts.[30]

As Matthew N. Lyons notes, the anti-imperialist tradition runs deep inside of Third Positionist fascism, finding inspirations in Francis Parker Yockey's writings, the Eurasian "Fourth Political Theory" of Aleksandr Dugin, "American first" isolationism, and the critiques of the role of capitalism in international conflict that is shared by both leftist anti-capitalists and Third Positionists.[31] According to Lyons,

> Wherever they come down on these questions, far-right anti-imperialists represent a false and dangerous alternative to the status quo. Their conflict with U.S. global power is real, but their aim is to reshape human oppression and exploitation, not abolish it. Some of them want a society defined by racial purity, some focus on patriarchy and religious obedience, others want to help superior individuals of different ethnic groups rise above the bestial minority.[32]

It is important to note the complexity of these issues and the fact that there can be superficial agreement between the left and the far-right for different reasons, but this does not signify a reason to cross the chasm and bond. In many cases, not challenging these similarities can allow the left to act as the decisive blow for the right. This was true with the "Lexit" contingent of the Brexit campaign, where some supporters on the left supported Britain's exit from the European Union, despite the opposition from organized labor and the clear racial implications of the U.K. Independence Party's propaganda.[33]

Syncretic Traditions

Third Positionist trends have inspired political movements that hold internal contradictions; they often look different than traditional racist organizations. Syncretic politics are ones that hold ideas often thought of as contradictory elements in concert, such as anti-capitalism and nationalism. Since a refusal of capitalism is often

30   "Counterpunch or Sucker punch?" *Meldungen Aus Dem Exil*," July 19, 2015, https://meldungen-aus-dem-exil.noblogs.org/post/2015/07/19/counterpunch-or-suckerpunch/. Web. 21 Jan. 2017.

31   Matthew Lyons, "Anti-Imperialism and The U.S. Far-Right," *Red Skies at Night* 3 (2017): 1–15.

32   Ibid., 17.

33   The "Left Leave" campaign would be the largest of these.

thought of in terms of egalitarianism and the destruction of classes, and nationalism is about the maintenance of traditional hierarchies, their congruence in a particular ideology would be considered syncretic politics. Once can see, however, that the perception that the particular political components are in opposition is only due to historical precedent, not material reality. Nationalist anti-capitalists, including various trends called "socialist," reject capitalism because of its destruction of their own mythic order, not because they want to upend stratification. This strange confluence is becoming commonplace, as fascism heads into the twenty-first century, fragmenting just as significantly as the left has.

In the early 2000s the fissures became apparent as National Anarchism rose to a serious position in far-right politics. Developed by former National Front radical Troy Southgate, National Anarchism attempted to create a nationalism that was opposed to the nation-state and in favor of an idealized series of tribal enclaves. It drew on a huge range of influences, such as the revival of Germanic paganism, and attempted to appropriate critiques from anarcho-syndicalism, post-left anarchism, and anarcho-primitivism.[34] In an attempt to "destroy the modern world," National Anarchists also opposed work as we know it today, mass industrial society, and political elites, yet they came at it from a Traditionalist perspective rather than an egalitarian one. In the U.S., this mantle was carried over by groups like the Bay Area National Anarchists, who put on workshops on tribal affiliation and were involved in both anti-war and anti-immigrant demonstrations. They were stridently traditionalist, opposed abortion, were "anti-Zionist," but they also wanted to be invited into the larger San Francisco anarchist community.[35]

The National Anarchist Tribal Alliance (NATA) of New York grew even larger, organizing "dual power" projects like subsistence farms. Like many syncretic Third Positionist groups, they are "prodding at weak points in the left"—such as the willingness of

---

34   It should be noted clearly that none of these trends in anarchism are uniquely problematic because of this association, but instead that fascists simply take parts of revolutionary critiques that they can use to further their own ends. This has been true of all revolutionary left traditions, from hardline Stalinism to anarcho-syndicalist labor ideas, deep ecological green anarchist trends, and different forms of nihilism.

35   Casey Sanchez, "California Racists Claim They're Anarchists," *Southern Poverty Law Center*, May 29, 2009, https://www.splcenter.org/fighting-hate/intelligence-report/2009/california-racists-claim-they%E2%80%99re-anarchists.

some left spaces to flirt with anti-Semitism, to passively condone non-white racial separatism, and to allow the kind of cross-political alliances common in anti-imperialist organizing. "They want a unity of opposites versus the center, all extremists versus the center," says antifascist researcher Spencer Sunshine.[36]

From the materials of these groups emerges a vision of the world with racially exclusive city-states, which choose tribal affiliation by a number of means. Some tribal groups would be whites only, some black only, and others multiracial. Some would be queer-normative, others would exclude gays; some would be capitalist and others communist. They would have "autonomous zones" for trade and exchange, and all would stand against "pernicious" Jewish control. Keith Preston, formerly a member of the anarcho-syndicalist organization the Workers' Solidarity Alliance and radical union the IWW, took these ideas further with the website *Attack the System*, which uses the term "pan-secessionism," to include all those "against the system," from white nationalists to anarchists, allying themselves in opposition to the state. *Attack the System* and NATA even invited non-white people to join their ranks, including writers such as Vince Rinehart, a Tlingit tribal member who supports various forms of indigenous nationalism.[37]

International Third Position

National Revolution takes a lot of these Third Positionist ideas in another direction, influenced by Russian fascist thinker Aleksandr Dugin, whose background in traditionalism and National Bolshevism tries to sync fascism and anti-capitalism from a uniquely non-Western perspective. Similarly, National Action (NA) revitalizes open neo-Nazism in the U.K. and Europe but is influenced by some elements of Autonomous Marxism and Situationism to develop a critique of the "Crisis of Modernity" and uses it to mobilize young people to action. Though relatively small—and banned as a "terrorist organization"—NA is growing as it recruits, with its revolutionary rhetoric and violent opposition to the liberal state, young people whose orientation might previously be toward insurrectionary left movements. Fascist groups that have incorporated

---

36   Spencer Sunshine, interview with author, December 5, 2016.
37   Jack Donovan and Vince Rinehart, "Episode #2 – Vince Rinehart," *Start the World*.

leftist strategies dominate many sections of the European far-right. German Autonomous Nationalists, for example, take inspiration from the Autonomen by showing up in Black Bloc dress ready to fight the police. In Ukraine, these disparate nationalist contingencies unite with a revisionist history of Ukrainian Free Territory revolutionary anarchist Nestor Mahkno. Makhno fought against both the reactionary forces of the czar and the incoming Bolshevik Red Terror, and he's now being reimagined as a Ukrainian nationalist leader pitted against Soviet communism. The anti-colonialist guerilla revolt of Che Guevara, the insurrectionary resistance of Mao, and the anarchist call for direct action, they argue, are implicitly about the violent assertion of essential identity.[38]

Borrowing from the left is a prevalent tactic, but it lacks the history and real connection to the original ideals. While they may share a revolutionary spirit, a disdain for the immiserating effects of capitalism, and some aspects of romantic utopianism, what defined left revolutionary movements was the destruction of authority, the cause of universal freedom, and blanket egalitarianism. While the fascist right can appropriate the critique, from a rejection of late-capitalist consumerism to the problems of suicidal environmental destruction, what defines revolutionary left movements is the fight for equality.[39]

Back to the Streets

In the U.S., White Aryan Resistance (WAR) mixed the skinhead aesthetic with Third Positionist critiques through the 1980s and 90s. Built by former John Birch Society and KKK member Tom Metzger, WAR focused on recruiting a foot-soldier contingent from the growing white supremacist skinhead milieu for a contemporary American Schutzstaffel (the paramilitary wing of the Nazis). Building relationships with groups like the Hammerskin Nation and appealing to a baser racism with their racial cartoon-laden newspaper, WAR identified the capitalist class as the primary enemy of the white race. Bringing in a former Trotskyist, Metzger abandoned his earlier rabid anti-unionist, anti-communism by developing a set of

---

38   Ross, *Against the Fascist Creep*, 198–227.
39   It is this syncretic quality that often leads to the most frightening evolutions in thought from people previously associated with left-oriented movements who then take on fascist qualities. That does not, however, mean that the left movements that share figures and areas of critique with the right have uniquely problematic features.

ideas that put opposition to international capitalism front and center, not just because of its supposed Jewish nature, but because of its destruction of the white working class.[40]

Taking cues from Identitarian groups in France, Identity Evropa has burst onto the U.S. scene. Primarily structured as a "fraternal organization" and a propaganda project, their key tenets include racialism, traditionalism, opposition to political correctness, and combating the fatal subversion of the West through cultural Marxism. Founder Nathan Damigo has networked so well with the growing Alt Right that Identity Evropa has become a "go to" organization for young people, especially those radicalized through campus "Students for Trump" organizations and online message boards.[41]

The American Third Position Party was launched in the U.S. in 2010, with an ostensibly "pro-white" platform opposed to free trade and immigration. The party ran filmmaker Merlin Miller and white nationalist professor Virginia Abernathy for president in 2012 and made it onto the ballot in three states. Founded by William Johnson—who penned the "Pace Amendment," which proposed that only non-Hispanic whites should retain American citizenship—the party was renamed the American Freedom Party (AFP) later to play on the success Johnson saw with the Tea Party. Despite the name, the party and its candidates rarely critiqued capitalism and seemed to recruit from the hard edge of libertarians, Patriots, and Constitution Party dissidents. Today the AFP has well-known white nationalists and Alt Right figures, such as Kevin MacDonald, James Edwards, and Tomislav Sunic, on its board.[42]

The Alt Right broadly fits into the Third Positionist framework, especially the meta-political efforts of *Radix Journal*, Counter-Currents Publishing, and Arktos Media. The Alt Right has traditionally been made up of ex-libertarians and pro-market ideologues, but they now reject those notions, believing instead that libertarianism leads to "degeneracy," a lack of collective identity, and miscegenation because of its lack of social authority. The Alt Right can be considered a "post-libertarian" ideology, and remains critical of free market ideas even if anarcho-capitalism and Austrian School capitalist economics were a part of its ideological development.

40   Ezekiel Raphael, *The Racist Mind* (New York: Viking, 1995), 74–91.
41   Nathan Damigo, interview with author, May 5, 2016.
42   "American Freedom Party," *Southern Poverty Law Center*, https://www.splcenter.org/fighting-hate/extremist-files/group/american-freedom-party.

Entry of Opposites

Fascism relies on contradictions. As a syncretic ideology, it proudly holds ideas together thought to be at odds. While Mussolini's fascist movement decried what we would call feminism, it also fought to give women an expanded role in the state by extending voting rights. WAR attacked feminism as a Jewish disease, but also thought that sexism had to be abolished and Aryan women to be raised up. These contradictions define the Third Positionist ideological position, which appropriates the left to further greater inequality. This creates the potential for fascist politics to find their way into left-oriented mass movement projects. With a desire to deconstruct assumptions about the world and centers of power, far-right ideas are often adopted in complex analysis uncritically.

Alexander Reid Ross has labeled this process, in which radical political cultures and movements on the left begin to adapt ideas from the radical right, "creeping fascism." Though the phenomenon is being dismissed as marginal, incidental, or new, it has been foundational to fascist movements since Mussolini's adaptation from the Italian Socialist Party. At a point when radical theory attempts to destabilize the basic assumptions of the social order, which all revolutionary movements do, the foundations of a "left" analysis, namely human equality, can become tenuous. The ideological compromises that movements have made in the past, such as allowing problematic coalition members during anti-war or anti-imperialist struggles, can allow far-right analysis to creep in.[43]

In 2016, the Brooklyn Commons became mired in controversy after the decision was made to host an anti-Semitic "9/11 Truth" speaker, Christopher Bollyn. The Commons is a café and working space rented at "below market-rate" by projects like *Jacobin* and the Marxist Education Project and often hosts speakers and events that have a progressive or radical bent. The owner, Melissa Ennen, was known to be a "9/11 Truther" herself and issued a statement that the space was to be used for controversial and conflicting views and was not a "safe space."

Bollyn has been employed by Liberty Lobby projects, such as the far-right publication that helped to center white nationalism and Holocaust Denial in conservatism. He has written recently for the *American Free Press*, focusing heavily on the conspiratorial role he saw for Jews in U.S. foreign policy, claiming that Israel was behind

---

43   Alexander Reid Ross, interview with author, January 15, 2017.

the 9/11 attacks. Building on a conspiracy theory that "unites the left and the right," Bollyn posited in the *American Free Press* that the attacks were orchestrated to allow military intervention as a Middle Eastern oil grab.[44] He has appeared on former KKK leader David Duke's radio show and is known for citing the forged *Protocols of the Elders of Zion,* alleging that Jews run financial and media systems worldwide.[45] Bollyn's talk at the Brooklyn Commons was, presumably, to be about alleged Israeli involvement in 9/11 and other acts of terrorism, playing on well-worn conspiracy theories about the role of Jews in violent world affairs. While this is not normally the kind of discourse the Commons would allow, since it is couched in the vitriolic language of conspiracy and because the group singled out were Jews, Ennen overlooked the speaker's past and refused to cancel the event. Unfortunately, it is not totally uncommon in radical circles that a shared political position—for example, criticism of Israeli nationalism and conduct—blinds some to other extremely problematic issues. Anti-Semitism rears its head in revolutionary left movements just as it does on the right, and politics framed as "anti-Zionist" overstep the boundaries of legitimate criticism and can extend to Jews, Judaism, or anti-Semitic conspiracy theories.[46]

In response to the announcement of this event, *Jacobin* and other tenants at the Commons issued a statement asking Ennen to reverse her decision.[47] The event continued anyway and protesters amassed outside, including a large Jewish contingent angry that a known anti-Semite would be hosted in a progressive space. Jewish Anti-Fascist Action was there to confront the willingness of left-oriented spaces to flirt with anti-Semitism. A new group called Common Decency was formed after the issue with the Commons, and it organized a boycott of the space. The project is using the

---

44   Michael, *Willis Carto and The American Far-right*, 231.
45   "Brooklyn Commons Hosting Anti-Semitic Truther Christopher Bollyn," *Jew School*, September 3, 2016, https://jewschool.com/2016/09/77362/brooklyn-commons-hosting-antisemitic-truther-christopher-bollyn/.
46   It should be noted clearly that criticism of, or outright opposition to, Israel is not anti-Semitic. However, citing those criticisms in terms of its Jewish character is, as is using false histories to minimize Jewish suffering, anti-Semitism, or to suggest a primacy of Jewry in problematic world affairs. The problems with Israel are imperialism and nationalism, not Judaism.
47   "Statement from Multiple Organizations on Christopher Bollyn Event at The Brooklyn Commons," *The Brooklyn Institute for Social Research*, September 4, 2016, https://thebrooklyninstitute.com/news/statement-from-multiple-organizations-on-christopher-bollyn-event-at-the-brooklyn-commons/.

campaign as a pilot for a broad-based community-organizing approach to antifascist issues.[48]

The earliest days of the environmental movement in the United States are stained by racism—an early advocate, Madison Grant, equated environmental protection with the preservation of formalized white supremacy. Many people know EF! as an environmental direct action group and for the anarchist character it took on in the late 1980s, but this came after a fierce resistance to the racist attitudes and masculinist behavior of many early founders. Judi Bari and the IWW were influential in this, and at a movement gathering in 1986, a group of anarchists challenged the racist machismo that permeated the group. That year, the *Earth First! Journal* ran a story called "Alien Nation," which called for closed borders, an idea long supported by EF! founder Dave Foreman who had a relationship with the white nationalist Tanton Network and, later, the Rewilding Institute. Early in EF!'s development, masculinist calls for violence were central, epidemics like AIDS were celebrated, and vulgar, racist language was used in arguments.

That year, 1986, anarchist EF! members came to the EF! rendezvous with confrontation in mind, and activists like Ed Abbey were unwilling to hear it. The group shut down Abbey, and he came back with what they called the "Buckaroo Squad," threatening campers with weapons and homophobic taunts and hailing to the "mountain man" aesthetic of heteronormative violence that Abbey and others had desperately tried to cultivate in their green cult of martyrdom. This confrontation exposed Abbey and the early generation of EF! as harboring a male-driven and white supremacist politic. From then on, the movement sought to develop an anti-oppression stance. Foreman continued to deepen his racialist understanding of the ecological crisis, writing for Californians for Population Stabilization and acting as a leader for Apply the Brakes, another immigration restrictionist organization—but by then he was a relative outsider to the EF! movement.[49]

---

48 Spencer Sunshine, interview with author, December 5, 2016.
49 "Dave Foreman Still Aligning with Bigots | Earth First! Newswire," *Earth First! Newswire*, September 30, 2011, http://earthfirstjournal.org/newswire/2011/09/30/dave-foreman-still-aligning-with-bigots/.

Faith, Family, and Folk

The fascist project has always tried to root itself in a transcendent, spiritual impulse. Much of the racism that permeates the fascist right is rooted in theories that utilize spiritual explanations for racial differences, rather than the falsified "data" of "racial science." The earliest construct for contemporary racism comes out of two key tracts from sixteenth century Spain and Portugal. The first, and dominant one, was that non-white people were "pre-Adamic," meaning they were humanoid mammals that arrived before proper people did. To square things with the Bible they placed these "creatures" as animals created before the true "Adamic" race. The second tract says that they are a degenerate people, and their failure to reach true "Aryanness" comes from their failing moral lineage. Both pieces were foundational in the creation of racial science, but both are mythic in their explanation and are maintained in many racialized interpretations of Christianity, Hinduism, and Neo-paganism.[1]

The early periods of Bavarian romanticism saw something *essential* about identity that went beyond the physical form; it was as true in spirit as it was in blood. As fascism advanced as a political response to the economic crisis after World War I, it did so out of the growing desire to find a strict identity founded in esoteric teaching, occult mysteries, and initiatory paths. While the NSDAP and Hitler moved in the direction of vulgar racial science, a feature of the Alt Right today, they had a parallel spiritual track that has had enduring influence. Identitarianism, various Third Position ideologies, and the various incarnations that we see popping up

---

1   Sussman, *The Myth of Race*, 13–25.

have deep roots in certain types of esotericism, which has provided special tools for fascism to build on and given it a unique appeal for people in transition, crisis, or on a quest for answers to life's big questions.

As was true of many eras of fascist ideological development, from the mystical anti-rationality of the Germanic volkish movements to the European New Right, Christianity is often seen as responsible for the disastrous effects of "modernity." As social ecologist Janet Biehl points out, Christianity seeks an end to alienation and toward a pure "essence," which is mirrored in identitarianism, Traditionalism, and Third Positionism:

> In the view of the "New" Right today, the destruction of the environment and the repression of nationalities have a common root in "Semitic" monotheism and universalism. In its later form, Christianity, and in its subsequent secularized forms, liberalism and Marxism, this dualistic, homogenizing universalism is alleged to have brought on both the ecological crisis and the suppression of national identity. Just as Judeo-Christian universalism was destructive of authentic cultures when Christian missionaries went out into the world, so too is modernity eliminating ethnic and national cultures. Moreover, through the unbridled technology to which it gave rise, this modern universalism is said to have perpetrated not only the destruction of nature but an annihilation of the spirit; the destruction of nature, it is said, is life-threatening in the spiritual sense as well as the physical, since when people deny pristine nature, their access to their "authentic" self is blocked.[2]

Part of this opposition is then a result of the "anti-Americanism" that runs through much fascist thought, in that they oppose the globalized systems of capitalism, "McCulture," and universalized spiritual identities. This is a reminder of the contradictions so present in the radical right milieu: that one sector can brand themselves patriots, à la the KKK of the 1920s, while another trend, such as National Revolution, can label themselves traitors to Western capitalism and imperialism.

---

2   Biehl and Staudenmaier, *Ecofascism*, 34.

God of Thunder, God of War

For those encountering neo-fascism today, the most common form of esotericism is neo-paganism. Mystics rediscovered the pre-Christian European religions during the early periods of capitalism, industrialism, and mass cultural orientation as a way for Europeans to find an identity for themselves that was rooted in their own uniqueness. This was a way to separate themselves from the "universalism" of Christian salvation, as well as its Jewish nature. Since the seventeenth century paganism, first with neo-Druidic study and then various other traditions, has been a testament to the romanticism that developed out of early industrialization and urbanization, which took its toll on agrarian life and unsettled deeply rooted communities. While these more traditional folkways should not be seen through rose-colored glasses, they still had a connection with neighbors and the commitment to a "life of the soul" that many pined for. This, paired with nationalism in many cases, inspired much of the aesthetic and religious basis that we saw in fascist movements in the twentieth century.

Heathenry, the Germanic-Nordic pagan religion, is the most common type of neo-paganism to be found in an explicitly racialized form. Odinism, as it has often been called, was developed by Else Christensen in the first half of the twentieth century as an explicitly racial religion, one that was equal parts anti-capitalism and tribalism. Christensen's background was rooted in anarcho-syndicalism, which she attempted to synthesize with the racial ideas that were coming out of Germany. She imagined tribal non-state communities founded on indigenous religions, which were racially exclusive and built on traditional craftsmanship and ecological sustainability. Odinism has gone on to be known as an explicitly racialized religion and sees Odin as the figurehead of the spiritual pantheon that is unique to those of Northern European people.[3]

What drives much of this movement is the early work of Carl Jung, who, at one point, saw the development of psychological archetypes as racial. In his influential essay "Wotan," Jung outlines the idea that Hitler and the Third Reich were the unrestrained spirit of Wotan (Odin) resurrected in the Germanic soul. In this perspective, the gods and goddesses of indigenous religions are unique to those with that ancestry. In the Jungian concept, the archetypes of the warrior, the pursuer of knowledge, and the conqueror are manifested in Odin,

---

3   Mattias Gardell, *Gods of the Blood* (Durham: Duke University Press, 2003), 165–70.

and other ethnicities and cultures have archetypes in their gods that are unique to their biological and spiritual character. This is the foundational idea that has driven much of the racialized heathenry, and it is what fuels European New Right scholars like de Benoist, who wrote in his seminal book *On Being a Pagan* that Europeans should identify with their pagan archetypes.

For many, the archetypes are not good enough, and they see them both as metaphors and, literally, as gods and goddesses, different spirits and impulses that are made religious and knowable through the images of gods and the stories of the lore. Heathenry is singled out because much of the theological work was done by and for this racialist purpose, as a way of providing a counter-cultural identity to whites. Building on the image of the Vikings, it countered modern narratives and argued that the true nature of Northern Europeans was that of a tribal warrior who prioritizes his "in-group" over his "out-group."[4]

In the U.S., a slightly less racialized version of heathenry named Asatru became dominant. It was more focused on magic and the unique interpretation of Icelandic lore. While Asatru did not champion the open Nazism of many Odinist groups, it maintained a "folkish" distinction in many kindreds, and asserted itself as the religion of the Northern European peoples through genetic privilege. The Asatru Folk Assembly and its founder, Stephen McNallen, maintain this idea, and the principles of Asatru are centered on its European identity and "answering a call" that comes deep from their ancestors. A focus on "reconstruction" and historical accuracy has reigned, and they attempt to bring Germanics back to the most "untainted" version of their tribal religion. Anti-racist heathens, who are the vast majority, share much of the archetypal vision and view on tradition and customs but the folkish community has been increasingly vocal.[5] Jack Donovan's Wolves of Vinland, a closed heathen group known for mixing tribal spirituality and the structure of a biker gang into a type of National Anarchism, and their recruitment tool, Operation Werewolf, is one of these, attempting to redefine the boundaries of heathenry by focusing on the violence and male virility of a tribally defined spirituality. Operation Werewolf reflects Wolves of Vinland founder Paul Waggener,

---

4   The best example of this narrative is found in: Stephen McNallen, *Asatru: A Native European Spirituality* (Minneapolis, MN: Runestone Press, 2015).

5   Mattias Gardell, *Gods of The Blood* (Durham: Duke University Press, 2003), 258–76.

who mixes his own brand of nihilist philosophy, exercise regimens, and black metal aesthetics. While the Wolves are a close-knit group that is hard to join, Operation Werewolf has worked as a tent that former skinheads, bikers, MMA fighters, powerlifters, and others moving to the fringes can unite under. Its decentralization and focus on what we could call "lifestyle fascism" presents a concerted meta-political threat as it is creating a close-knit subculture of rightist men who were unable to find shelter in insurrectionary organizations on the wane.

Paganism is dominant among non-Christian white nationalists and has a deep influence on even secular nationalist philosophy, arts, and aesthetics. Fascist neofolk music is centered in a similar romanticism of Europe's past, and everyone from NPI to the *Daily Stormer* venerate the Nordic gods of Odin, Thor, and Freyja despite not believing in them in a literal sense. The most violent interpretation, known as Wotanism, was developed by The Order terrorist, and former Aryan Nations member, David Lane and still proliferates among skinheads and white supremacist prison gangs. Other than just seeing racialism as a component of their spirituality, Wotanism sees racial identity and warfare as the driving focus of it and uses apocalyptic warrior language to justify mass violence in the name of racial preservation and expansion.[6]

Though not nearly as prevalent, there have been racialized interpretations of Celtic and Welsh paganism, traditions more closely associated with leftist interpretations and Wicca. Reconstructionism itself has come under fire as a concept as it is so closely allied with nationalists looking for identity. Rodnovery's connection to Russian nationalism, Hellenism with Greek nationalism, orthodox Shinto reconstructionism in Japan, and Hindu nationalism all draw connections between the "native faith" and the national identity, which centers ethnic identity in sectarian conflict. The spiritual foundation here is not found in a particular tradition's lore and customs but in the uniquely modern idea that spirituality is particular to the metaphysical psychology of a particular ethnic group. This has increasingly driven political movements in many countries, where a strong meta-politic has to be developed in order for the citizenry to accept nationalism.

---

6   Nicholas Goodrick-Clarke, *Black Sun: Aryan Cults, Esoteric Nazism and the Politics of Identity* (New York: New York University Press, 2002), 269–77.

Book of Shadows

Outside of heathenry and ethnic paganism, Left Hand Path (LHP) traditions differ in their rejection of conventional morality. Posing in opposition to the "universal morality" and the redemption offered by what they call Right Hand Path religions, LHP traditions make up various different strands of thought including Satanism, Thelema, the Temple of Set, and various Middle Eastern and Hindu sects. While the term "Left Hand Path" is not a great dividing line for actually studying religion, those who use it often make up different esoteric paths that venerate the self. Though the vast majority of contemporary LHP people denounce racism, there are groups that have notoriously mixed the religion and racism. The Order of Nine Angels advocated a type of "Satanic Nazism" that proposed eugenics in the form of human sacrifice. The Joy of Satan, similarly, shared members with known Nazi groups and advocated a Gnostic reading of Biblical scripture that reframed Yahweh as the evil "Jewish" God that people had to overcome to discover their true destiny.

The National Socialist Liberation Front (NSLF), originally founded by hippie-dropout-turned-fascist revolutionary Joseph Charles Tomassi in 1974, was modeled on Yockey's own European Liberation Front as a "propaganda of the deed" project. It was taken up by the occult-minded James Mason, who used Satanism and an obsession with Charles Manson to advocate for a new type of terror war against the globalizing commercial influences of the "Zionist Occupation Governments" in NSLF's newsletter *Siege*.[7]

Thelema, the esoteric religion developed by infamous occultist Aleister Crowley in the early twentieth century, focuses heavily on the discovery of "True Will" in participants and the use of formal ritual magic and the worship of archetypal gods, often of Mesopotamian and Egyptian origin. A marginal attorney and Libertarian Party of Florida Senate candidate made waves in 2015 as his mix of Thelema and nationalism brought the support of skinhead groups like the American Front. Augustus Sol Invictus, the name given to him in a religious ceremony, had many high-profile incidents that drew media attention, like going on a desert spirit quest and sacrificing a goat on camera. Invictus's own politic is one that aligns with many LHP adherents, which is a "Will to Power" desire for themselves. Invictus believes that human sacrifice to the gods unites a nation, and he worships "pan-European" gods, believing that all

---

7   Ibid., 217–28.

European gods were just different names for the same transcendent forces. He became active in supporting various fascist organizations, including speaking at the National Socialist Movement conference and the reformation event for the American Front, whom he also defended in court against terrorism charges.[8]

While Hinduism is not an essential part of the American fascist movement, the white savior of Nazi Vedas remains important for the meta-political underpinnings. Savitri Devi was a French-born Greek who turned to the Hindu myths in a search for a more authentic and non-Semitic spirituality. Following the Indo-Aryan mythology about the Caucasian origin of the Vedas, Devi believed Hinduism was an ancient Aryan religion, even if contemporary Indians had been ruined through race mixing. Following the Vedic cycle of ages and search for avatars, Devi saw Hitler as the reincarnation of the Hindu god Vishnu, who many in Hindu nationalism venerated and saw as a model for how to treat the Muslim population in India. Both during and after the war, Devi became a focal point for international fascist projects, living the life of a nationalist aesthetic committed fervently to her own brand of heretical mystic Hinduism.[9]

While race is only one component of these religions, their beliefs are centered on human inequality and the necessity of domination. If you strip fascism of its racial components, which some ideological currents do, the belief in the cruelty of formalized hierarchy and violence is still implicit. If these occultist paths reject equality and a basic respect for universal human dignity, which is part and parcel for the rejection of historic "religious" morality inside of the LHP movement, then it intersects so clearly with fascism that it is difficult to come to its defense even though it denies bigotry.

Men Among the Ruins

While the spiritual paths of paganism and occultism have presented a strong spiritual counter-narrative to liberal Western thought, it is the syncretic nature of traditionalism that has influenced the Alt Right/ New Right the most. Traditionalism is a perennial philosophy that

---

8   Shane Burley, "Fascism Against Time: Nationalism, Media Blindness, and the Cult of Augustus Sol Invictus," *Gods & Radicals*, March 24, 2016, https://god-sandradicals.org/2016/03/24/fascism-against-time-nationalism-media-blindness-and-the-cult-of-augustus-sol-invictus/.

9   Nicholas Goodrick-Clarke, *Hitler's Priestess* (New York: New York University Press, 1998).

sees all religions as coming from a single "divine source," similar to theosophy. The traditionalism of people like mystic philosopher René Guénon and Evola held that the spiritual traditions themselves—the hierarchies and militant social structures—were divine as well, and those traditional stratifications were sacrosanct for maintaining aristocratic divine rule.

Evola positioned himself to the right of European fascism, criticizing it for not maintaining traditional hierarchical life clearly enough. Influenced by Hindu and Tantric mysticism, Evola subscribed to the Vedic "theory of ages," which breaks down world cycles into four distinct ages and sees our current period of "degeneracy" as a part of the Dark Age, or Kali Yuga. Society was most healthy when stratified, and through the ages different Vedic castes had ruled, with the Brahmin caste of priestly aristocrats as the destined leaders, rather than the lowest caste of workers who have come to dominate in the twentieth century through Marxism. The world is then created in a spiritual image, with different types of people intended to rule over others, based on perceived innate qualities. Evola found Tantrism as an alternative to what he saw as the egalitarian and democratic values of modernity, where initiatory spiritual orders are a hierarchical alternative to the modern world of technology. In Evola's flagship book *Against the Modern World*, he outlines a complete rejection of the current state of the world, in part because the "lesser races" of the Global South have access to Aryan nations. The alternative to the universal cosmopolitanism of the contemporary world is the world of Tradition, the spiritual foundations that lie underneath and promise transcendence through inequality. Since the end of the Kali Yuga and the return to the Golden Age are inevitable, he proposes an absolution from politics and instead advocates becoming "aristocrats of the soul," a proposal that still fuels many inside of Neoreaction and the New Right.[10] While Evola certainly had a race realist understanding of racial groups, he also believed that a "spiritual race" underlies this and that even someone who had a non-white body could rise to become an Aryan by virtue of their warrior spirit. Jews took a special place of scorn and, despite being entranced by Hebraic Kabbalah, he thought that the Jewish soul was particularly degenerate when "secularized." Consistent with his belief in the power of myth, he acknowledged that while the *Protocols of the*

10   Ibid., 54–67.

Elders of Zion was a forgery, it still accurately described the way that Jews undermined the West.[11]

The extent of Evola's influence on modern neo-fascism cannot be overestimated. Evola is a motivating ideologue in groups like the National Anarchist-leaning Wolves of Vinland, in their rejection of modernity and "return" to tribal values.[12] While his extensive esoteric spirituality is often not ported over directly, the Alt Right greatly values his analysis, and Counter-Currents, Arktos Media, and the National Policy Institute are foundationally centered in his worldview. While Evola decried neo-paganism as "idle nature worship" and thought it was illegitimate because it "lacked a chain of initiation," it has still been incredibly influential inside of folkish paganism. Journals like *TYR* use the Evolian term "Radical Traditionalism" and publish excerpts of Evola's books alongside articles by nationalist pagan theorists like Colin Cleary, who writes about reclaiming ethnic religion. This is largely a testament to the lack of consistency and the breadth of work on the radical right, and therefore Evola tends to permeate wherever the fascist tradition attempts spiritual depth, since they hold few philosophers.

Evola's influence has been made terrifyingly material in the decades of violent "revolts" he has inspired. The neo-fascist militant organization Ordine Nuovo was founded by a student of Evola, Giuseppe Umberto "Pino" Rauti, and intended to developed a class of "political soldiers" and "warrior aesthetics" that would reinforce state power by handing it to violent agents of the government.[13] Directly tied to the revolutionary Traditionalist ideology at play in the 1969 bombing at Milan's Piazza Fontana,[14] Nuovo also attacked an antifascist march in 1974, murdering eight activists.[15] Terrorist organizations in an international network of fascist groups see their revolutionary origin in Evola and feel the need to reclaim a warrior life and strike out against the world—rhetoric that often found allies on the left in those who looked to "break the spell" of international

---

11   John Morgan, William Neville, Richard Spencer, "The Idea Is Our Fatherland," podcast audio, *Radix Journal*, MP3, 47:21, Dec 12, 2014, archived at https://player.fm/series/the-radix-podcast-radix-journal/the-idea-is-our-fatherland.

12   Paul Waggener, interview by Greg Johnson, Counter-Currents Publishing, February 3, 2016, http://www.counter-currents.com/2016/02/greg-johnson-interviews-paul-waggener-2/.

13   Goodrick-Clarke, *Black Sun*, 67–68.

14   Ross, *Against the Fascist Creep*, 86.

15   "Italy Jails Far-Right Militants for 1974 Brescia Bombing-BBC News," *BBC News*, July 23, 2015, http://www.bbc.com/news/world-europe-33633872.

consumerism. Environmental radicals have been especially vulnerable to this type of ideological infiltration, as we saw former Earth Liberation Front prisoners Exile and Sadie begin professing Evolian-inspired traditionalism that focused on hidden spiritual qualities of race and its connection to the natural world.[16]

While many of these fascist esoteric ideas are often not taken literally, they are seen as a metaphorical understanding of a material phenomenon. As Greg Johnson points out, the spiritual ideas are often seen as metaphorical understandings of racist and anti-Semitic ideas that need an emotional grounding, which moves beyond verifiable history and science. Johnson, as the publisher of Counter-Currents, has been instrumental in publishing fascist spiritual scribes from Radical Traditionalism to fascist occultism to ethnic paganism, yet he sees them as metaphorical components of a scientific phenomenon that is explicitly racial and hierarchical.

> I think that ultimately the context in which you have to appreciate myth and metaphysics is a somewhat naturalist and somewhat pragmatic approach to these things. Meaning, you can understand, naturalistically, the motives that give rise to religiosity and you can give pragmatic accounts of its utility.[17]

For years thinkers like Evola were a great example of the canon from which the fascist right drew, unbeknown to modern conservatives. In a 2014 speech that rocked the Catholic world, Steve Bannon, the former *Breitbart* CEO and senior White House advisor, cited Evola, along with Russia New Rightist Aleksandr Dugin, drawing a connection between traditionalism and his attraction to an aggressive twenty-first-century nationalism with tactical roots in Leninism.[18] Evola's influence in more "mainstream" areas of fascist crossover continues because of the intellectual depth of his work, but the ideas themselves go further than most on the far-right. Bannon wants revolution, to reshape society on the basis of a believed spiritual order that necessitates a violent assertion of marginalized people into areas of servitude, poverty, and persecution. While the

---

16   "Former ELF/Green Scare Prisoner 'Exile' Now a Fascist," NYC ANTIFA, August 5, 2014, https://nycantifa.wordpress.com/2014/08/05/exile-is-a-fascist/.

17   Greg Johnson, interview with author, 2016.

18   Jason Horowitz, "Bannon Cited Italian Thinker Who Inspired Fascists," *New York Times,* February 10, 2017, https://www.nytimes.com/2017/02/10/world/europe/bannon-vatican-julius-evola-fascism.html?_r=0.

complexity of Evola's mystical ideas are little understood beyond adepts committed to Aryan mysticism, his ideas of the persistent nature of tradition have come to define an area of the right that is looking for a coherent tradition of identity and innate inequality beyond the bounds of Western conservatism.

Similar to Evola, Miguel Serrano has seen a revival over the last twenty years, though his Gnostic ideas about the Aryan race are more convoluted, theologically confusing, and, therefore, more marginal. Here, the Jews are seen as the race of a lesser ethnic god who attempts to challenge the great Aryan gods for hegemony, destroying the material plane with universalism.[19] The secular understanding of this has been revived in the Alt Right, where the "destructive nature" of the Jews is taken back many millenniums in an attempt to trace the loss of racial consciousness in whites to the influence of Jews, even if the spiritual narrative is only metaphoric.[20]

Children of Zion

Because of America's overwhelmingly Christian demographic, U.S.-based white nationalist groups have traditionally, strategically built inroads with the Christian right. Built on the axis of anti-communism of the 1950s, organizations like the John Birch Society were able to intensify the politicization of Christianity as an anti-liberal force and helped to radicalize many prominent leaders in the white supremacist movement.[21] While Christianity has often been used to justify whatever institutional oppression is at play during a historical period, from the inquisition through Chattel slavery and Jim Crow segregation, it was after World War II that it became a tool to radicalize conservative Jesus-loving groups into the neo-fascist movement.

Playing on rural racism and the legacy of Christian anti-Semitism, the Christian Identity (CI) movement became a huge opportunity for Nazis when they found a narrative originally coined as "British Israelism." CI synthesized some of the most radical

---

19 Goodrick-Clarke, *Black Sun,* 179–186.
20 Mike Enoch, "Between Two Lampshades: Mike and Cledun's Passover LARP Extravaganza," *The Right Stuff,* April 11, 2015, http://therightstuff.biz/2015/04/11/between-two-lampshades-mike-and-cleduns-passover-larp-extravaganza/.
21 This includes people like White Aryan Resistance founder Tom Metzger, Creativity Movement founder Ben Klassen, and National Alliance founder William Pierce, among many others.

racial thinking of neo-Nazis with fundamentalist Christianity, centering white Europeans as the "chosen people." This undermined the idea presented by the Scofield Reference Bible and understood broadly in American Christianity: that the Israelites of the Old Testament were the ancestors of today's Jews. Instead, CI asserted that it was, in fact, white people that were the real Israelites of the Bible, and they then migrated through Europe and became the Western white nations. The Jews, in contrast, were a demonic tribe who were created in a schismatic birth of Cain through insemination of Eve by the Devil in what is often called "Dual Seedline Theory." People of color are actually pre-Adamic peoples, animals that, unlike proper white humans, do not have souls. Jews then attempt to destroy the chosen white people through race mixing and, of course, degeneracy.[22]

This radical interpretation quickly fueled the most violent recesses of the white nationalist movement, centering on Aryan Nations, the Church of Jesus Christ-Christian, and many fourth-generation KKK and militia organizations. Their eschatological view of "race war" fueled some of the most frightening acts of terrorism over the last quarter of the twentieth century. The terrorism of The Order—including the killing of Jewish radio-host Alan Berg and a Missouri State Highway Patrol officer—was some of the most pronounced of the 1980s. Eric Rudolph, who went on the run in 1998 after allegedly bombing gay bars and abortion clinics, and Buford Furrow, who opened fire at a Los Angeles Jewish Community Center, were tied to the identity movement and Aryan Nations. Even more violent, the Phineas Priesthood developed out of the identity movement, using a twisted interpretation of the Phineas story from the Bible to develop "self-anointed warriors" who would then kill "race mixers." This label has been applied to a number of attacks over the last couple of decades, including an eight-person cell in Spokane, Washington, accused of a series of bombings.[23]

Today Christian Identity has largely faded because of its association with violence, bizarre conspiracy theories, and the working-class rural character of the movement that is even further losing its financial stability. The most well-known Christian Identity organization, the Aryan Nations compound, was shut down

---

22		Martin Durham, *White Rage* (London and New York: Routledge, 2007), 66–72.
23		"Christian Identity," *Anti-Defamation League*, n.d., https://www.adl.org/education/resources/backgrounders/christian-identity.

in a $6.3 million lawsuit settlement against the organization. In 1998, a woman and her son were driving by the compound outside of Coeur d'Alene, Idaho, when their car backfired, inspiring the jumpy guards that surrounded the place to open fire on the vehicle. The lawsuit effectively destroyed the church and militia wing, and along with the death of Reverend Richard Butler, the luminary racist running the operation, the organization and movement devolved into infighting.[24]

More recently, Kinism showed up as a viable option for white racists looking for a biblical justification for ethnic nationalism. Owing more to the racism of Southern churches during Jim Crow segregation, Kinism came out of Presbyterian Calvinism. Kinism holds that a person's primary duty is to one's family, which they interpret as expanding in concentric circles to include "nation" and "race." While they do recognize people of color as equally human, they do not believe that they should share communion with them, thinking instead they belong to separate paths in Christ. This thought flourished to some extent in Southern nationalist and Alt Right organizations, including with Scott Terry and Matthew Heimbach of the Traditionalist Youth Network. Heimbach made waves when he first formed the White Student Union at Towson University and went on to become a celebrity in the white nationalist movement. Scott Terry turned heads when he advocated for slavery at a panel at the Conservative Political Action Conference.[25] Both went on to be guests and writers for *Tribal Theocrat*, a Kinist podcast and website, which argues that the Bible preaches ethnic separatism, that it is historically and scientifically justified, and that Christians have a duty to oppose "egalitarianism" and race mixing.

Orthodox Christianity has also seen a revival, with TradYouth members like Heimbach and Matt Parrot joining the church. This has helped them connect with Russian fascists and Greek Golden Dawn members, as the Orthodox Church has a much larger role in far-right politics in those countries. Heimbach was ex-communicated from his Orthodox Church after a confrontation with a counterprotester he attacked with an Orthodox cross,

24 "Aryan Nations," Southern Poverty Law Center, n.d., https://www.splcenter.org/fighting-hate/extremist-files/group/aryan-nations.

25 "The New Neo-Nazis: How Matthew Heimbach Is Building a Racist Network Across The US," *It's Going Down*, September 30, 2015, https://itsgoingdown.org/the-new-neo-nazis-how-matthew-heimbach-is-building-a-racist-network-across-the-us/.

but he has since connected with churches in Eastern Europe that have validated his racialist stance.[26]

Over the last fifteen years, Christianity has waned as a dominant influence in the far-right. This has happened primarily in the more "hip" circles of the Alt Right, as traditional Christianity is viewed as a political failure and lacking in strong philosophical dimensions. Paganism, specifically heathenry, however, has grown massively in the fascist right. The Christianity that remains is fusing with traditionalism. Neoreaction, for example, has many Catholic and Orthodox Christian members, but their interpretations are largely Evolian and perennial. The traditional Christian members who have remained in the racialist movement have usually been relegated to the rural organizations like the KKK and militia-hybrids, which are often scoffed at by the more highbrow "suit-and-tie" fascists.

All Praise Kek

The Alt Right's "Cult of Kek" best represents the metaphorical spiritual ideas of the right. The term "Kek" was a piece of jargon essentially meaning "LOL" from the MMORPG World of Warcraft, a term that was ported over to Alt Right message boards because of its intersection with gaming culture. The term was similar to an Egyptian frog god immortalized in hieroglyphics, appearing strikingly close to the favorite Alt Right meme Pepe. Some on the Alt Right, both literally and metaphorically, began referring to Kek as an ancient Aryan god of chaos (they believe ancient Egyptians were white), destroying the old order and helping to replace it with one where whites dominate. This traces back to the metaphorical understanding of gods as particular forces of nature or spiritual influences, similar to racialist understandings of heathenry. Kek has become one of the most venerable symbols across the far-right today, one that connects those who revel in 4Chan lingo with committed white nationalists looking for a coded alternative to the swastika. Like any good symbol, it has the ability to communicate to their base while also appearing less caustic to the "normie" public viewing it from the outside.[27]

---

26   Musonius Rufus and Matthew Heimbach, "Rebel Yell 119: Trad Youth, Matt Heimbach," podcast audio, *The Right Stuff*, MP3, 1:42:59, May 27, 2016, https://radio.therightstuff.biz/2016/05/27/rebel-yell-119-trad-youth-matt-heimbach/.

27   "Kek and Christ," *The Right Stuff*, December 16, 2016, http://therightstuff.biz/2016/12/13/kek-and-christ/.

Spiritual Warfare

Fascism is not the logical conclusion of any spiritual path, no matter how historically reactionary or steeped in the institutional oppression of marginalized people. Instead, the open nature of most spiritual paths and its flirtation with spaces of power allow it to channel ideas that people intend to inlay with significance. The same Catholic Church fueled the social climate that built interwar fascism as well as Liberation Theology and the Catholic Workers Movement. What religion provides is a unique identity, tactical set, and meta-politics that can be useful for inspiring followers to go much further than would be coaxed by materialist political gains, and that can shift both right and left.

Religious groups have traditionally been one of the most central antifascist projects, both because churches are center to people's social lives as well as their starting point for engaging with social issues. Those inside of spiritual paths are a massive constituency who can meaningfully confront fascism on their own terms and where it affects them personally.

One of the most prescient of these intercommunity confrontations is inside of paganism, with heathenry becoming well known as a battleground between the folkish and antiracist camps. Because racists have done so much of the theological work, it requires rethinking the foundations from a non-ethnic viewpoint. Over the past several years, heathenry has begun to see a reckoning take place with antiracist heathens taking a stand.

The group Circle Ansuz made a huge impact on this discourse in its short life by presenting an anarchist-specific interpretation of Germanic heathenry. They created a synthesis they called Heathen anarchism—a choice to see the faith in its historical reality as both inspired and flawed:

> There are two main pillars that serve as the foundations of Heathen anarchism. The first is the justification based on historical data, the social practices of the ancient Germanics, and modern archeology. The second justification is rooted in the most commonly accepted creation epic, the Voluspol, and in the spiritual truths inherent in cyclical cosmology.[28]

---

28 "The General Theory of Heathen Anarchism," *Circle Ansuz*, July 4, 2013, https://circleansuz.wordpress.com/2013/07/04/the-general-theory-of-heathen -anarchism/.

They saw the egalitarian practices in the Viking spiritual culture as inspirational but incomplete, and they rejected a romantic rewriting of history. Instead, the cyclical nature of the spirituality, the individualism and anti-hierarchical relationship to the gods, and the anti-imperial traditions of heathenry against the expansive colonization of European Christianity provide inspiration.[29] They took the "warrior spirituality" implicit in some of heathenry as inspiration in a battle against fascism and made confrontation with fascist influences in countercultural spaces a key component of their platform. Before going dormant, they had "kindreds" (religious formations) in San Francisco and Portland and also allowed for general "at large" membership, in an effort to mimic the structure of general heathen organizations, providing a real alternative for religious heathens who wanted the spiritual community.

Over the past several years, heathen organizations around the country have begun to go from passive acceptance to explicit rejection of folkish heathenry. When McNallen passed on the leadership role of the Asatru Folk Assembly to a new generation, they began taking to social media proclaiming their allegiance to traditional gender roles and "white men and women." McNallen himself has become an increasingly controversial figure, seeing blowback for his relationship with the Alt Right and anti-immigrant stances. In response to the Asatru Folk Assembly's behavior, heathen organizations around the country have issued statements denouncing the folkish interpretations, drawing a line in the sand. The Troth, the largest heathen organization in the U.S., has always had a "universalist" stance on inclusions but in 2016 finally issued a statement unequivocally saying that heathenry was not an ethnic religion and was instead open to all believers.

Many joined together for the Declaration 127 campaign, which cited the 127th declaration in the Havamal, a book of Viking quotes used as a holy book in many heathen kindreds. The declaration reads, "When you see misdeeds, speak out against them, and give enemies no frid [peace]." Blogs and organizations around the U.S. signed on, saying that it was a heathen imperative to speak out against racists in their religion. They have committed to not work with organizations that have discriminatory policies, like the Asatru Folk Assembly, especially since many of the racialist heathen organizations sell many of the religious items and books that pagans use in spiritual communion.[30]

---

29   Ibid.
30   "Declaration 127," available at: http://declaration127.com/.

Organizations like Heathens United Against Racism (HUAR) have been taking this work a step further, organizing publicly against racialist paganism *as heathens*. In an attempt to unite antiracist heathens, they are further marginalizing the folkish voices that have dominated public perception of the faith. On May Day 2016, Beltane on the Germanic pagan calendar, they held the Light the Beacons event, a chance for antiracist heathens to light fires, including candles and bonfires, and to share it publicly as an act of antiracist defiance. This was inspired by the bonfires held in Germany on May 8, 2015, celebrating the seventieth anniversary of the defeat of Nazism.[31] HUAR relies heavily on a social media convergence to create a strong anti-racist heathen counter narrative. Their "Stephen McNallen Doesn't Speak for Me" campaign had heathens from around the world posting photos of themselves holding handmade signs, explaining their background and why McNallen and his folkish clique do not share their heathen voice.

Beyond just attacking this tendency internal to heathens, the relationship that many pagans have had to this racialist sector has created a culture of resistance inside many pagan communities as well. The website *Gods & Radicals* has asserted an anti-capitalist understanding of paganism, attempting to connect those walking a spiritual path to a uniquely Marxist and anarchist perspective. This has meant taking explicit stances against fascism, which feeds on paganism due to their shared devotion to gods. After one of the editors, Rhyd Wildermuth, published a short profile on the New Right and the figures that often use paganism as a spiritual justification for fascist politics, he was accused by large swathes of the folkish community of a villainous "witch hunt."[32] This reflected his experience as an organizer of the Many Gods West polytheist conference in Olympia, Washington, where panels on fascism in paganism were denounced as divisive.[33]

Religious organizations have often been leaders in left struggle, even if dominant factions of the same religions have sided with the forces of reaction. Christian leaders across the United States came

---

31   "Light the Beacons," *Facebook Events*, May 1, 2016, https://www.facebook
       .com/events/135921890127980/.
32   Ryan Smith, "Understanding the New Right and Our Movement,"
       Through the Grapevine, April 27, 2016, http://www.patheos.com/blogs
       /throughthegrapevine/2016/04/understanding-the-new-right-and-our
       -movement/.
33   Rhyd Wildermuth, interview with author, March 31, 2016.

together as abolitionists, even participating in many of the violent revolts against slavery, as the institution was an anathema to the message of Jesus. Inside of the civil rights movement historically black churches that served as hubs of organizing, from the Birmingham Bus boycott to the founding of the Student Nonviolent Coordinating Committee, took on the South with money from the Southern Christian Leadership Conference, which continued the lunch-counter sit-ins that had begun in Greensboro, North Carolina, and Nashville, Tennessee.

Organizations like ISAIAH out of Minnesota have continued to use the faith community as a progressive bulwark to organize around a range of issues, from the working-class crisis in the Midwest to principles of diversity. With the Twin Cities' long legacy of Somali and Muslim immigration, ISAIAH has focused on organizing white Christian communities in support of immigrant and refugee rights in the state, especially important at a time when Republican politicians have built a base in many white Churches on outlandish fears about what their Somali neighbors have in store for them. In December 2016, ISAIAH rallied with a hundred faith leaders and thirty congregations against the proposed mass deportations and Muslim registry that the president-elect was promising in his first one hundred days in office.[34]

Fascism attacks religious minorities in much the same way that it targets color and sexual identity, and because of that, there is a critical place for organizations made up of targeted religious minorities. B'nai B'rith International, the oldest Jewish organization in the world, has a record of creating Jewish institutions, from daycare centers to retirement homes. It has also made anti-Semitism a major target by acknowledging the ongoing danger Jews face, and it has used this experience of anti-Semitism to do international trainings on bigotry for children, and to create materials that confront the threats to young Jews. This commitment is what led to their development of the Anti-Defamation Commission in the U.S., which targets international human rights abuses. Similarly, the Anti-Defamation League has been one of the stalwarts of fighting anti-Semitism and fascism internationally (more on this later). While confronting fascism and its anti-Semitic components has been a feature of most large

---

34   "Faith Communities Across Minnesota Declare Their Place of Worship 'Sanctuary' for Immigrants Seeking Refuge," Isaiah: Faith In Democracy, December 7, 2016, http://isaiahmn.org/2016/12/faith-communities-across-minnesota-declare-their-place-of-worship-sanctuary-for-immigrants-seeking-refuge/.

Jewish organizations, this does not mean that they have an entirely acceptable politic. The Jewish Defense League has been one of the most militant movements in the West to confront violent anti-Semites, gaining ire for posting public ads offering payment for the murder of confirmed neo-Nazis and bombing Islamist mosques. At the same time, they are viciously nationalist in defending anti-Palestinian genocidal policies and are the U.S. creation of neo-fascist Israeli politician Rabbi Meir Kahane who believes that Israel should be cleansed of non-Jews.[35]

Muslim American organizations have taken on a special role here with the rise of Islamophobia, where state agencies and politicians are putting the fantastical fears of the far-right into policy. With the resettlement of refugees, a general wave of reactionary fear has come from Central and Western European nations and is only compounded by America's growing scapegoating of Muslims, which ramped up after the 9/11 attacks and during the amorphous "War on Terror." The Council on American-Islamic Relations (CAIR) is the best-known American advocacy organization that confronts Islamophobia, often providing legal council to those facing discrimination, speaking out publicly on issues of Muslim profiling, and lobbying in favor of Islamic issues in the U.S. CAIR joined other Muslim organizations and the ACLU to end the "confronting violent extremism" program, which is a mirage intended to create a climate of suspicion about Muslims. The Desis Rising Up & Moving–South Asian Organizing Center (DRUM) out of Queens, New York, is another of these groups confronting the rise of Islamophobia from a uniquely Muslim immigrant population. They have come together to organize in response to the programs started years ago that target Muslim immigrants and worship centers, and as Trump makes good on his promise to further marginalize Muslim immigrants their work takes on a frightening urgency.[36]

In the face of the rapidly growing fascist right and Donald Trump and his appointees' control over state mechanisms, many Jewish and Muslim organizations are bridging a gap that has divided them for decades. The Islamic Society of North America and the American Jewish Society came together in 2016 to form a new

35   "Jewish Defense League," *Southern Poverty Law Center*, Jan. 30, 2017. https://www.splcenter.org/fighting-hate/extremist-files/group/jewish-defense-league.

36   Abiade, Kalia. "How Muslim Activists are Organizing against Islamophobia in the Face of President Trump," *Inthesetimes*, December 22, 2016, http://inthesetimes.com/features/trump_left_resistance_islamophobia.html.

project—The Muslim-Jewish Advisory Council—to expand rights for religious minorities and to "develop a coordinated strategy to address anti-Muslim bigotry and anti-Semitism in the U.S." This could develop further with more organizations that see a common far-right adversary that is accusing Jews and Muslims of being key actors in the "Death of the West," with Jews often being caricaturized as the masterminds and Muslims as the "invaders" coming to destroy white hegemony.[37] More militant organizations, like MuJews Antifa, attempt to create unity as well, building on a common experience of fascist menace, as bomb threats on synagogues and mosques were rampant in the early months of 2017.

The far-right requires some type of spirituality because it needs to define itself as being "beyond politics." Even if this is just taken metaphorically, it has always helped fascist ideologies define themselves, which puts religious people in both a troubling and advantageous position. The ability to confront this violence from inside a spiritual community provides leverage and could reach across religious and racial divides to develop the type of community that creates a barrier to reactionary movements.

---

37   Maltz, Judy. "Trump Effect: Jewish and Muslim Organizations Form New Alliance - U.S. Election 2016," *Haaretz*, N.p., November 14, 2016, http://www.haaretz.com/world-news/u-s-election-2016/1.753161.

American Patriots

The story started with two ranchers. Dwight and Steven Hammond had been ranchers in Harney County, Oregon, for decades, and had been convicted in 2011 of arson and poaching on federal land they had been using for years. Like many in the area, the Hammonds had a long and contentious relationship with the Bureau of Land Management (BLM), and they held the opinion that land use matters should be taken away from the federal government and given over to local control. Similar to a form of libertarian economics, the federal government and environmental protections are seen with extreme suspicion as they could interfere with land rights, and Patriots prefer a mythic past where ranchers and other property owners had free reign over the landscape. The Hammonds served a brief sentence, which the federal government quickly appealed since its brevity violated its mandatory minimum sentence, and were ordered back to prison to serve the rest of their five-year mandatory minimum.

In 2014, Ammon and Cliven Bundy, ranchers and Patriots from Nevada, led an insurgency of militia groups after the BLM seized their cattle for grazing on federal land without paying grazing fees. This happened after a long ideological battle over the use of federal lands, in which the wealthy Bundy family said the fees were an overreach by the federal government. Hundreds descended on Nevada and, after pulling guns on federal agents, the government backed down and there were few consequences. The Bundys won.

Emboldened, the Bundys put out a call for Patriot support of the Hammonds, whether or not they planned to turn themselves in to serve their sentence. Ammon Bundy contacted the Harney

County sheriff, Dave Ward, and threatened mass civil unrest unless he intervened. This led to a march of hundreds of far-right protesters in the rural town of Burns, Oregon, and afterward, in a grocery store parking lot adjacent to the march route, the Bundys and several supporters created a new plan. They were going to occupy the nearby Malheur Wildlife Refuge and make demands, including the distribution of all federally owned lands to loggers, miners, and ranchers. They planned on staying in this heavily armed occupation for years if that is what it took.[1]

The Black Helicopters

The Patriot movement of today has its roots in the white supremacist Posse Comitatus of the 1970s. Movement founder and Christian Identity minister William Potter Gale believed that the Constitution was founded for and by white Christians and was perverted through a Jewish-controlled federal government. He was the first to institute the concept of "citizen's grand juries," a model for various fake courts and legal proceedings that movement members use to single out federal employees and judges. By 1976, the FBI tracked Posse Comitatus numbers at anywhere between 12,000 and 50,000 members. By the time the 1980s farm crisis erupted and small family farms saw mass foreclosure due to inflation and a shift toward corporate agribusiness, Posse Comitatus, the earliest formation of what we would now label the "militia movement," was on the scene to provide an anti-Semitic conspiracy narrative about a tribal elite in control of land and finance through the state. While, in recent years, the movement has shifted away from the explicit white nationalism of Posse Comitatus, much of the underlying logic, conspiracy theories, and political narratives rely on the same basis of thought.[2]

The 1990s saw the three most significant events triggering growth of the new wing of the Patriot movement. They were the 1992 standoff with Christian Identity affiliate Randy Weaver at Ruby Ridge; the raid on the Waco, Texas, compound of the Branch

1   Conrad Wilson and Dave Blanchard, "What Happened in Harney County: This Land Is Our Land," podcast audio, Oregon Public Broadcasting, MP3, 40:58, August 31, 2016, http://www.opb.org/news/series/burns-oregon-stand-off-bundy-militia-news-updates/occupation-trial-podcast-this-land-is-our-land/.

2   Spencer Sunshine, *Up in Arms: A Guide to Oregon's Patriot Movement* (Scappoose, Oregon: Rural Organizing Project, Political Research Associates, 2016), 13–16.

Davidians in 1993; and the passage of the Brady Bill in 1993–94, which added a five-day waiting period for handgun sales. The right seized on these events and created a climate of fear where Patriot groups were portrayed as moderates, and Americans worried their guns would be seized by the government. This allowed white nationalists like Louis Beam, a Christian Identity adherent known for advocating violent revolution, to organize projects like the United Citizens for Justice. At an October 1992 meeting of militia activists, which came shortly after the blunder at Ruby Ridge, a coordinated effort was made to form a "white Christian Republic" through the use of vigilante violence. By the fall of 1994, groups like the Michigan Militia boasted ten thousand members across three-quarters of the state's numerous counties. A survey found that 55 percent of state and local judges questioned admitted to some level of harassment from Patriots and supporters. Threats against federal judges tripled.

It was this growth in the movement that led to the passage of laws to address "common courts"—the fake courts often used by militia members—in twenty-seven states. The massive growth of the militia movement included crossover into the GOP, a shift seen with the election of California state senator Don Rogers, whose radical right ideas about the Tenth Amendment got him invited to speak at a Christian Identity event. The argument about the Tenth Amendment became an important part of the Patriot movement from then on, as they asserted that, per the constitution, all federal land should be "returned" to the states and/or counties.[3]

The growth of the Patriot movement hit its zenith in 1996, just after the bombing of the Oklahoma City federal building by Timothy McVeigh and Terry Nichols, both deeply embedded with the fringes of the Patriot movement and with ties to Christian Identity. Inside of McVeigh's getaway vehicle, investigators found copies of *The Turner Diaries*, a pseudo-anonymous book written by National Alliance neo-Nazi leader William Pierce about a coming race war.

Though government probes were bungled in the years that followed, the Patriot movement still saw a dramatic decrease in size and influence. That is, until Obama was elected and their numbers once again skyrocketed.

---

3   Daniel Levitas, *The Terrorist Next Door* (New York: Thomas Dunne Books/St. Martin's Press, 2002), 301–14.

The Militias on the Ground

Today, there are a number of regional Patriot and militia organizations, but the two most prominent nationwide projects are the Oath Keepers and the 3%ers. Alabama militia member Mike Vanderboegh invented the 3%ers in 2008 and uses decentralized structures to harbor fear of federal investigation and informants. The name comes from the erroneous idea that only 3 percent of early colonialists were willing to stand up and fight the British, and they see themselves as the inheritors of that legacy in the battle against a tyrannical federal government. Building their reputation on a tendency for violence and a tenacity of rhetoric, the 3%ers were prominent in the Malheur standoff as they claim a thousand members in Oregon alone.[4] The violence of the 3%ers is not just rhetoric, and there are numerous examples, including the 2015 shooting of Black Lives Matter activists in Minnesota.[5]

The Oath Keepers, on the other hand, are a slightly more centralized project, complete with non-profit status and a founder, Stewart Rhodes, who was a former aide to Ron Paul before he was fired and disbarred. Though claiming only 40,000 members nationwide (the ADL believes it is closer to 2,000 or less),[6] the Oath Keepers recruit people with backgrounds in the military, law enforcement, and other "official" positions to follow their declaration of "Orders We Will Not Obey." These include disobeying the orders of an encroaching fantasy authoritarian socialist state that would capture all of the guns, end privacy rights, arrest right-wing activists, use martial law to invade states, and convert American cities into concentration camps.[7]

Strategically, the 3%ers employ what some have labeled an "inside/outside" strategy, where they have embedded themselves in some rural local governments while at the same time trying to challenge state institutions externally. Part of this strategy is to create "dual power" structures where their groups provide services that the state would normally be tasked with, but because of rural budget cuts, a lot of services have dried up. Where emergency services may be absent or dangerously late in many parts of the country, Patriot

---

4   3%ers claim 85,000 members nationally, but this number is likely highly inflated.
5   Sunshine, *Up in Arms*, 17–20.
6   "Oath Keepers and Three %ers Part of Growing Anti-Government Movement," Anti-Defamation League: https://www.adl.org/education/resources/backgrounders/oath-keepers-and-three-ers-part-of-growing-anti-government.
7   Sunshine, *Up in Arms*, 17–20.

networks have begun doing patrols and providing emergency support, which only helps to grow the image of their legitimacy. This works well with the false governmental bodies they form—including Committees of Safety that are intending to look like an executive branch, or the false "grand jury indictments" where they put various federal government employees "on trial" before often engaging in violent threats. Adopting a racial tone, their efforts have also included border patrols looking to "catch" undocumented migrants.[8]

Much of the growth of the Patriot movement came from tapping into existing far-right networks and pushing them toward armed action. This meant bringing sovereign citizens, pro-gun advocates, anti-tax protesters, anti-abortion extremists, and dominion theology Christians together with white nationalists who had been lingering in the rural sector. Its ideological foundations, which are mainly based in conspiracy theories, can be traced back to white nationalist institutions like the John Birch Society. The project has always been founded on the idea that the "pure" American government, created by the Founding Fathers, has been perverted by various subversive elements that are going to use their growing power to put down those who represent the interests of "real America."[9] Within this rhetoric, their racism is often covert rather than overt; they deny systemic racism as an issue and instead see the true oppressed class as rural white farmers, miners, ranchers, and loggers. Their preference would be a radical right government, highly decentralized and stripped of social welfare tools that are meant to address inequality.

In 2014, Oath Keepers went to Murrieta, California, to block immigrant buses on their way to detention centers, trying to halt any attempts by migrants to create homes in their communities. While anti-immigrant sentiment is rampant, Islamophobia is often open and unhidden. This was taken to extremes with John Ritzheimer's "Global Rally for Humanity" against Islam, which happened shortly before they headed to Harney Country for the Malheur occupation. Blaine Cooper, another Malheur occupier who had also been a part of the earlier Sugar Pine Mine occupation—a battle with the BLM over two miners' rights that drew militia support just nine months before the Malheur standoff began—posted videos of himself wrapping a Koran in bacon before setting it ablaze. Both immigration and Islam act as slightly socially acceptable

8   Ibid., 40–42.
9   Berlet and Lyons, *Right-Wing Populism in America*, 300.

forms of othering: creating a collective American identity by defining an out-group that is "not one of us."[10]

Even still, the racialist connections are real and tangible. During the 2016 Malheur occupation, people like Andrew Anglin from *The Daily Stormer* repeatedly posted in support, while well-known Holocaust denier John Friend came to the refuge to interview the militiamen. TradYouth, which has courted the militia movement in many Midwestern states, voiced support, while trying to say that it was leftist contradictions that caused the armed troop to be labeled terrorists. From *Occidental Dissent* to *Taki's Magazine* to the infamous *Stormfront*, the far-right was unified in their blushing fascinations with the Bundys' cause.[11]

According to antifascist writer Spencer Sunshine, the Patriot movement "represents the most aggressive form of the most toxic mainstream politics and tactics" and uses both legal and non-legal means. With the GOP's far-right shift over the past thirty years, especially when it comes to federal land use issues, libertarian economics, and populist social conservatism, the politics of the militia movement are only really distinct in their associations and volume.[12]

While to some they appear more moderate than the foaming mouths of neo-Nazis rallying in front of Americanized swastikas, their historical record has also shown that the militias have an extremely high potential for violence. In the two years before the murderous bombing of the Oklahoma City federal building there were three bombings of federal property meant for the Forest Service or the Bureau of Land Management.[13] After the Oklahoma tragedy, Eric Rudolph bombed the New Women All Women Health Care Clinic in Birmingham, Alabama, in January of 1998, killing two and permanently injuring a nurse. This bombing was then linked to the 1996 dirty bomb at the Olympics in Atlanta, Georgia. Rudolph was tied directly to the anti-abortion and militia-affiliated Army of God and the Christian Identity movement.[14] Along with their use of fake courts, they are often linked to regional acts of terrorism when "carrying out" the decisions of

---

10   Sunshine, *Up in Arms,* 27–28.
11   Spencer Sunshine, "Will the History Books Record How Neo-Nazis Made Eyes at the Bundy Militia?" *Truth Out,* January 27, 2016: http://www.truth-out.org/news/item/34575-will-the-history-books-record-how-neo-nazis-made-eyes-at-the-bundy-militia.
12   Spencer Sunshine, interview with author, 2016.
13   Levitas, *The Terrorist Next Door,* 313.
14   Zeskind, *Blood and Politics,* 459–463.

these various counter-state bodies. Federal employees take on special risk, as does progressive opposition.

In a 2014 survey conducted by the *New York Times* and the Police Executive Research Forum, of 382 agencies involved in law enforcement, 74 percent labeled militia projects as one of the top three terrorism threats. They identified these Patriot groups as more than double the "threat" of "Islamic extremism." Since 9/11, there have been 337 attacks from Patriot-affiliated people, causing 254 deaths, compared to only a fraction of that number from the much-maligned Muslim community.[15]

These are also some of the groups most likely to increase their numbers because of the environment in which they grow: the budget-starved rural areas of the country that are only getting poorer. Across the country, as neoliberalism shrinks public budgets, union jobs dry up, manufacturing is offshored, and agribusiness snuffs out family farms, the rural economies are shuddering with no hope in sight. This crisis presents radical opportunities just as it does financial pain, yet these areas have largely shifted toward right-wing narratives about "globalism," immigration, and the role of the federal government in betraying the working-class left behind. The far-right's use of conspiracy rhetoric, implicit racism rather than explicit white nationalism, and a tacit support from some areas of the Republican Party, has made them an attractive avenue for many sectors of the far-right looking for influence. During the tense heat of August's election, Trump met with Elko County, Nevada, Commissioner Demar Dahl, who stood out in the movement to transfer land away from the federal government, back into county control and into the hands of exploitative industries. At this posh fundraising dinner, the two discussed the concept of land transfer, a brazen show of support by Trump for the radical fringes of the Patriot project.[16] This climate could lead to the growth of Patriot influence inside local governments, but a Trump betrayal on key issues, as well as his inability to bring back rural jobs in manufacturing or extractive industries, could also lead them to desperate acts of violence.

---

15   Charles Schanzer, "The Growing Right-Wing Terror Threat," *New York Times*, June 16, 2015, https://www.nytimes.com/2015/06/16/opinion/the-other-terror-threat.html?_r=0.

16   Tay Wiles, "Trump Met with a Leader of the Land Transfer Movement," *High Country News*, October 17, 2016, http://www.hcn.org/articles/trump-met-with-a-leader-of-the-land-transfer-movement.

The greatest demonstration of Patriot growth was the wave of occupations, starting with the 2014 confrontation in Nevada and then eventually with militia groups from around the country descending on southern Oregon in an effort to make the Hammond verdict an example of federal "overreach." After the occupation and federal trial, an acquittal verdict sent a message to militias everywhere that these sort of armed takeovers were consequence-free. Many compared the Malheur occupation and the result of the Bundy trial with the treatment of the Standing Rock protesters at the Dakota Access Pipeline who, despite coming unarmed, were subjected to harsh treatment with security dogs, dispersal gas, and water cannons.

A left that has prioritized urban struggles in the battle for numbers has largely abandoned rural America. There is a false narrative about the inherently conservative nature of many Midwestern states and rural farming areas, but this is reasonably new. Instead, the turn toward the right has often come in the absence of a true left opposition. Groups that are seeing the militias as a real threat are trying to meet this force head on.

Toward a Racial Insurrection

The imagery that is conjured when one thinks of the radical right is dotted with burning crosses and steel-toed Doc Martens. This is the result of sensationalism and America's lurid fascination with the right. The history of America is one of racial violence, first of settler colonialism and the systemic genocide of First Nations peoples followed directly by the assault on the humanity of black Africans. Over the years, many institutions of public violence were destabilized and uprooted, while inequalities were normalized within capitalism, such as with segregation, and the white public's angry bigotry remained largely unchanged. As formal white supremacy eroded, those who saw their white privilege as security in an increasingly fragile order mourned its loss.

All fascist movements are revolutionary to a degree, since they need to fundamentally overthrow key elements of the state and economic order, as well as undermine the underlying values that give those systems legitimacy. They have a new vision for social structures, one that privileges tribal group members and attempts to codify inequality, either in state policy or rigid social guidelines, and this requires washing away the sweeping effects of capitalism and liberal multiculturalism. The violent right movements are the ones that have captured most people's consciousness. For those who are not engaging with fascist movements regularly, these violent movements are the ones most recognizable since their politics are in your face and cannot be deferred, confused, or tempered. This presents problems *and* opportunities for communities that see these ideas, even when presented merely as philosophical arguments, as a physical threat. These white racialist groups are associated with clear acts of violence—from the lynching of black people across the south to the attacks on synagogues in Midwestern cities—so it is easy to argue that their ideas are inseparable from violence. On the other hand, it also creates a caricature of how white nationalism develops, making it harder to identify the more covert fascist projects or to single out the way that white supremacist attitudes and social structures pervade our daily reality.

One of the primary objections to these philosophical currents is their implicit violence, both from their political methodology, which requires mass violence against marginalized peoples at multiple levels, and also the increased systemic violence implicit in the systems they propose. While murderers like Dylann Roof are part and parcel of white nationalist movements, and that violence will only increase as those ideologies gain footing, the philosophies themselves are codified violence, an attempt to use the failures of the liberal state to provide an alternative that would privilege few and would take the worst atrocities of capitalist modernity and flip them into explicit tyrannies. Even for the most moderate-toned white nationalists, those who are especially prevalent in the "non-violent" argumentation of the Alt Right, their vision is intensified persecution and genocidal bloodletting. Those who are open about the violent nature of their politics, rather than attempting to couch it in electoralism, meta-politics, or academics, can be labeled "insurrectionary" since they are basing their strategy on the efficacy of violent acts, the need for egregious violence against various agents of the despised social order.

In the U.S., there are two tracks for what I am labeling "insurrectionary" fascist movements, and both list violence as an organizational priority. These are the Ku Klux Klan and neo-Nazis, the latter often meaning skinhead organizations. While violence is a distinguishing factor of these groups, they could very easily be broken down along the lines of class as well. These are generally working-class organizations, coming from low-income areas of the South, the Midwest, and poor areas of the Rust Belt. There is a reason why the National Socialist Movement was headquartered in Detroit, and why the KKK grows in some of the poorest areas of Mississippi and West Virginia. The Alt Right, as with many forms of Third Positionist and esoteric fascist ideas, inspire a more middle-income and college-educated crowd, while neo-Nazi literature cuts straight to the heart of the issue. There is no reason to obscure the bigotry, there is no use for attempts at crossing over into the mainstream. The honesty of their approach sets them apart, and it is their association with the "white trash" part of poor America that has helped to make the general public view them with revulsion.

Racist Americana

The Ku Klux Klan is a uniquely American invention, coming out of the post-Confederate struggle to maintain brutal plantation slavery and white dominance. It has continued through multiple generations as an institution revived primarily by rural whites to battle integration and civil rights during the height of racial tensions and the capitalist subversion of labor. Six former Confederates first founded the KKK not six months after the final surrender of Robert E. Lee to the Union armies of the North. Created as a social club by Nathan Bedford Forrest, a man whose likeness is immortalized on murals and statues across the Deep South, the organization was built along fraternal lines and evolved into a paramilitary force meant to battle the integrationist power of Reconstruction. Engaging in "night rides," evolving out of the antebellum "slave patrols," the KKK became known for acts of extreme violence and terror meant to scare freed slaves from integrating into spaces of social and political power. They were eventually banned and pushed underground in 1871 as the government refused to tolerate the subversive nature of the growing "invisible government," which threatened the state in the South.

In 1915, the KKK was revived at Stone Mountain, Georgia, a rock-carved monument to the generals who fought for "Southern independence." This Second Generation of the KKK came amid a flurry of immigration, where 23 million people from Southern, Central, and Eastern Europe flooded into the U.S., changing the demographics from its Anglo-Saxon base. D.W. Griffith's movie *Birth of a Nation*, adapted from the 1905 book *The Clansman*, revised the true history of the KKK's murderous rampage, filtering it through a lens of American romanticism as a group of Southern gentlemen protecting white women and civilization from the "bestial Negro." By 1921, the KKK had 100,000 members, swelling to as many as 4 million members by some estimates. (This would be around 15% of the voting-aged population of the U.S.) Focused on degeneracy such as alcohol use during Prohibition as well as black crime, mis-cegenation, and the sinister threat of Catholics and Jews—who they believed owed their loyalty to a foreign state—the KKK rose to such prominence that they had governors, mayors, senators, clergy, and business leaders in their ranks. Detroit, far from the South and set to boom with the manufacture of American automobiles, was a Klan stronghold with 80,000 registered members. While a hatred of blacks was not the most prominent part of the Klan as a political institution in those years, they lynched thousands of black people across the South. By the end of the 1920s, the Klan was depleted by controversies and their own financial mismanagement.[1]

By the time its Third Generation emerged in 1954, their white nationalist movement had already taken a huge blow in public perception because the logical conclusion of their politics—the Holocaust—had come into full international view. As the civil rights movement began and the landmark *Brown v. The Board of Education* ruling promised the end of school segregation, the Southern Klan returned to their paramilitary roots, and they murdered civil rights activists and engaged in mass bombings, including twenty-seven bombings in 1959 alone.

> The Ku Klux Klan represented, in some ways, the lower class white response to this integration. They were not trying to stop it by political means. They were not trying to stop it by economic means. They were trying to stop it by violence and intimidation.[2]

The violence during the 1950–60s civil rights movement was at the level of sectarian conflicts often discussed with horror in other countries, including extensive retaliatory lynching and the bombings of black churches, with no child spared. While it took years to be publicly exposed, its history is now seen as one of the most significant periods of terrorism inside the borders of the U.S., with the United Klans of America (UKA) attempting to take the more disorganized attacks into the realm of organization that made the 1920s Klan so influential. Amid the failure of the pro-segregationist camp and the FBI investigations against Klan killings, their numbers dropped from their Third Generation peak of 40,000 members

---

1   Berlet and Lyons, *Right-Wing Populism in America*, 95–103.
2   *Ku Klux Klan: A Secret History*, directed by Bill Brummel, performed by Paul Thomas, David Chalmers, and William Banks (1998; Dobson, NC: History Channel), DVD.

and more than thirty coordinated organizations under the UKA banner.[3]

The Fourth Generation marked the real decline of the KKK as an influential organization and its descent into the recesses of violent fringe white supremacy where it is today. David Duke, America's best-known modern KKK member, hand-delivered the organization into this world. After many years working in neo-Nazi organizations like the National Socialist White People's Party and protesting what he saw as Jewish communist influence in the government, Duke took over the Louisiana-headquartered Knights of the Ku Klux Klan, one of the many groups that were taking up the "official" legacy of the KKK. Duke wanted it to go mainstream with public campaigns to shift perception of the Klan to a "white civil rights" organization. At the same time, Duke "Nazified" the Klan, bringing in strong anti-Semitic and white nationalist ideas that were more familiar to explicit fascist ideologues. For years the Klan was focused on specific mobilizing issues rather than an overarching ideological framework, but Duke wanted to bring the ideas of neo-Nazis to the front. In doing so, he launched many white nationalist leaders, like *Stormfront* founder Don Black and White Aryan Resistance leader Tom Metzger. Duke's own corruption and embezzlement of Klan funds also set the precedent for the culture of crime that would continue through later generations of the Klan, often connecting their outlaw lifestyle with drug running, bank robberies, and the edges of the economy.[4]

Boots and Braces

The skinhead culture that came out of Britain the 1960s–70s was a working-class "dockworker" culture of young people inspired by Jamaican music and multiracial solidarity, but the attraction of National Front politics to this base also recruited a "Stormtrooper" neo-Nazi cadre that were in direct opposition to the anti-racist principles of the original identity. "White Power" skinheads ended up receiving more attention than their anti-racist Trojan counterparts, and this was due to the massive stream of street violence that has rocked cities on both sides of the Atlantic since they first made a home for themselves in tight Levis and red-laced Doc Martens.

---

3   Ibid.
4   Tyler Bridges, *The Rise of David Duke* (Jackson: University Press of Mississippi, 1994), 35–65.

What came out of these skinheads was more a gang culture than a seasoned political operation, but that does not mean they did not have the ability to pull in huge numbers from disaffected areas. Local gangs like East Side White Pride in Portland, Oregon, or Keystone United in Pennsylvania moved between densely packed urban arenas to music venues, art spaces, and gun shows in an effort to violently target multiracial couples, queers, and immigrants. This led to a culture of seemingly random violence, where most political acts were spontaneous and as bloody as they were disorganized.

Starting in the 1990s, Volksfront attempted to create a confederation of skinhead gangs that had previously been poorly coordinated. This new gang was based in Portland, which, despite its reputation for liberal politics, has had a long history of active racist organizing and neo-Nazi clashes. Originally formed by Randal Lee Krager while he was in prison for putting an African American man into a coma, the gang had been known for violence such as the 2003 Tacoma, Washington, attack where three Volksfront members beat a homeless man to death under a bridge. Online music distribution services, something that has always been a huge part of the skinhead culture, funded the operation. Since it started primarily as a music scene, skinheads differentiated themselves from the anti-racist punk scene by their Rock Against Communism project and their particular brand of "White Noise," which set aggressive and profanity laden racial violence fantasies within generic "Oi!" punk sounds. By 2013, Volksfront was seeing its end after aggressive campaigns by anti-racists and the public horror shows like when Volksfront acquaintance Wade Michael Page opened fire on a Sikh Temple in Oak Creek, Wisconsin, killing six people.[5]

Similar to Volksfront was the American Front, which differentiated itself as a "thinking man's" skinhead gang. The members had ties to prominent neofolk music acts and pagan occultists, and generally were known for a strong Third Positionist leaning that integrated the work of the ENR and Aleksandr Dugin with a strong critique of capitalism and colonialism. In 2012, members were arrested as part of a probe from the FBI's domestic terrorism investigations, they were charged with weapons possession, illegal paramilitary training, and conspiracy to commit hate crimes.[6]

---

5   "The End of Volksfront?" Southern Poverty Law Center, November 20, 2013, https://www.splcenter.org/fighting-hate/intelligence-report/2013/end-volksfront.

6   Henry Curtis, "Informant Exposed Osceola Hate Group: American Front

One member, Marcus Faella, was prosecuted for attempting racial conflict in 2014, and on appeal hired now infamous attorney Augustus Sol Invictus. On a judge's orders the American Front was disbanded, but in 2016 Invictus was invited to Vancouver, Washington, to speak at the alleged reformation of the organization. After a confrontation with Rose City Antifa the next day, he was barred entry into Canada where he was set to speak at another American Front-organized event. While they are still said to be growing, there is little to indicate if they have a future as a prominent organization.[7]

Keystone United, formerly the Keystone State Skinheads out of Pennsylvania, have also tried to cultivate a dual impression as both a white power gang and an aboveground project geared toward racial organizing. They have been instrumental in building larger skinhead-centric events like Hatefest and Hammerfest, while also joining up with comrades from the Traditionalist Worker Party for coalition projects. Their attempts to recruit from crossover spaces has been limited by their history of street violence, such as the 2003 conviction of three members who beat a black man with chunks of pavement in Scranton. Like many of these sorts of formations, its membership has overlapped with almost every white supremacist organization in the country, from Aryan Nations and the National Alliance to David Duke's former "NGO," the National Association for the Advancement of White People.[8]

The most prominent nationwide skinhead gang is the Hammerskin Nation, which operates across multiple states. While they list six official chapters in the U.S., and locals in twelve additional countries, their exact numbers—thought to be in the hundreds—are hard to estimate. Their growth has come from a public presence on internet message boards, a formal "supporter" system, and public concerts like the annual Hammerfest. Their violence is legendary, something they wear on their sleeve (and brag about on their website), and it has become the "go to" group for racialists who lionize the "White Power Skinhead Lifestyle."

Arrests Part Of Broader FBI Investigation," *Orlando Sentinel*, July 18, 2012, http://articles.orlandosentinel.com/2012-07-18/news/os-informant-exposed-hate-group-osceola-20120718_1_race-war-undercover-informant-osceola.

7   Shane Burley, "Fascism Against Time: Nationalism, Media Blindness, and the Cult of Augustus Sol Invictus," *Gods & Radicals*, March 24, 2016, https://godsandradicals.org/2016/03/24/fascism-against-time-nationalism-media-blindness-and-the-cult-of-augustus-sol-invictus/.

8   "Keystone United," Southern Poverty Law Center, https://www.splcenter.org/fighting-hate/extremist-files/group/keystone-united.

While skinhead gangs like the Hammerskins and SacTown Skinheads in Sacramento, California, make up very real threats of violence in those communities, their political power and size has waned dramatically. While these two wings of the movement, the KKK and the neo-Nazi skinheads, are staple segments of the movement, there are many organizational types that do not fit into that binary. Aryan Nations was a revolutionary project that engaged in violence, both through individual members and organizationally as a group, but its character was closer to the militia movement and a religious organization than a neo-Nazi gang.

A History of Violence

It is undeniable that tactically and organizationally, the insurrectionary projects, from the urban youth skinhead gangs to the revolutionary rural groups, are weak compared to the more aboveground and well-considered fascist projects and parties. The inability to create mass movements leads them to a constant recycling of organizational failure and insurrectionary responses, never succeeding in driving cultural change independent of the radical core. That further lends to a culture of "lone wolf" violence, as these hiccups of mass murder usually happen when they create a revolutionary fervor through ideology and rhetoric and then cannot support those ideas through effective organizing models. It is their failure to see through goals that has led to suicidal acts of violence, which have been venerated by each successive generation of insurrectionary white supremacists.

Much of this comes from the model of "leaderless resistance" advocated by Louis Beam. Similar to the way that many on the ultra-left reject formal organization for fear that it will limit the revolutionary potential of the working class, far-right leaderless resistance advocates a more extreme vision including murders, bank robberies, and acts of terrorism meant to destabilize the current order, rather than resorting to the more conservative compromises of movement building that requires mainstream appeals.[9] This plays out in the fashion of lone wolf violence, where "leaderless" Aryan warriors take the violence into their own hands to murder

9   Louis Beam, "Leaderless Resistance," *The Seditionist,* February 1992, http://www.louisbeam.com/leaderless.htm.

politicians, "race traitors," and non-whites. People like White Aryan Resistance founder Tom Metzger advocated this:

> Always start off small. Many small victories are better than one huge blunder (which may be the end of your career as a Lone Wolf). Every little bit counts in a resistance. Knowledge is power. Learn from your mistakes as well as the mistakes of others. Never rush into anything, time and planning are keys to success. Never attempt anything beyond your own abilities, failure could lead to disaster. The less any outsider knows, the safer and more successful you will be.… I have never said their [sic] will never be a time when all small cells and lonewolves may evolve into a highly structured but ruthlessly militant organization with steel hard leaders. That time is not now and will not be for the foreseeable future. No present leader including myself will be leading that phase. We are only to prepare the way. Hopefully what we say and do now will make future victory possible.[10]

Lone wolf violence has been persistent over the past thirty years in the U.S., as illustrated by attacks like the bombing of the Oklahoma City federal building or the mass shootings at Jewish community centers or the killing of a security guard at the U.S. Holocaust Memorial Museum in June 2009.

While these acts are typically portayed as outside the confines of the organized white nationalist movement, there are formal organizations propping up most of the people suspected of these atrocities—not to mention propaganda, meeting space, music, and all other cultural elements that are needed to support angry trigger men and their morbid fantasies. Roger Griffin notes this as "groupuscularisation," the seemingly diffuse and tiny formations that, together, make up the sizable new formation of the fascist movement rejecting the political structures of the interwar period, in favor a new model that attempts to gain the same palingenetic fascist ideological goals through the "uncivic space" of alternative organizational praxis.[11] The result is far from a lone wolf; there is an ideological and social network that props up these acts, and with the internal logic and explicit strategy of many white nationalists,

---

10   Tom Metzger, "Laws for the Lone Wolf," StormFront, https://www
      .stormfront.org/forum/t708050/.
11   Roger Griffin, "Fascism's New Faces (and New Facelessness) in the 'Post-
      fascist' Epoch," 192.

the violence is the intended path, rather than simply the unintended results of angst meeting revolutionary thinking. This was especially true in the 1988 murder of twenty-eight-year-old Ethiopian student Mulugeta Seraw on the curb of an inner city Portland, Oregon, street. Members of East Side White Pride, a local skinhead gang, beat Seraw to death with baseball bats. While disorganized and packed with alcoholic fury, the group was pushed from fantasy to action knowing they had the support of Tom Metzger and Dave Mazzella, a subcultural leader of disaffected racist youths.[12]

The Order may be the most sweeping example of the organizing revolutionary trend spinning off from an aboveground group, which, in this case, was the Aryan Nations. Led by Robert Jay Matthews and David Lane, who later founded the Wotanist current of racialist heathenry, the group traveled across the country robbing banks and businesses, distributing the money to well-known white supremacist organizers like Frazier Glenn Miller, who later went on to kill three people in shootings at a Jewish daycare and retirement home. Order members murdered raucous talk radio show host Alan Berg who had spent months antagonizing Nazis on air. His death was intended to send a chilling effect through the Jewish community and act as inspiration to other lone wolves.

Though not nearly as political as the skinhead gangs, the white supremacist prison gangs have grown in size, as they are able to extend their reach from the inside when prisoners get released and need support on the outside. While the Aryan Brotherhood is heavily documented in sensationalized reality television programs, little known regional groups like the European Kindred in the Northwest are linking up to run drugs, both on the inside and the outside.

While these groups often straddle the line between underground paramilitary-style operations and public political groups, many are trying to make the most revolutionary currents mainstream, and these ideas are made more palatable in this political climate with Donald Trump and the Alt Right. The National Socialist Movement, the largest and most well-known neo-Nazi organization in the U.S., has often been derided as "Hollywood Nazis" because of their slavish allegiance to the swastika and veneration of the Third Reich. Though they have often had public rallies and events, they are taking a further step toward mainstreaming their message by dropping the

---

12   Elinor Langer, *A Hundred Little Hitlers* (New York: Metropolitan Books, 2003).

swastika as their public symbol in favor of the Odal Rune, the magical Nordic alphabetical symbol that translates to "heritage."[13] This does not mean that the NSM is backing away from its revolutionary aims, as it created a confederation called the Nationalist Front that hosts sixteen additional organizations, including the reformed Aryan Nations, the Racial Nationalist Party of America, and the Nordic Order Knights of the KKK.[14]

Over the last two years, the Traditionalist Youth Network and its political party wing, the Traditionalist Workers Party, has provided a more mainstream "activist" orientation for the working-class racist constituents who are often affiliated with neo-Nazi, KKK, or militia organizations. In August 2016, TradWorker joined together with 3%ers, the Soldiers of Odin, and other Patriot and skinhead groups to host an Indiana area "pro-Trump" event and picnic. In June, TradWorker had co-hosted an event with the Sac-Town Skinheads and Golden State Skinheads in Sacramento, California—an event that saw violent clashes between skinheads and anti-racist protesters. Matthew Heimbach, unlike many Alt Right and other racialists, has tried to bridge these groups, attending *American Renaissance*, National Policy Institute, and Stormfront annual conferences and KKK cross burnings. TWP has joined the call of the Nationalist Front, a coalition of some of the more extreme racist organizations including White Lives Matter and the National Socialist Movement, and that alliance has further cemented them in the insurrectionary camp.

While it may be easy to label these violent groups as separate from the Alt Right and other nationalists, they have always existed along the same continuum in direct coordination with one another. *American Renaissance*, as the most prominent "race realist" publication and conference in the U.S., regularly has insurrectionary white nationalists in attendance, from Aryan Nations and skinhead members to David Duke and Don Black. Groups like the Wolves of Vinland, though aesthetically different than most violent American racialist organizations and sharing many high profile members of the Alt Right, still uses rhetoric and organizational structures that mimic

---

13   "NSM Announcement Nov., 2016," National Socialist Movement, November 4, 2016, http://www.nsm88.org/nsmnews/NSMAnnouncement_Nov_2016.htm.

14   "Press Release: Historic Alliance Formed by U.S. White Nationalists," National Socialist Movement, April 26, 2016, http://www.nsm88.org/press/ NSM_PressRelease_HistoricAllianceformedbyUSWhiteNationalists_ april_2016_.htm.

the tribal warfare of motorcycle clubs. Groups like the American Freedom Party have brought together the street warfare of Golden State Skinheads with Alt Right staples, like the *Political Cesspool* host James Edwards, who also sits on the party's board. The Council of Conservative Citizens (CofCC), which also hosts people like Edwards and *American Renaissance* founder Jared Taylor, has also acted as a bridge between the Southern organizations with a history of violence and the more public segregationist contingents. Their messaging has always been about the apocalyptic nature of "black crime," stoking racial tensions with trumped-up statistics, out of context stories, and disproven "scientific theories." Dylann Roof, who murdered nine people in a historically black church in Charleston, South Carolina, cited the CofCC's website as his inspiration, saying it taught him the "problem" that blacks posed to the white majority. After James Harris Jackson stabbed a black homeless man with a large sword in New York City, police discovered that he came to the Big Apple "with plans to kill black men in relationships with white women." On his social media accounts he followed videos by people like Richard Spencer and Alt Right provocateur RamZPaul, who is best known for his satirical *YouTube* videos and stand-up routines, as well as "fashwave" music like "Cyber Nazi," which takes an ironic view of 80s synth-pop and dubs in the voice of Trump and other historical racists.[15] Similarly, in 2011, Jared Lee Loughner opened fire on Congresswoman Gabrielle Giffords, wounding thirteen and killing six others. When investigated, *American Renaissance* was found at the front of his internet activity.[16] The rhetoric of the Alt Right, though coded, is tied to the extremist mind-set that has fueled the same lone wolf and terrorist violence that has colored the entire history of white nationalism.

In every Alt Right gathering you can trace a history of white supremacist terrorism as these contemporary racialist institutions have a direct connection to earlier generations of white supremacist organizing, and it is their ideas about the sub-human nature of non-white people, the insidious parasitism of Jews, and the danger of feminism

---

15   Ben Norton, "White Supremacist Who Traveled to New York to Murder Black Men Followed Extremist Racist Online Groups Who Support Trump." *Salon*, March 24, 2017, http://www.salon.com/2017/03/24/white-supremacist-who-traveled-to-new-york-to-murder-black-men-followed-extremist-racist-online-groups-who-support-trump_partner/.
16   Sussman, *The Myth of Race*, 279.

that drives them to respond with violence. Even while figures on the Alt Right, like Richard Spencer, often speak against the use of violence, their ideas of ethnic cleansing are implicitly genocidal and they create a critical step in the dehumanization of non-white people, which is necessary for the trigger to be pulled. The Alt Right has the same ideas, the same historical vision, but puts them into a twenty-first century context with bigger budgets and more thoughtful media strategies.

Even the campus world of the Alt Right is laden with a history of racist violence. At the University of Wisconsin, for example, Daniel Dropik was looking to form an Alt Right-specific student organization to combat what he called a climate that was hostile to students and faculty of European ethnic background and traditional values. Dropik had been convicted of setting fire to black churches in 2005, an act of "racial retaliation" that got him a sentence of five years in federal prison.[17]

The notion that above-ground racialist organizations will likely remain non-violent has been disproven repeatedly as these organizations descend into acts of bloody murder, often even while trying to maintain a public propaganda wing. In 1979, the Workers Viewpoint Organization, later known as the Communist Workers Party, had been organizing textile workers in the South and developing an anti-racist strategy in the community. With Klan opposition growing in the area, protesters began their "Death to the Klan" campaigns by shutting down a screening of *The Birth of a Nation* by a local Klansman in China Grove, North Carolina. In November 1979, there was a large mobilization intent on confronting the KKK in a largely African American area of Greensboro, North Carolina. Despite having police informants in their group, members of the Klan formed the United Racist Front and opened fire on the protesters in a ninety-second hailstorm of bullets. When the dust settled, the "Greensboro Massacre" saw five people dead, murdered by members of the KKK, the United Racist Front, and the National Socialist White People's Party. Though NSWPP member Harold Covington went on to be a public figure, especially famous for his "Northwest Imperative" advocacy of moving whites to the Pacific Northwest, they still ended up with

---

17   Erin Corbett, "Student Trying to Form University 'Alt-Right' Group Was Once Convicted for Arson of Black Churches," *Raw Story*, January 26, 2017, https://www.rawstory.com/2017/01/student-trying-to-form-university-alt-right-group-was-once-convicted-for-arson-of-black-churches/.

five corpses on the picket line and the Klansmen were acquitted of murder charges.[18]

18   "Greensboro Massacre (1979): The Black Past: Remembered and Reclaimed," *BlackPast.org*, http://www.blackpast.org/aah/greensboro-massacre.

Mainstreaming

Observing the language of historical perspectives, discussions about the economic projects of the Confederacy, and the supposed on-going "anti-Southern" discrimination of the post-Reconstruction American political world, it was almost difficult to pick up on the key theme: race. The Council of Conservative Citizens' yearly conference was a meeting point for those across several political distinctions, the strongest of which was a belief that the South could "rise again." What separated the CofCC from other organizations that maintained a cadre of white nationalists was that it invited Republicans from state and federal government to speak to their organization about "traditional Christian values." In 1993, the organization hosted Mike Huckabee, and Republican congressman Bob Barr gave their keynote address in 1998. Former Senate Majority Leader Trent Lott has addressed the CofCC five times. Since its founding in 1988, they have hosted dozens of major Republicans and included Southern regional GOP politicians as official members, including state legislators and elected judges. This all happened despite its openly racialist stance, which venerates the antebellum South and promotes a segregationist view of race.

Coming out of the White Citizens Councils that fought desegregation with a militant fervor during the 1950–60s civil rights movement, the project came together to continue to raise alarmist fears about immigration, affirmative action, and school busing. Birthed by former White Citizens Council organizer Gordon Lee Baum in 1988, with members from the original segregation days, the organization became a home where white nationalists, neo-Confederates, and KKK members could don a suit-and-tie and drop the racial slurs in favor of polite ethnic scapegoating.[1]

Fascist movements have never been able to stand on their own with rhetoric and ideas that run counter to the moral contract held by most of society. While white supremacy is systemic in modern America, overt appeals to racial nationalism are still met with responses of horror, memories of the violence boiling under the surface. What these movements need is crossover points, politics, and projects that take some of their key ideas, modernize and dilute them, and give them access to the mainstream. Paxton offered this as an intrinsic part of the fascist strategy: the ideologues must find a larger coalition, and a "mainstreaming" faction is that gatekeeper to the broader culture. In the days of segregation, the White Citizens Councils and eventually the campaigns of Barry Goldwater and George Wallace provided that.

Memories of a Blessed Parish

Starting in the 1980s, in response to the growing hegemony of Neoconservatism inside the GOP, a new movement developed out of a dissident strain of American conservatism. As interventionist foreign policy and growing social spending became the order of the day, hitting a pinnacle in the George W. Bush administration, there was an impulse to look deep into the past and resurrect a vision of America that was based in nostalgia for the 1950s. Paleoconservatism, as Paul Gottfried would name it, was an attempt to reinstate in America an Old Right form of conservatism, one that was isolationist and "America First." This vision of conservatism's past was largely mythological as paleoconservatism was uniquely modern even if it fetishized the post-WWII American landscape, a standard feature of fascism. While it did not have big money like most avenues in the conservative movement, it created some lasting institutions like the Rockford Institute and its magazine *Chronicles*.

What was most obvious about paleoconservatism, besides its tacit alliance with hard-right libertarians, was that, by contemporary standards, it used the language of racial arson. Seeing itself as critical of unrestricted free-market capitalism, paleos often stood against

1   "Almost Acceptable: The Curious Case of the Council of Conservative Citizens," *Anti-Fascist News*, July 25, 2015, https://antifascistnews.net/2015/07/25/almost-acceptable-the-curious-case-of-the-council-of-conservative-citizens/.

"mass immigration" as a force created by economic elites to undermine white workers. Special ire was saved for non-white immigrants they accused of "failing to assimilate." Often tied to deeply religious people, increasingly Catholic, the movement also skewed Southern, with a nostalgia present for the monoracial and ordered structures of early Southern generations.[2] The pinnacle of this movement was the 1992 presidential run of iconoclastic right-wing politician Pat Buchanan, who, like Donald Trump, used a degree of economic populism to draw from the white working class. Taking many of the talking points that made David Duke a formidable challenger just a year earlier in the Louisiana governor's race, Buchanan railed against Third World immigration and trade deals, saying that he was explicitly an "American nationalist." Many Beltway conservatives avoided Buchanan's fiery rhetoric, as well as the fact that his rallies were more likely to have bikers than men in well-tailored suits.[3] Buchanan went on to found the *American Conservative*, a right-wing publication that broadened out from its Paleo base yet still ported over many of its non-traditional conservative stances like the opposition to the 2003 invasion of Iraq.

Paleoconservatism has also acted as a stop-over point for white nationalists looking to mainstream, or even for traditional conservatives moving in the other direction. Sam Francis, a well-known paleoconservative columnist for the *National Review* and *Washington Post*, was among these ranks, critical of capitalism from a "traditionalist" perspective. Francis was difficult to pin down in his earlier years, often making dog whistle appeals to racial solidarity and fears about non-white immigration and crime. In 1992, he found himself indebted to Buchanan's language of the "Middle American Radicals," considering the angry racialism of conservative and rural areas a "political class" with a revolutionary rightist character. This group was going to act as the inverse of Marx's vision of the proletariat, instead rising up against the "anarcho-tyranny" of liberalism.[4] That dog whistle was clarified as he joined the 1994 *American Renaissance* conference where he discussed the need to develop a "white identity."[5] This started Francis's decline in the conservative movement, eventually seeing him dropped from mainstream conservative organs

---

2   Hawley, *Right-Wing Critics of American Conservatism*, 181–203.
3   Zeskind, *Blood and Politics*, 277–88.
4   Ibid., 288–93.
5   Sam Francis, "Inequality: Natural, Political and Social," AmRen Conference, 1994, https://www.youtube.com/watch?v=AWFcqJgqgMQ.

of thought. He went on to continue his support of *AmRen*, edited the CofCC's newsletter *The Citizen Informer*, and was the center of the formation of the National Policy Institute. Paul Gottfried also followed suit, becoming an ideological mentor for the Alt Right as he ran the H.L. Menken Club, contributing to various publications run by Richard Spencer, and writing fawning books on fascism.[6]

Right of the State

As George Hawley describes, there are two key traditions of capitalist libertarianism in America. The far-right usually had crossover with the more hardline anarcho-capitalism types, with organizations like the Cato Institute and *Reason Magazine* eventually siding with cultural liberalism.[7] Much of this loose coalition came less from pure ideological agreement and more from cultural affiliation and common enemies, where the anti-tax movement of the 1980s and 1990s became a great entry point for skinheads, Patriots, and others "against the system" to enter the politics of the semi-mainstream right. Regional parties like the Libertarian Party of Florida have acted as an incubator for these types of edge politics, and include members like Augustus Sol Invictus. Many on the right saw Ron Paul's 2008 presidential run as an opportunity, primarily to go after institutions like affirmative action and welfare. Much of Paul's hard right past was made apparent during the controversy when his newsletters from the 1980s were made public, and overtly racist claims made about black crime and AIDS survivors were singled out. Photos of him standing with *Stormfront* founder Don Black didn't help, nor later did a 2008 picture of him with Richard Spencer. What this said was less that Ron Paul had strong ideological bedfellows with white nationalists and more that, in the edge of right-wing American politics, it is much easier to get into a room with libertarians than it should be.

The Illuminati

Since the John Birch Society attempted to root out "communist subversion" in the 1950s, the vast world of conspiracy acted as a

---

6   "Sam Francis," Southern Poverty Law Center, https://www.splcenter.org/ fighting-hate/extremist-files/individual/sam-francis.

7   Hawley, *Right-Wing Critics of American Conservatism*, 146–52.

mainstreaming institution in its own right. While theories about shadow governments should be enough to preclude someone from mainstream politics, there has always been an element of conservatism in America that has feared subversion. The Republican obsession with Eurasian communism took most of the focus of this for decades, and later the far-right used tragedies like the assassination of John F. Kennedy to show "proof" of Soviet meddling in American affairs.

What fascist ideologues often get out of conspiratorial thinking is the destruction of "previous assumptions" in a person. Their theories on race and, especially, the "Jewish question," necessitate certain levels of conscious conspiracy, a malevolent elite seeking to destroy white identity. To this end they have found that the various channels of conspiracy theory have been a good stopping point as, no matter how seemingly marginal, the world of conspiracies still has more mainstream currency than fascism does. Since September 11, 2001, this thinking has only increased, as the 9/11 Truth Movement suggested that a secret elite was orchestrating "false flag" attacks in the U.S. This type of thinking was also incredibly important in the early 1990s, as Holocaust Denial became an avenue for the far-right to embed anti-Semitic narratives. Approaching it similarly to Creationists who want to "Teach the Debate," they attempted to sow doubt in key facts about the Holocaust in order to, first, relieve interwar fascism of its burden of genocide and, second, to identify international Jewry as a powerful tribal group manipulating world affairs. They had moderate success with campaigns like the university-focused Committee for Open Debate of the Holocaust, which ran ads in campus publications. In 1988, they had one of their biggest breakthroughs as the trial of Holocaust denier Ernst Zundel in Canada sought to find experts to disprove the "official story" of the Holocaust. Here they hired an unlicensed engineer, Fred A. Leuchter, to go to Auschwitz and see if the buildings there were actually used as gas chambers. Without the expertise to do so and after fumbling the available tests, Leuchter put out the erroneous *Leuchter Report* that described the "impossibility" of the official narrative. Experts have debunked the *Leuchter Report* across the scientific fields, and after his affiliation with neo-Nazis ended his spurious career creating execution devices for American prisons, he continued his work speaking at anti-Semitic conferences.[8]

---

8   *Mr. Death: The Rise and Fall of Fred A. Leuchter, Jr*, directed by Errol Morris, performed by Fred Leuchter Jr., Robert Pelt, and David Irving (1999; USA: Universal Studio), DVD.

In 1993, Jewish academic Deborah Lipstadt wrote the definitive book on the history of Holocaust Denial, *Denying the Holocaust*, where leading "revisionist" historian David Irving was identified as a liar. Before finally coming forward as a revisionist, Irving had a long career as a World War II historian, publishing controversial works that sold well enough for him to travel around town in a luxurious Rolls Royce. This success, despite a background in far-right politics, including a public debate on the merits of immigration alongside British Union of Fascists founder Oswald Mosley. Irving is also credited with referring to himself as a "mild fascist" and described Hitler's mountain vacation home "a shrine for me."[9] While he often denied accusations of anti-Semitism, Irving's own public speech often betrayed him:

> What I've done is nothing compared to what they [Jews] do every day...And they will be paid back in kind. What happened after Weimar—that last time they were allowed to acquire so much power—is nothing compared to the reckoning that awaits them.[10]

Irving later sued Lipstadt for libel, but was publicly roasted by her attorney and ended up paying heftily in her counter-suit. In many European countries it is against the law to publicly declare the Holocaust a myth, so Irving eventually did two years in an Austrian prison, effectively ending any mainstream credibility he had.

While Holocaust Denial remains socially toxic, 9/11 Truth has provided an incredible avenue for continuing anti-Semitic narratives. This is especially true of the allegations that it was various Israeli agents responsible for the attack, making it appear as though it was Muslims so the U.S. would carry out Israeli-inspired foreign policy in the Middle East. This continues the long-standing rubbish that Jews hold allegiance to Israel rather than the U.S.

While many conspiracy theories have been consciously sanitized of their overt anti-Semitic character, they often still retain the same internal logic. The labeling of Rothschilds or other Jewish-identified families as the "financial elite" plays back to the idea that it is a specific group of people, ethnically Jewish or otherwise, that run world affairs, rather than the institutions of capitalism that develop

---

9   Nicholas Fraser, *The Voice of Modern Hatred* (Woodstock, NY: Overlook Press, 2001), 101.
10   Ibid., 97.

a ruling class. At the same time, other conspiracy theories, such as AIDS denialism, hides its far-right roots while appealing to African American communities most affected by the epidemic. While conspiracy theories about the government's role in "inventing" HIV have become popular among the most affected black prisoners in mass incarceration, the figures that developed the ideas did so from a place of radical social conservatism and xenophobia. When their policy solutions are boiled down, from William Douglass to Lyndon LaRouche, they all deal with the criminalization of queers and sex workers, the closing of the border, and the close policing of sexual behavior. The driving factor here is their skewed, far-right social lens, from which bizarre theories are constructed and then sold back to the very people who they intend to victimize.[11]

It has been this understanding of global politics that has developed the world of Alex Jones and *Infowars*, the largest conspiracy platform acting as a crossover point for white nationalism today. While often referred to as an Alt Right media outlet, Jones instead has made it a one-stop shop for conspiracies, unproven alternative health cures, and now a kind of angry American nationalism. Jones first got his start during the Patriot fever over the ATF blunder at the Waco, Texas, compound of the Branch Davidians. He has developed an ever-changing set of theories that intermix Masonic and Illuminati narratives. In recent years, his operation has grown substantially and he has moderated his views, but with Donald Trump's presidential campaign he turned *Infowars* into an explicitly civic nationalist project that spends most of its time attempting to bait leftist protesters. In doing this, Jones has made incredible friends in the far-right, especially among the Patriot subculture that has always been looking over its shoulder for fear of a tyrannical federal government. *Infowars* correspondents have even called themselves Alt Right at times, but their lack of ideological consistency and affiliation with white nationalism indicates that this is likely an attempt at hip branding, and they have been labeled "Alt Light" instead.

Borderlands

With immigration as the key "crossover" political issue for white nationalists, it is no wonder that anti-immigrant political organizations

---

11   David Gilbert, *AIDS Conspiracy Theories: Tracking the Real Genocide* (Montreal: Kersplebedeb, 2002), 18–24.

have been an avenue to influence the GOP. Immigration, which to them is an ethnic invasion unseating the racial citizens of the country, is the defining political issue since it is one of the few issues in contemporary politics that they maintain a clear connection to—and their demographic loss could signal defeat before they are even able to define themselves as a movement. The American Immigration Control Foundation (AICF) and the Federation for American Immigration Reform (FAIR) are the largest of these. John Tanton, who has close ties to *American Renaissance* and other race realist and white nationalist leaders, founded FAIR. In 2008 alone, FAIR was featured almost five hundred times in the mainstream media and he has made dozens of appearances before Congress since 2000. This is all while receiving $1.2 million in funding from the neo-Nazi-affiliated Pioneer Fund and featuring Council of Conservative Citizens members in their television show. Kris Kobach, the secretary of state of Kansas, worked for FAIR's legal wing, where he authored the pilot for Arizona's radical SB 1070 legislation, which required that people suspected of being undocumented show papers.[12] Kobach, who also worked to end "birthright citizenship" and published a book opposing anti-apartheid work, was shortlisted for attorney general under Donald Trump and was later considered for the secretary of homeland security spot, where he was proposing measures almost identical to Trump's eventual "Muslim travel ban."

The focus on Muslim immigration specifically has been an issue that has defined far-right parties in Europe—like Marine Le Pen's Front National France—because of an increased rate of immigration from Middle Eastern countries, due to proximity and logical position during the refugee migrations of recent years. The increased Muslim populations in France, the U.K., and Germany have incited underlying racial tensions, which the far-right has made the defining point of their campaigns. The internationalist arm of the far-right has melded this concept in the U.S., where a history of terrorism is an easy trigger point for the right to use against Islam. Groups like ACT for America, with their June 2017 "March Against Sharia," was instrumental in this, reframing Islamophobia as a refutation of Islamic Law, which they believed ramps up "Islamization of the West" and the U.S. specifically. In this way they can use liberal values of secularism and multiculturalism to denigrate Muslims, and then to signal to anti-immigrant, anti-refugee groups for the implementation

---

12   Sussman, *The Myth of Race*, 287–95.

of travel restrictions. Identity Evropa and other Alt Right groups were in attendance at the marches, but after some of the violence at recent Alt Right-sponsored "Free Speech" events, some of the Patriot groups were wary of their presence. Nonetheless, these moments of anti-immigrant sentiment are the perfect mixer between the two camps as they largely have the same racist motivations, and the only difference is their level of intensity.

As Trump sets his sights on becoming more of a Beltway conservative, the immigration issue remains the primary connection between him and the white nationalists clamoring for a seat at the table. His increased deportation orders and the Southern border wall are both ways to enter into the discussion, first framing immigration as a violent criminal issue, then allowing the extremity of the solution to be an entry point for even more radical positions. The *Radix Journal* produced ironic "Trump's Deportation Force" posters, and a meme from the Chan side of the Alt Right suggested that deportations should be a community affair. Even if Trump does not execute significantly bigger deportation numbers than the Obama administration, he has increased the culture of anti-immigration that robs neighbors of compassion and solidarity.

Whitelash

What would later be called a "whitelash" began as Barack Obama headed into the White House and began to unveil his landmark piece of legislation, the Affordable Care Act.[13] By the time Obama came in for his second term in office, Patriot membership had jumped by 755% and explicitly white supremacist organizations had risen to their highest number in years.[14] As he was still in his first term, a new movement developed under coded language that preferred to target "taxes" and label Obama a "socialist." The Tea Party, which stood for Taxed Enough Already, exploded onto the national scene shortly after his election, using theatrical clothing and incendiary language to argue about perceived government overspending. While there were moderate libertarian talking points in much of the official literature, the ground-game was about racial signaling, often buying into

---

13   Whitelash has been used to describe a white backlash to the gains for marginalized people that may cost them superficial privileges, such as priority in hiring.
14   Mark Potok, "The 'Patriot' Movement Explodes," *Intelligence Report*, March 1, 2012, https://www.splcenter.org/fighting-hate/intelligence-report/2012/patriot-movement-explodes.

racist theories that Obama was a secret Muslim born in Kenya. This hard-right atmosphere was also seen as an opportunity for white nationalists to get involved, with people like the American Freedom Party's William Johnson speaking at Tea Party events. The Arizona Tea Party even hosted regional neo-Nazi politician, J.T. Ready, who organized volunteer border patrols and publicly celebrated the "success" of Nazi Germany.[15] The problem with this movement, however, was that it almost immediately baked itself into the GOP and developed an affinity for the Americanist propaganda white nationalists were abandoning. For many on the emerging Alt Right, it lacked a focus on immigration and white identity and instead was still too correlative to "color-blind" Christian evangelism.

Donald Trump, on the other hand, fit perfectly. It would be wrong to blanket the Trump campaign as white nationalist even with its strong allegiances. White nationalism, as an ideology, tends to be both consistent and explicit: they want to achieve their goals and those goals have to be made known. Instead, Trump is a right populist who has taken the playbook of Buchanan, Duke, and Goldwater and repackaged it with fame and success, dotting in an angry personality that Americans love to hate. What the fascist right saw in Donald Trump was an ally on key political issues, specifically immigration. If Trump could successfully halt Mexican and Middle Eastern immigration, especially legal immigration, then this could slow demographic shifts that, if left unchecked, would make later white nationalist political moves impossible. At the same time, they saw what many on the left also viewed with horror: Trump had become a shorthand for an angry white identity. People were chanting "Build the Wall" at their Mexican neighbors. They were calling Black Lives Matter protesters violent terrorists. They were pulling off the hijabs of Muslim women. They were finally saying they didn't care. It was this climate that white nationalists viewed with hope because, as Richard Spencer often says, white people have to "think of themselves as *a people*" before they can become a nation.

The question out of the Trump campaign is how much these ideas permeated the base, especially traditional GOP strongholds like Christian evangelicals. Students for Trump chapters became a

15   Stephen Lemons, "Neo-Nazi J.T. Ready Speaks at Phoenix Tea Party Event, as Does Tasered Tempe Pastor Steven Anderson," *Phoenix New Times*, July 6, 2009, http://www.phoenixnewtimes.com/blogs/neo-nazi-jt-ready-speaks-at-phoenix-tea-party-event-as-does-tasered-tempe-pastor-steven-anderson-6499351.

mixing point for open white nationalists, libertarians, and young Republicans looking for an alternative to the stuffy Brooks Brothers atmosphere of most College Republicans. Now that the Alt Right has used this climate to become increasingly public, it may end up with fewer ideologues using these Trump crossover groups, as they believe they can drop the "crossover" organization in favor of acting openly as Alt Right. They are attempting to blur the lines between white nationalist and Trump Republican—even neo-Nazi website *The Daily Stormer* labeled itself as the "number one Republican" site after Trump's victory.[16]

Alt Light

In today's crossover political atmosphere, the "Alt Light" has entered the primetime. In years past, people like Pat Buchanan played on their fame in GOP party politics as a signal to respectability, and it was their celebrity mixed with nationalism that allowed for their niche. Party politics have less cachet in a world where the Republican president of the U.S. has almost no affiliation with his own party. Instead, it is people like Milo Yiannopoulos who are creating the mainstreaming platform that the far-right can use as a stepping-stone. As mentioned earlier, Milo made a name for himself at the hard-right website *Breitbart*, creating click-bait articles intended to mock the left and marginalized identities. While labeled a journalist, his prime celebrity and income seem to come from speaking tours where he gives comically insulting speeches loaded with bigotry. Often going after fat and transgendered people specifically, Milo has created a cult of personality on college campuses where he gives students permission to mock and degrade those outside of "respectable norms," all while insulating himself from criticism because of his own gay identity.[17] At a December 2016 campus appearance of his "Dangerous Faggot Tour," Milo openly mocked transgender woman Adelaide Kramer, calling them a "tranny" and saying that he would have sex with them since they "weren't passing."[18] Milo's own racism has, again, been explicit as he

---

16   Before that, it had labeled itself as "The #1 Alt Right, Pro-Genocide" website.
17   Jack Hunter, "Meet Milo Yiannopoulos, the Appealing Young Face of the Racist Alt-Right," *The Daily Beast*, May 5, 2016, http://www.thedailybeast.com/articles/2016/05/05/meet-milo-yiannopoulos-the-appealing-young-face-of-the-racist-alt-right.html.
18   Diana Tourjee, "Trans Student Harassed by Milo Yiannopoulos Speaks Out," *Broadly*, January 3, 2017, https://broadly.vice.com/en_us/article/trans-student-harassed-by-milo-yiannopoulos-speaks-out.

commonly rails against Black Lives Matter, and then backtracks by stating he will only have sex with black men. In this discourse he relies on the flipside of anti-black racism, where he fetishizes black masculinity and jokes that he brings color swatches to dance clubs to see if someone is "dark enough" for him to have sex with.

In an attempt to bring more gay men over to supporting Donald Trump, Milo co-founded Gays for Trump and held a party during the Republican National Convention. Pamela Gellar, a noted Islamophobe who ran the "Draw Muhammad" contest in Texas, an offensive jab at the Islamic prohibition on creating images of the prophet, joined him. This is perfectly fine for Milo, as he has made his appeals for gay support of Trump almost exclusively on Trump's promised ban on Muslim immigration. Without hiding his contempt for Islam, Milo had denounced the left for leaving queers vulnerable to the "anti-gay" Islamic religion. As he took the podium at the RNC party he was wearing a rainbow-tinged "We Shoot Back" tank top, referencing the mass shooting at the Pulse nightclub in Orlando, Florida. In the crowd were Richard Spencer and other Alt Right leaders, all of whom look past Milo's flamboyant sexuality in search of a spokesperson.[19] Shortly after Milo's appearance in Berkeley was canceled amid an explosive action from Bay Area counter-organizers, a video surfaced of him defending the sexual abuse of young boys by Catholic clergy. He was then asked to resign from *Breitbart*, his book was canceled, and the entire Alt Right—from Richard Spencer to the *Daily Shoah*—put the final nail in his coffin.[20]

Organizations and figures that are mainstreaming nationalist messages are generally short-lived in their crossover phase. The process by which fascists develop a relationship with a mainstreaming institution often creates tension, as the reason there is any crossover appeal is that they lack ideological unity with their white nationalist acquaintances. Those institutions are given an unspoken mandate to get off the fence, to pick sides. The tradition then is often for the far-right to ride a wave toward the mainstream only to be betrayed by their mainstreaming institutions before they make it to

19   Natalia Barr, "There Was a Gays for Trump Party at the RNC & It Was Terrifying," *Out*, July 21, 2016, http://www.out.com/news-opinion/2016/7/21/there-was-gays-trump-party-rnc-it-was-terrifying.
20   Dorian Lynskey, "The Rise and Fall of Milo Yiannopoulos – How a Shallow Actor Played the Bad Guy for Money," *The Guardian*, February 21, 2017, https://www.theguardian.com/world/2017/feb/21/milo-yiannopoulos-rise-and-fall-shallow-actor-bad-guy-hate-speech.

the finish line. Paleoconservatism never allowed white nationalists to gain any real access to the GOP, and instead those organizations backtracked against accusations of racism, and major figures were purged from the conservative movement when they flew too close to the untouchables. The Alt Light started creating a strong boundary between themselves and the ideological core of the Alt Right, seeing just how far this toxic class of renegades is willing to go. Milo was the first to do this after publishing articles at *Breitbart* profiling the Alt Right, giving them exposure yet also reducing their less palatable talking points to mere memes and offensive jokes. He later went on CNBC and defined the Alt Right as "free-market capitalism" and "freedom, equality," which pushed Alt Right staples like the *Daily Shoah*, *The Daily Stormer*, and *Fash the Nation* to sever ties.[21]

During the November 2016 NPI conference, cameras from *The Atlantic* caught the end of Richard Spencer's speech where he yelled "Hail Trump, hail our people, hail victory!" He was met with multiple stiff-armed Roman Salutes, a "Seig Heil" declaration that showed the real constituency of the crowd. This, along with overtly racist and anti-Semitic statements in his speech, led to a massive roasting in the press, which was compounded as the NPI behavior split the Alt Right. Alt Light leaders like Paul Joseph Watson, the popular *Infowars* correspondent, and Mike Cernovich immediately denounced Spencer, with Cernovich suggesting that Spencer was an agent provocateur possibly working for the government. The move also brought condemnation from the core of the Alt Right, forcing people like Andy Nowicki of the *New Alternative Right* and Greg Johnson of Counter-Currents to ponder if Spencer killed the Alt Right "brand" entirely.[22] These battles continued through the "Free Speech" rallies that followed, ACT for America's "March Against Sharia," and the growing feuds between the core of the Alt Right and organizations like the Oath Keepers. Without the Alt Light, it is difficult to see how the Alt Right could gain any possible respectability, especially now that journalists have created protocols for how to address them and to qualify them as a white supremacist movement.[23]

---

21   Milo Yiannopoulos, *Milo Yiannopoulos: What the 'Alt-Right' Is Really About*, CNBC, September 8, 2016, http://video.cnbc.com/gallery/?video=3000549601.

22   "Let's Watch as the Alt Right Implodes," *Anti-Fascist News*, December 4, 2016, https://antifascistnews.net/2016/12/04/lets-watch-as-the-alt-right-implodes/.

23   "Editors' Note: Think Progress Will No Longer Describe Racists as 'Alt-Right,'" *Think Progress*, November 22, 2016, https://thinkprogress.org/think-progress-alt-right-policy-b04fd141d8d4#.xkpmaifog.

Many crossover organizations shift to the right, however, losing their middle ground stance altogether. This was true of the CofCC, as it has become explicitly a white nationalist organization, even going as far as running ads on Christian radio stations declaring their support for "racial purity as God's chosen order."[24] CofCC took an even bigger hit after the murders committed by Dylann Roof, who, in his "manifesto," cited his education in racial matters from the CofCC website, which mainly stacks misleading articles on "black crime" and attempts to characterize black people as genetically abhorrent when compared to whites.[25] CofCC board member Jared Taylor made matters worse by attempting to reframe the organization in media interviews after the fact, further cementing the group in the world of violent white supremacy.

The Proud Boys, the "Western Chauvinist" gang created by *Vice* founder Gavin McInnis, has also straddled the line between Alt Light and Alt Right. While operating similarly to Identity Evropa, and even proving more ready for violence at "free speech" rallies, they seemed to be taking up the open racialist mantle of the Alt Right. Instead, they have intentionally avoided racialist language and have even recruited gay, transgender, and non-white members. When given the choice, they have chosen to side with Alt Light figures in disputes with white nationalists, cementing them into the civic nationalist camp.[26]

Other projects, like the anti-immigration website *VDare*, has spent years trying to bring different branches of conservatives together to write about immigration, but their inclusion of "race realists" like Steve Sailer and other white nationalists has shifted the center of the website firmly into the world of far-right politics. At *The Right Stuff*'s "TRSlemania," a private convergence of affiliated regional groups, the "Seig Heils" were screamed, and all pretense was dropped as the Nazism became so overt that hotel staff had to call the police. This made sense since *The Right Stuff*, though popularized through its meme warfare, has made a name for itself with the anger that supports their extreme brand of white nationalism.

---

24   These ads are featured on almost every episode of the white nationalist *Political Cesspool* show, which is featured on a Christian broadcast network.

25   Dylann Roof, "Dylann Roof's Manifesto," *New York Times*, December 13, 2016, https://www.nytimes.com/interactive/2016/12/13/universal/document-Dylann -Roof-manifesto.html.

26   Kyle Chapman, interview with author, June 4, 2017.

PART II

Ending Fascism

Twentieth-Century Resistance

Under Oswald Mosley, the British Union of Fascists (BUF) antagonized England—even during the German bombing raids of the Second World War. Mosley was interned in prison in 1940 and was absent from the nationalist scene for years while the BUF was outlawed. He was released in 1943, and in 1947 he was ready again to lead his fascist comrades, forming new organizing committees with people from disaffected areas of British cities where postwar immigration was heaviest. A group of largely Jewish veterans, named the 43 Group, threw bricks at windows during Mosley's "Union Movement" meetings and, later, forged tickets to get inside and confront the fascist cadre directly. Using a "wedge formation," they would rush the stage to tip over the speaker's platform, knowing that, at that point, the police would likely shut down the event entirely. Drawing from the communist and anarchist militancy that formed the antifascist committees before and during the war, the 43 Group left the door open to "anyone who wants to fight fascism and anti-Semitism," building "intelligence" departments that researched fascist organizations and "commando" committees that would confront fascist formations. The increased numbers of disruptions put many off of the nationalist cause, as they felt that it was simply not worth the retribution they were facing.[1]

While many in the 43 Group thought its militancy would decimate Mosley's appeal in industrial areas, some felt a legislative push was necessary, hoping to target anti-Semitic and racist speech for

---

1 Mark Bray, *Antifa: The Anti-Fascist Handbook* (Melville House, New York: 2017): 41–44.

state repression. The militants would "reject the legislative route because of their revolutionary anti-state politics," while trying to remain open to a mass participation by various political strands united in fighting fascism and anti-Semitism. Similar debates are happening today.[2] These debates and conflicts over strategies and tactics are "ever present," driven by the persistent need to fight fascism's shifting face.

The story of American fascism is useless unless framed in the world it endangers, and this is not a story of helpless victimization, but instead a collective survivorhood marked by refusal. So far, I have outlined fascism—from the development of white nationalism to the coinage of the Alt Right, from its spiritual appropriation to its false science—but a partisan narrative views it as the left experiences it: through antifascism. This is an attempt to capture pieces of these enduring movements. From the early history to the present, we see generations of resistance to fascism that are even more diverse than their opposition. We will look at the various movements that have confronted fascism's rise, with a special eye to the U.S. and how mass movements have changed the tools of organizing with shifting approaches.

This second half of the book shifts the gaze, reframing the narrative to the partisans. These sections will look at antifascism, not just as a monolithic political force defined in singular narratives, but also as a mission and strategic outlook from the masses who participate. This could not, and should not, be seen as an exhaustive look at all the ways that fascist movements have been resisted since World War II, but instead snapshots of the ways that different communities, approaches, ideologies, and tactical frameworks have fought it. The intention is to show antifascism from a variety of contexts since, as history plays itself out, the struggle will be as multitudinous as the composition of the class confronting it.

Antifascism in the U.K. can be traced back to 1924 with the formation, by the Communist Party of Great Britain, of the People's Defense Force (PDF), which began confronting the first Britain fascist organization, British Fascist Ltd.[3] On October 7, 1923, organized communists disrupted the first meeting of the British Fascists, and the PDF was created in 1924 to go after the increasing fascist street threat. With communists heading this antifascist organizing,

---

2   Ibid, 41.
3   Originally named the British Fascisti.

militancy was front and center from the earliest days of resistance.[4] After the electoral defeat of his New Party—a right populist political party—Oswald Mosley toured Europe, meeting with Mussolini and Nazi officials. He returned home and formed the BUF in 1932, attracting thousands with the organization's anti-Semitism and anti-immigrant rhetoric. The main strategy of the antifascists at the time was disruption. Antifascists would engage with both public and private events, fighting with the Nazi sympathizers who chanted slogans like "To hell with the Jews." With Hitler rising in Germany, working-class Jews started turning to Communist Party radicals who presented the only concrete threat to fascism. Antifascist organizations were formed across the U.K., largely by the labor movement, structured by professions like, for example, the British Cab Drivers Antifascist Committee and the King's Cross Railwayman's Antifascist Group. Membership of the BUF peaked at 40,000, but after a massive confrontation with coordinated antifascist groups it dropped to merely 5,000 in 1935. The antifascists robbed the Blackshirts, the militant fascist rank-and-file, of their middle-class respectability and peeled away the layer of supporters who were not committed enough to withstand the fight.[5]

The conventional wisdom in the U.S. has been that organizations of Italian and German immigrants, less assimilated than WASP families who go back hundreds of years, were the most prone to early fascist ideas because of national kinship. The German-American Bund (Amerikadeutscher Volksbund) is the most famous of these. Formed in 1936, the German-American Bund had tens of thousands of members in seventy regions around the country. The best estimate is that, in the 1920s, about 5 percent of the U.S. immigrant population took part in "Blackshirt activities," inspired by the battle for national identity happening in early twentieth-century Europe.[6]

The same immigrant communities also formed some of the strongest antifascist responses to the phenomenon that they were also seeing in their homelands. Italian anarchists and trade unionists, committed to the shop-floor labor battles of the 1920s, focused on fascism as they saw fellow Italian immigrants forming American

4   David Hann, *Physical Resistance: A Hundred Years of Anti-fascism* (Zero Books, Reprint Edition, 2013), 12–15.

5   Ibid., 24–62.

6   Alan Taylor, "American Nazis in the 1930s—German American Bund," *The Atlantic*, June 5, 2017, https://www.theatlantic.com/photo/2017/06/american-nazis-in-the-1930sthe-german-american-bund/529185/.

incarnations of the Partito Nazionale Fascista (Italian National Fascist Party) after Mussolini's "March on Rome" in 1922. By 1923 there were some 20,000 stateside Italian fascists operating within forty regional organizations under Mussolini's thumb. Carlo Tresca, an Italian anarchist known for his later battles against mafia infiltration of unions, started the paper *Il Martello* (The Hammer), which destroyed the heroic narrative of fascist mythology. The Il Martello Group developed a nationwide strategy with fundraisers, antifascist boycotts, and the smuggling of radical literature into Italy once the presses there were smashed. In collaboration with Communist Party leaders, they created the Antifascist Alliance of North America, in which anarchist principles of direct action led to enormous counter-actions, including physical engagement, during fascist mobilizations. The precedent had been set, from New York to Minneapolis, and the anarchist movement was part and parcel with antifascism, and that meant a "no platform" approach long before that terminology was coined.[7] This idea, as will be elaborated later, is that fascist activity, including fascist speech, is to be disallowed by organizers, thwarting their attempts at recruitment.

As World War II broke out, the resistance movements engaged in armed struggle against genocide. After the Popular Front of leftists won the Spanish elections in 1936, General Francisco Franco united with the fascist Falange and staged a coup. Upwards of 35,000 volunteers from fifty-three countries joined the Stalinist International Brigades to fight Franco, and in the northern areas of Aragon and Catalonia, anarchist organizations and unions staged not just a rearguard action in defense of the Republic, but instead a "three-way fight" against both fascism and the bourgeois state.

In Germany, the failed socialist revolution of 1918–19 led to massive attacks on social democrats and communists, yet when the Nazis really came to power in 1933, there were 150,000 communists engaged in illegal resistance against the Brownshirts. In association with the now-outlawed Communist Party of Germany (KPD), committees were created to take on the Nazis directly. These were known as Antifaschistische Aktion, or shortened to "Antifa." The dual flag in the now famous logo used internationally for militant antifascist organizations came from the tacit alliance between the Marxists and the social democrats, a difficult relationship given the

7   Andrew Cornell, *Unruly Equality: U.S. Anarchism in the 20th Century* (Oakland: University of California Press, 2016), 94–96.

decades of revolutionary tension that preceded the creation of the Schutzstaffel.[8] After the war, party members reactivated these networks and developed Antifas in most cities, attracting thousands. They went after Nazi war criminals still evading capture or even censure in postwar Germany, as well as the fascist partisans who continued to ideologically align themselves with National Socialism.

The narratives about resistance during the war have centered on Allied forces, overlooking resistance that occurred internally. In 1943, the Warsaw Ghetto of Poland was one of the largest strongholds of Jews who were interned on their way to the network of concentration camps, with a swelling population of 490,000. Jews in the ghetto organized "self defense units" and when the full "liquidation" of the camp's population to the surrounding extermination camps happened, the Jewish partisans fought against the Nazis with minimal arms. Militarily the effort fell short, as the Nazis vastly outgunned their opponents, but they acted in the spirit of resistance, not willing to surrender to the German machine.[9]

Since World War II, neo-fascist projects, attempting to revive their perspectives and aims in new conditions, have met stiff resistance. The potential for fascism to take root is a fact of history, and its fruition must not be repeated. The tactics have changed just as the fascist threat and the radical left has, each evolving through conflicting visions of the future. The center of antifascism has always been resilient communities, those that are resistant to fascist incursion because of the strength of multiculturalism and their sturdy social networks. Victory requires mutual dependence and a collective vision of the future grounded by unity. Fascism recenters the anger of crisis away from the powerful elite to the "other," whether that is based on skin color or national origin or sexuality. The left finds power when the community unites.

---

8   While the logo originally showed two different red flags to indicate the communists and the social democrats, today's image features a red flag against a black flag to signify unity between communists and anarchists in antifascist organizing.

9   William A. Pelz, *A People's History of Modern Europe* (London: Pluto Press, 2016), 154.

Fascism Without Adjectives

Fascism is always shifting, changing, and interpreting the world in a multitude of ways. The term "Fascism Without Adjectives" comes from an episode of the post-left Crimethinc podcast, which reluctantly used the term to describe a call for far-right unity from enigmatic white nationalist Matthew Heimbach.[1]

> Whether you are a Christian authoritarian like myself, a Constitutionalist, a fascist, a National Socialist, or whatever stripe of white Traditionalist, just acknowledge that it is time to throw off the shackles of the poisoned American mind-set, time for a new unity within our folk and new ideas for a new age.[2]

Heimbach's was a call for fascists of all stripes. It calls for fascism no matter what your specific cultural background or pet cause is. For the dominant faction, this is clearly race, but for the "Manosphere" it has been gender, for religious and social conservatives it is sexual orientation, and for many of the tribal masculinist organizations, this includes a war on a diversity of body types. Fascism is intersectional, it sees the need to reclaim privilege and establish hierarchy in the myriad of ways that people experience identity. Division and boundaries form the mission—between white and black, men and women, fat and thin, healthy and sick, smart and stupid, strong and weak. Difference cannot be celebrated horizontally; it can only be ranked vertically.

1   "#11: Never Forgive and Never Forget," The Ex-Worker, CrimethInc., October 8, 2013, https://crimethinc.com/podcast/11.
2   Matthew Heimbach, "I Hate Freedom" Trad Youth, July 2013, archived at http://archive.is/4PKNI.

An effective left opposition has to be equally intersectional. It must see itself as the inverse of the fascist quest for power by analyzing how oppression stems from systems of hierarchical inequality. The countering of white supremacy, both interpersonal and systemic, needs to be linked up with the repression of women, the violence against trans bodies, the further marginalization of fat people, and the continued assault on immigrants.

While there are multiple approaches to antifascist organizing, from direct engagement to state advocacy, the barriers are coming down in favor of maintaining a broad-based mass movement. While antifascist organizations still find it necessary to publicly confront fascist organizing, most are seeing a need to move beyond subcultural affiliation. This has meant expanding the term "antifascist" to include people with various abilities, levels of commitment, and interests, so that multiple channels of resistance can be mobilized. Many of the organizations emerging or evolving today use a diverse range of tactics, and may mix pressure campaigns, mass mobilizations, research, and doxxing with the traditional walls of confrontation that antifascism has been known for.

Information and Organization

Fascism will always be an extremist threat, as violence is a cornerstone of its ideology. In recent decades, a large non-profit infrastructure has been built to keep tabs on the white nationalist movement. While there is a diversity of opinion on how to deal with this threat, there is a long history of research and a big body of work that has been useful to a range of antiracist projects. The Anti-Defamation League was founded in 1913 through the Independent Order of B'nai B'rith to confront bigotry, anti-Semitism, and what they saw on the horizon as a "crisis of human rights." They have worked as an educational and information resource, focusing heavily on the insurrectionary wing of the neo-Nazi, KKK, and white nationalist networks. They have traditionally worked closely with law enforcement to go after terrorist plots, aiding in high-profile incursions like the Alcohol, Tobacco, and Firearms raid in Crockett County, Tennessee, where three neo-Nazis were stockpiling weapons with the hope of assassinating then-presidential candidate Barack Obama.[3]

---

3   "ADL Applauds Law Enforcement for Preventing Killing Spree and Obama Assassination Attempt," October 7, 2008, Anti-Defamation League, http://archive

A similar project, though larger in size and scope, is the Southern Poverty Law Center (SPLC), an institution that has mixed extensive research and reporting on hate groups with training, direct organizing and exposure, and legal aid and lawsuits dedicated to shutting down the largest racialist organizations in the U.S.

Their Klanwatch project looked to expose and shut down Klan chapters that were increasing their violent rhetoric. The founder of the SPLC, Morris Dees, challenged the United Klans of America (UKA), whose federation of Klan locals made its legacy in the guerilla warfare of the 1960s. After nineteen-year-old Michael Donald was murdered in 1981 in Mobile, Alabama, by UKA members in retaliation for a mistrial of a black murder suspect, Dees went after them. Filing a lawsuit stating that the organization itself was responsible for the violence inflicted by its members, the four-day trial in 1987 saw multiple Klansmen explaining that they were instructed in these acts of barbarity. The jury delivered a $7 million verdict against the UKA, shuttering the most enduring Klan organization in the country, and the victim's mother ended up with a 7,000-square-foot building that had housed one of the most notorious white supremacist organizations in history.[4]

Thus the SPLC created a model for getting large settlements for victims of hate crimes and for bankrupting the organizational infrastructure of white nationalism. After the 1988 murder of Mulugeta Seraw by members of East Side White Pride in Portland, Oregon, the SPLC wanted to use the same model to confront the growing skinhead street war. Though decentralized, they set on how Tom Metzger and his project, White Aryan Resistance (WAR), had used a rhetoric and strategy of gang warfare to create a climate of murderous rage. Dave Mazella was sent to Portland by WAR to crystalize the foundering political mission of murderers Kyle Brewster, Steve Strasser, and Ken Mieske of East Side White Pride. The lawsuit was a nationwide sensation, sending a shiver of fear through racialist organizations bent on recruiting from the skinhead scene. The SPLC was eventually successful, taking Metzger's home and forcing him into bankruptcy. Though WAR persisted, it was never able to achieve its former glory, and along with a series of serious convictions for skinhead activity, the movement took a major hit.[5]

.adl.org/presrele/extremism_72/5380_82.html#.WGHih7YrKgQ.

4   Langer, *A Hundred Little Hitlers*, 272–77.

5   Ibid., 303–355.

Militant Antifascism

Distinct from liberal organization is militant antifascism, a model that directly engages with fascist forces only if needed. This is arguably the original conception of antifascist resistance, which came out of a period when fascists presented not just a material threat but also a growing global one. The realities of World War II, combined with the consciousness of the historic colonialist project of white supremacy, led many to the conclusion that symbolic actions were insufficient and that the state could not be relied upon to be the arbiter of human rights.

Militant antifascism came in the wake of the European response to the rapid growth of fascist parties in the 1960s–70s, with organizations like Anti-Fascist Action rushing the National Front's street demonstrations with thousands of supporters. In the U.S., the historical struggles against chattel slavery, Jim Crow, and U.S. colonialism informed a new type of project. The John Brown Anti-Klan Committee (JBAKC) was formed by those radicalized in the civil rights and anti-war movements of the 1960s, those who witnessed state repression of the black power movement, which often resulted in comrades locked up under false pretenses or with egregious sentences. When prisoners in New York began communicating with organizers on the outside that the KKK was organizing prison guards, few believed them. When scrutinizing the corporate papers for the New York State KKK, organizers found that some of the leadership of the prison guard union were indeed members.[6]

It was on this basis that the JBAKC was formed. They confronted the KKK directly, while also tying them publicly to the larger issue of white supremacy as historically stewarded by the police. In Austin, Texas, a group of white organizers were working with the Brown Berets, a militant Chicano organization, and the Black Citizens Task Force (BCTF) around the exploitation by wealthy white people of a neighborhood of color that sat adjacent to a popular summer boating lake, forming an organization that affiliated with the JBAKC. Chapters were eventually established in Kentucky, Chicago, San Francisco, New York, Austin, TX, and western Massachusetts.[7]

Just as antifascist organizations have historically done, and have later defined themselves by doing so, they homed in on research about local groups in order to bolster local organizing. In the days

---

6   Lisa Roth, interview with author, July 2, 2017.
7   Linda Evans, interview with author, July 2, 2017.

before easy internet research, this sometimes meant going inside of these groups for information. In Texas, for example, they maintained a post office box that was filled monthly with their subscriptions to racist literature from various organizations. When *Stormfront* founder and KKK leader Don Black was on trial in Dallas for exceeding his permit to public land, which he was using to train racist paramilitaries, JBAKC members came to the courthouse and pretended to be interested students so that Black would open up to them. Later, a female member went to Louisiana and posed as a fan of David Duke for research, attending a meeting of his NGO, the National Association for the Advancement of White People. He was so impressed he offered her a job.[8]

Open about its presence in Texas, the Klan held major public rallies, which the JBAKC answered with over a thousand people to overwhelm the Klan event. "It is really, really important for people to not allow these events to just happen unchallenged," says Lisa Roth, a JBAKC organizer out of New York. "The principle is that you never let these people enter the public sphere and do their thing unopposed. And then the tactics you use to make that happen can be anything."[9]

In the Napa Valley of California, they did just that. When Aryan Woodstock was announced on private land in 1989, the JBAKC came down to address the Napa City Council, asking that they revoke the permit of the "hate rock" festival. Understanding that the council would likely use a "free speech" argument and refuse to intervene, media coverage of their presentation allowed them to connect with locals in a way they couldn't have done before as they were based nearly fifty miles away, in the Bay Area. While the festival went on, they brought a roaring crowd of five thousand to the gates in the pouring rain.[10] As well as challenging the Klan, in their communities, the JBAKC succeeded in raising consciousness about the threat of insurrectionary and ingrained white supremacy, even using street theater and focusing on university appearances of political figures.[11]

SHARP and Anti-Racist Action
Skinheads Against Racial Prejudice (SHARP) was formed in 1987 in New York as an antiracist organization designed to confront the

---

8   Ibid.
9   Lisa Roth, interview with author, July 2, 2017.
10   Ibid.
11   Linda Evans, interview with author, July 2, 2017.

growth of neo-Nazis skinheads in American music culture, drawing from the original multiracial skinhead crews that were the bulwark against Nazi infiltration of working-class punk scenes in the 1980s in England. In places like Portland, Oregon, neo-Nazi skinhead gangs, often associated with WAR or the American Front, had seen massive growth by recruiting at music venues. "You could just drive down the street and point out Nazi gang members, there were hundreds of them," remembers Tom, an early member of SHARP. Developing from the traditional working-class skinhead culture inspired by ska and reggae, SHARP members' politics were all over the map, but their commitment to ending racism in these subcultural spaces bound them together. In Minneapolis, an antiracist skinhead crew known as The Baldies had been working to eliminate the presence of the White Knights, a white supremacist gang, starting in 1982. Seeing the need to expand the reach of antiracist organizing in urban areas, they helped to form what would become the Anti-Racist Action (ARA) network that had its first nationwide meeting while Tom Metzger was fighting his civil lawsuit from the SPLC.[12]

Focused on direct engagement where fascists were doing their recruiting and laying siege, ARA created a format for committed organizers intermixing physical resistance with larger movement and coalition building. Points of unity were developed, which outlined not just the strategic orientation for the project but also the ideological foundation that identified that oppressions intersect and can be bolstered through state institutions.

1. We Go Where They Go: Whenever fascists are organizing or active in public, we're there. We don't believe in ignoring them. Never let the Nazis have the streets!
2. We Don't Rely on the Cops or the Courts to Do Our Work For Us: This doesn't mean we never go to court. But we must rely on ourselves to protect ourselves and stop the fascists.
3. Non-Sectarian Defense of Other Antifascists: In ARA, we have lots of different groups and individuals. We don't agree about everything and we have the right to differ openly. But in this movement an attack on one is an attack on us all. We stand behind each other.
4. We Support Abortion Rights and Reproductive Freedom: ARA intends to do the hard work necessary to build a broad, strong

---

12   "Tom," interview with author, 2016.

movement against racism, sexism, anti-Semitism, homophobia, discrimination against the disabled, the oldest, the youngest and the most oppressed people. We intend to win![13]

Like SHARP, ARA's focus was on direct engagement with neo-Nazis. It was a tactic that stripped away the less committed people from the skinhead gangs and made it difficult for them to find a platform. It was the same strategy used by the 43 Group in Britain. ARA was more intensely political than SHARP had been, inspired directly as they were by anarchist and feminist politics, and many were involved in the Love and Rage Revolutionary Anarchist Federation.[14] In Portland, a culture of violence had brewed as the neo-Nazi organizations brandished weapons and targeted antiracist organizers on the streets and at their homes. In 1993, the shooting of neo-Nazi Eric Banks in what many still allege was a confrontation between skinheads and antiracists was the culmination, until Volksfront was formed.

In Portland, ARA found common ground with the Coalition for Human Dignity, and this bridged a political divide since the Coalition often focused on educating politicians and seeking their intervention about the threat of racist violence in the streets. While the racist skinhead scene has shrunk dramatically, the growth of groups like the PNW Wolfpack in Olympia, Washington, the Northwest Knights of the KKK, and the subcultural recruitment efforts of Operation Werewolf is troubling.

By 1997, there were 1,500–2,000 people associated with ARA across almost two hundred chapters—incredible for an organization founded on a "We Go Where They Go" principle of direct engagement with an increasingly violent wing of the neo-Nazi movement. This forced racist organizations like the World Church of the Creator to operate almost entirely undercover, and every attempt to hold a public event was met by an opponent ready to escalate. Due to the pressure put on by ARA, the "Creativity Movement," which was building a racist cadre focused on revolution, all but collapsed, with

13 "Anti-Racist Action's Points of Unity," *Beating Fascism: Anarchist Antifascism in Theory and Practice*, ed. Anna Key et al. (London: Kate Sharpley Library, 2006), 33.

14 The Love and Rage Anarchist Federation was a North American anarchist network-turned-federation that existed from 1989 through 1998. It was influential in building ARA as a political movement across the U.S. Wayne Price, "A History of North American Anarchist Group Love & Rage," *Northeastern Anarchist* #3 (Fall 2001).

the Pontifex Maximus eventually going to prison for conspiring to murder a federal judge, and different factions jostling for control of their movement.[15]

Antifa

Directly engaging with threatening white supremacist groups—which means the willingness to demonstrate publicly and interfere with their operations—has been taken up internationally under the banner of Antifa. Much of Antifa's tactical set is inspired by "militant antifascism," which uses direct engagement with fascist groups; opposes "parliamentary antifascism" that seeks to ban far-right groups and parties; and is distinct from "liberal antifascism," which uses less confrontational movement building.[16] This perspective is outlined in the "launch statement" of the International Network of Militant Antifascists, which does not seek a return of the status quo through its organizing, but posits antifascism as part of a larger revolutionary struggle:

> As the fascists attempt to gain credibility through electoral strategies, the task for militant antifascists is to out radicalize them in the battle for hearts and minds of working class communities. We stand for the physical and ideological confrontation of fascism and we are not fighting to maintain the status quo. We see the challenges facing us as a three cornered fight, between the militants, the fascists and the state. We recognize that the ultimate guarantee against the far right penetrating the mainstream, is a strong politically independent working class movement.[17]

That statement was written in October 1997, when Anti-Fascist Action hosted the first international conference for militant antifascists, which brought together organizations from across Europe and North America to build the International Network of Antifascists. Minneapolis ARA gave a presentation showing the continuity between the European groups that had been developing alongside fascist parties since before World War II.[18]

In the U.S., the first organization to use the Antifa moniker was Rose City Antifa (RCA). In 2007, the Hammerskin Nation and

---

15   Anna Key, *Beating Fascism*, 46.
16   M. Testa, *Militant Antifascism* (Oakland: AK Press, 2015), 5–6.
17   "International Militant Antifascist Network," *Antifa Forum* #3 (1998): 42.
18   Ibid.

Volksfront were attempting to reconcile the years of bloody feuding in a private event to be held at a veterans' hall in the suburban town of Sherwood, Oregon. A group called the AdHoc Committee Against Racism and Fascism came together to force the event's cancelation, but with racist violence on the rise the antiracist organizers decided they had to make their project permanent.

"Fighting for contested spaces, where there is right entryism into leftist spaces" is a key part of their strategy, and they often target music venues and social movements where white nationalist projects feel they can recruit and shift the discourse in favor of a Third Positionist synthesis. There is crossover in many subcultural and activist spaces, from Oi! punk shows that may appeal to racist skinheads as well as antiracist ones, or political spaces that flirt with conspiracy theories, and this is where groups like RCA intervened. This was true, for example, in RCA's campaign against Tim Calvert, a 9/11 Truther whose anti-Semitic connections and ideas went under the radar because of his ostensibly "leftist" pedigree, as a member of a popular bike collective. RCA stood apart from other groups by developing an organization committed to diversity, with women in leadership roles, and keeping closed membership and tight security. Going forward, RCA became notorious for putting out well-researched information and getting racists fired and evicted from their homes. With their long campaign, they were a key factor in seeing Volksfront finally disband. "What broke that organization was just being tenacious."[19]

Rose City Antifa is a part of the larger Torch Network, an offspring of the early ARA network that nationally coordinated regional groups.[20] There were, for years, only a few organizations that did this work, and it is common to find groups that mix this direct confrontation with larger movement building, combining strategies to approach the chameleon of fascism in their cities. Since Donald Trump's election and the rise of the Alt Right, groups identifying with Antifa have grown exponentially. Today, in most cities around the country, there are organizations claiming the mantle of ARA/ Antifa, using a mix of confrontational strategies with research and doxxing, and even working with community partners to build a mass movement against fascism. The label "Antifa" is broadly used to identify an antifascist movement that does not denounce militancy but may interpret it in broad ways.

---

19   Crow, founding member of Rose City Antifa, interview with author, 2016.
20   The Torch Network has 12 participating regional organizations. TorchAntifa.org.

New York City Antifa stands out as one of the oldest projects using this approach. They do not act in public under the group name but focus heavily on research. Contested spaces continue to fuel a great deal of their direction as they confront organizations that attempt recruitment in spaces commonly associated with the left. Through confrontation with far-right groups like the National Anarchist Tribal Alliance of New York, NYC Antifa has succeeded in thwarting attempts at entryism into the radical spaces that countercultural fascists often set their sights on. The antiracist organizers involved have also seen the significant cost that Antifa activists face when direct confrontation—often violent engagement—is the priority. One organizer with New York City Antifa notes that supporting imprisoned activists can use up the movement's limited resources:

> When there are more prisoners, Antifa activists will end up doing less work on the ground and more prison support. Being imprisoned also has an effect, not just the prisoner, but on their families and friends. And, especially right now, Antifa groups have a lot of room to expand by getting involved in larger community organizing projects.[21]

The suggestion here is less about moving away from the militant resistance to fascism, but instead determining what effective organizing looks like. The ability of movements to reproduce themselves necessitates the ability for those involved to keep projects going, to do work over years, to recruit new generations of people, and to expand struggles. More moderate groups may be less comfortable working with Antifa-signified ones, choosing to temper rhetoric and strategy so as to appeal to a broader coalition—an example of the liberal compromises that many organizations take. At the same time, direct confrontation has proven effective, both in the convergence of mass actions where large groups of antifascists confront major white nationalist groups in public formation, and when individuals are confronted in public, such as when Augustus Sol Invictus was hosting a meet-and-greet in a bar and was subsequently evicted by the establishment and his supporters run off.

Militancy has been a critical part of antifascists' success for years, including when the threat of losing means mass institutional

---

21   Anonymous member of NYC Antifa, interview with author, 2016.

violence, and it was those militant organizations that have been actively developing the work through struggle. For this type of organization, a cadre formation is necessary rather than a mass movement approach, since strict anonymity has to be maintained. Security culture then pervades this style of organizing, because of state repression as well as the threat of violent reprisal from neo-Nazis. NYC Antifa has preferred to work with a trusted set of colleagues that prioritize concrete research, focused doxxing, and a homing in on fascist events happening in their city. Replacing recruitment with training, they hope to empower interested people to form their own groups, and even to create more diverse models that draw on larger community organizing strategies.

Doxxing

The use of doxxing, the release of information about specific white nationalists, has been an incredibly potent tool for antifascist organizing, as it plays heavily on the fact that most nationalist activists cannot afford to be outed to their professional or social networks. Their personal information is often publicized, triggering social consequences that create a specter for those attracted to the fascist cause.

Rose City Antifa's campaigns have used this approach, taking on one person at a time. After making their information known to community members, it's then shared where the offender's affiliations has real consequences. When the American Freedom Party was attempting to take root in Portland, showing up at local gun shows and even anti-war protests, their members' personal and employment information was made public. Each member was exposed, one at a time, and then a strategy of escalation was employed at their workplace, causing them to be fired. The point here is simple: to continually raise the cost of participating in organized fascist formations, to destabilize those organizations by interrupting the lives of the people in them, and then to watch them dissolve.

As Nathan Damigo began rising to prominence in the Alt Right scene with Identity Evropa, Northern California Antifa began a long-standing research project on him that exposed his radicalization in prison by white supremacist gangs and the extent of his violent past. This helped to destroy the moderate image he hoped to cultivate, and then they took that information into the larger community where Identity Evropa was recruiting, making it difficult for Damigo to continue at the University of California, Stanislaus. The public doxxing of Identity Evropa members has had this effect, discouraging the College Republican types that were targets for recruitment. If participation in groups like Identity Evropa is proven to have serious consequences, such as losing a job or becoming estranged from one's family, then the Alt Right's mission is lost since it cannot insert the ideology into the community. While the Alt Right desperately tries to create an infrastructure to support those who have lost their public lives, such as *The Right Stuff*'s attempt to shift to a paywall format to bankroll Mike Enoch after he lost his career, it is not possible to maintain a middle-income life and continue as a public nationalist pariah.

In the age of social media, reality television, and the normalcy of public shaming, passive doxxing is rarely effective. While antifascist activists can face reprisal, the effective use of doxxing by the left against fascists has led to an "Anti-Antifa" culture of social media accounts that monitor antifascist communication and attempt to research and doxx those who they label broadly as "Antifa." This has led to dozens of Facebook and Twitter accounts that provide the names and images of thousands of people, most of whom have almost no connection to antifascist organizations. Mass information dissemination robs doxxing of its effectiveness, ceasing to identify anybody since it identifies everybody. They do this partly because the Alt Right has little experience with real organizing, and therefore individuals in diffuse social networks can appear to them as dedicated participants. Instead, effective use of information dissemination requires a few primary approaches, including proof of legitimacy and the focused use of the material itself.

For years a prime strategy for organizers confronting creeping white nationalism was to focus heavily on exposure and education. The ADL and the SPLC marked their growth on this strategy, where they would create large dossiers on specific movements and their leaders to make them notorious. In 2005, Kevin Lamb was fired from his position at the right-wing journal *Human Events* after the SPLC called the editorial staff to tell them he was moonlighting at the white nationalist *Occidental Quarterly*.[22] The One People's Project, members of the Torch Network, and other antiracist organizations also focus on researching specific individuals who would normally

---

22   "Occidental Quarterly," Southern Poverty Law Center, n.d, https://www. splcenter.org/fighting-hate/extremist-files/group/occidental-quarterly.

go anonymous online or would continue to stay in the shadows even when committing horrifying acts of racist violence. While large NGOs used to dominate this work, the growth of radical organizations has decentralized it and made public exposure more rapid, common, and consequential.

For many activists, the revelation of a person's information may come along with a call to contact their place of work, which often results in them being fired. This is a major concern for the growing white nationalist movement where people like Matthew Heimbach have been unable to hold down a middle-income job since becoming a public figure.

While Alt Right groups' public presence has grown heavily, the vast majority of their social networks want to operate in private. Daryle Lamont Jenkins of the One People's Project notes how the aging membership of most white nationalist organizations spelled a slow death for their movement just a few years ago, but groups like Identity Evropa and *The Right Stuff* network focus almost entirely on the recruitment of young Millennials because "they need to survive somehow." Though the leadership and a small cadre have been quickly exposed by doxxing projects, identifying the larger, anonymous mass would be highly effective, as few would want to join ranks, knowing their reputations would be tarnished before they even enter the job market.[23]

"That means they have something to hide, and we have to reveal it," says Jenkins. "There is no such thing as a public Nazi not getting the opposition." This exposure has heavy consequences, which makes being in the quiet layer of these movements seem like a more and more risky proposition, even if they do not willingly carry banners or pose for pictures.

The Great Shuttening

The internal policies of the social media platforms fascists rely on have made them incredibly vulnerable, especially since their ideological core and speech violates long-established rules on hate speech. Facebook was the first to come in and regulate, suspending accounts of violators regularly. Twitter, on the other hand, took longer to catch on and required the organized pressure of antiracists watching as fascist messages only amplified.

---

23   Daryle Lamont Jenkins, interview with author, September 1, 2016.

Milo Yiannopolous came to fame during the Gamergate controversy where groups of men harassed female reporters online for the offense of advocating gender equality.[24] This fame brought him to *Breitbart* where he continued to rise as a Twitter celebrity, harassing women like African American actress Leslie Jones to such a degree that she feared for her safety.[25] His behavior and his legions of supporters brought the controversy out into the open as a backlash formed, and Twitter heard the complaints and permanently severed his use of the platform.[26] Since then Alt Right people like Ricky Vaughn and Richard Spencer have on-and-off Twitter bans, and the company started flagging racial slurs. In response, Alt Right people began calling black people "Googles" and Jewish people "Skypes" to both go under the radar and mock the Twitter algorithm.[27]

Most podcasts rely on major distribution platforms like iTunes and SoundCloud, which is where the majority of people download their podcasts. Because of their "terms of service," mass complaints have gotten the *Radix Journal Podcast* and others dropped from iTunes syndication, and SoundCloud has dropped *Fash the Nation*, the *Daily Shoah*, and many other Alt Right podcasts.[28] This forces them to build their own platforms, which can distribute podcasts for their core audience, but it will not have the Web 2.0 component that brings their message to audiences far beyond their cult reach. The same principle has proven true for payment

24   Kristen Brown, "The Ultimate Troll: The Terrifying Allure of Gamergate Icon Milo Yiannopoulos," *Fusion*. October 27, 2015, http://fusion.net/story/220646/ the-terrifying-allure-of-gamergate-icon-milo-yiannopoulos/.

25   Kristen Brown, "How A Racist, Sexist Hate Mob Forced Leslie Jones Off Twitter" *Fusion*, July 19, 2016, http://fusion.net/story/327103/leslie-jones -twitter-racism/.

26   Abby Ohlheiser "Just How Offensive Did Milo Yiannopoulos Have to Be to Get Banned from Twitter?" *Washington Post*, July 21, 2016, https://www.washingtonpost.com/news/the-intersect/wp/2016/07/21/ what-it-takes-to-get-banned-from-twitter/?utm_term=.f766e1d5f076.; Jessica Guynn, "Twitter Suspends Alt Right Accounts" *USA Today*, November 15, 2016, http://www.usatoday.com/story/tech/news/2016/11/15/ twitter-suspends-alt-right-accounts/93943194/.

27   Alex Kantrowitz, "Racist Social Media Users Have a New Code to Avoid Censorship" *Buzzfeed*, October 1, 2016, https://www.buzzfeed.com/alexkantrowitz/racist-social-media-users-have-a-new-code-to-avoid-censorshi?utm_ term=.wbVXYKyeVd#.peqZ6dqb04.

28   Seventh Son, "The Daily Shoah Episode 61: Canceled!" *Daily Shoah*, December 1, 2015, http://therightstuff.biz/2015/12/01/the-daily-shoah-episode-61-cancelled/.; Jazzhands McFeels, "Fash the Nation Week 61: Dedicated Violators," *Fash the Nation*, October 15, 2016, http://fashthenation.com/2016/10/ fash-the-nation-week-61-dedicated-violators/.

platforms like PayPal, which stopped the *Daily Shoah* from receiving donations.[29] PayPal went a step further in 2017 by financially limiting various Alt Right and men's rights websites, as well as tools like WeSearchr. YouCaring, GoFundMe, and other sites, which are heavily relied on by Alt Right instant-celebrities, have also followed suit, continuing to limit the scope of their finances.[30] T-shirt companies have dropped these Alt Right groups after being told what the graphic content signifies. A huge wave of pressure is being applied to corporations that have open platforms that the Alt Right uses.

The Alt Right defines itself over these platforms—which in turn allows them access to mass culture—but this leaves them extremely vulnerable to outside pressure. This means we must identify who is using what platforms and organize contingents to do large-scale notifications, applying steady pressure, in a systematized way, until social media and publishing platforms become veritably unusable for the Alt Right. (Richard Spencer has even noted that this is likely in their future as they see Alt Right Twitter handles disappear and their materials drop from websites.[31]) This is similar to campaigns that have attempted to have "white noise" Nazi music dropped from iTunes distribution or the more successful effort to remove Confederate material from Amazon. As Spencer's concerns suggest, if you can't find their material on Google, if you can't read it on Twitter, and if you cannot buy it on Amazon, do they even exist? Even websites like Reddit have begun to ban Alt Right subreddits like "r/AltRight," and their attempts to move over to alternative platforms like Voat are futile.[32]

Spencer's response mirrors left-wing complaints against corporate censorship: declare these services a public utility. This is an important debate as it outlines both a strategy and a potential

29 "Bank Blocked: The Daily Shoah Gets Banned on PayPal," *Antifascist News*, March 15, 2016, https://antifascistnews.net/2016/03/15/bank-blocked-the-daily-shoah-gets-banned-on-paypal/.
30 Blake Montgomery, "PayPal, GoFundMe, and Patreon Banned a Bunch of People Associated With the Alt-Right. Here's why," *Buzzfeed*, August 2, 2017, https://www.buzzfeed.com/blakemontgomery/the-alt-right-has-a-payment-processor-problem?utm_term=.xgZdQgGA3#.jfmN50XJv.
31 Richard Spencer, "The Great Shuttening [Video]," *Radix Journal*, February 16, 2016, http://www.radixjournal.com/blog/2016/2/16/the-great-shuttening-video?rq=shuttening.
32 Bryan Menegus, "Reddit Says Goodnight to 'Alt-Right' Community [Updates]," *Gizmodo.com*, February 1, 2017, http://gizmodo.com/reddit-says-goodnight-to-alt-right-community-1791895544.

unintended consequence, which is that the same pressure could be put on social media to drop left voices. While certain standards, like overt racism, are used as dividing lines today, it could easily shift to other types of speech and organizing if the social mood changes. This has already happened as Patreon decided to disallow antifascist website *It's Going Down* from using their service, in a similar way to how they restricted white nationalist websites like Occidental Dissent.[33]

This attack on the Alt Right media infrastructure only intensified after the Unite the Right rally in August 2017, where Alt Right groups linked up with KKK and neo-Nazi contingents, forming a race riot that attacked protesters and ended when a Vanguard America associate murdered a protester with his car. Social media, web hosting, financial services, email providers, and just about every platform publicly rejected Alt Right and white nationalist figures in the largest ideological removal in history.

Protecting the Community

After the 1979 shootings in Greensboro, North Carolina, many criticized the Communist Workers Party for its arrogance in bringing the Klan to a black community without the proper precautions. It was with this incident in mind when the John Brown Anti-Klan Committee was formed, naming their monthly newsletter after the Greensboro chant "Death to the Klan."[34] At the same time as the Greensboro massacre, a march of Klansmen in Texas was interrupted when two thousand protesters showed up ready to engage the hoods. The JBAKC took the lesson that a community self-defense project and a mass organizing model needed to be combined, where white antiracists needed to step up in support of black neighbors securing their neighborhood. For much of the late nineteenth and early twentieth century, the mass migration of African-descended people from the South to places like New York, Michigan, and California were refugees escaping the paramilitary terrorism of the KKK. The JBAKC fought against a resurgence of the Fourth Generation of the KKK, especially in places like Chicago where Klan graffiti was prevalent. They continued to overwhelm Klan and skinhead gangs like Romantic Violence at public

---

33   "Patreon Caves to Tim Pool and Alt-Right, Bans IGD," *It's Going Down*, July 31, 2017, https://itsgoingdown.org/patreon-caves-to-tim-pool-alt-right-bans-igd/.
34   Their newsletter was later named after the popular chant, "No KKK, No Fascist USA," which is still used today in antifascist circles.

appearances, despite the racists showing up with wooden shields lined with razor blades.[35]

This community self-defense model inspired groups like ARA, which protected communities from racist violence while building a cross-racial antifascist movement. The idea of community self-defense has evolved from a more reactive response to fascist movements, to arguments for community defense networks in light of police shootings like projects such as those proposed by the Malcolm X Grassroots Movement. In what they call a "movement for survival" they identify two types of networks: New Afrikan or Black Self-Defense Networks (of specifically black members to defend against violence, both from the police and white terrorist organizations) and People's Self-Defense Networks (of multiracial constituencies to do the same).[36]

After the rise of racist violence in the wake of Trump's election, many community self-defense groups have formed—specifically due to the sense that the casual racism inside many white communities has heightened and might move from words to action. In Rochester, New York, the appearance of KKK graffiti and threats against queers and Jewish institutions inspired the formation of the queer gun club Trigger Warning. They teach LGBT people how to use firearms safely, how to respond to possible threats, and about the legalities of gun ownership.[37] In suburban Washington County, Oregon, the group WashCo Solidarity has started the "Lighthouse" program to deal with incidents of racial intimidation. By identifying participating businesses, they create a list of "safe places" where a person being threatened can go to receive shelter. Then a responder will come to meet the individual and escort the person home or to a safe house.[38]

Community defense expands beyond the immediate threat presented by reactionary street forces, moving into the institutionalized inequalities and state violence that fosters white nationalism to begin with. For antifascism to not simply return the community to the liberal status quo means expanding the types of threats it can respond to based on the lived experience of the community. Their responses

---

35   Alexander Reid Ross, "'Death to the Klan' and Armed Antifascist Community Defense in the US," *It's Going Down*, https://itsgoingdown.org/death-klan-armed-antifascist-community-defense-us/.

36   "The Black Nation Charges Genocide! Our Survival Is Dependent on Self-defense!," *Red Skies at Night* 2, No. 5 (2015): 2–4.

37   Jake Allen, interview with author, December 9, 2016.

38   John Robb, interview with author, January 10, 2017.

might even be to offer protections against state actors acting as vanguards of racialized policies. As ICE increases its brazenness in targeting undocumented immigrants, a community defense network can warn and protect some of its most vulnerable neighbors.

In New York City, an anarchist community space called The Base launched a rapid response network (RRN) to deal with the dual threat of neo-Nazi organizations and ICE raids, and twenty-two other cities in the U.S. are focusing on rapid response to ICE incidents. This new sanctuary movement prioritizes the interruption of deportations, something that many cities are committing to in their local governments given the rhetoric of mass deportations that Trump rode to power on. The Community Action Team NYC carries on this work by creating a formal structure that can move between different parts of the city to physically intervene during ICE round-ups.[39]

The U.S. Southwest—where the crackdown on immigrants of color only increased under President Obama—reactionary militants and state actors have been unified on policing the border. With events like the enacting of Arizona's SB 1070 law—partially written by Tanton Network affiliate Kris Kobach—which forced law enforcement to stop anyone suspected of being an undocumented immigrant, and border areas like El Paso, Texas, becoming increasingly militarized, the far-right has cheered. During a period of increased violence from drug cartels from 2006–8, the Border Patrol expanded their presence in border cities, implementing a police state and coercing support from communities living in fear of street terror. This climate allowed a rebirth of the Minutemen movement, civilian vigilantes who police the border and pretend to be a citizen's wing of the Border Patrol. In El Paso, they sabotaged travel routes that immigrants used to get over the border from Juarez, including destroying water and other supplies left by human rights organizations. While Minutemen did not have formal connections with the Border Patrol, there was a tacit support as they often went to the rural areas that official patrols missed. Indigenous and Latinx farmworker and community organizations began a program to confront this vigilante contingent, doing "what we need to do to defend our community." They instituted

---

39   Natasha Lennard, "Antifascists Will Fight Trump's Fascism in the Streets," *The Nation*, January 19, 2017, https://www.thenation.com/article/antifascist-activists-are-fighting-the-alt-right-in-the-streets/.

"Minutemen Watch" based on the Cop Watch model, making sure that the vigilantes were not allowed to operate with impunity.[40] Café Mayapan, a food market organized by indigenous organizers, acted as a hub, and the Centro Sin Fronteras workers center, the Mecha De Utep student movement, and La Mujer Obrera was formed as a nerve center for a community seeing the dual siege of the state and landowners using nativist language as an excuse to further enforce border violence.[41]

The creation of community self-defense organizations is not a new concept, yet people are adapting older models to the new situation. The Portland Assembly did this with their "Antiracist Neighborhood Watch" guide, which uses a broad-based community organizational model in connection with existing antifascist organizations willing to intervene in fascist intimidation. This involves regular community meeting schedules, focusing on regional issues, and creating a framework for developing skills to increase participation. Mixing neighborhood watch posts, communications positions, a rapid response phone tree for perceived threats, and a clear map of safe houses and community geography, the model can create a foundational community organization that is specific to a particular physical location and can expand beyond singular dangers to encompass issues like housing instability, food insecurity, or infrastructure repairs. The unified community, observing its own unique character and needs, is what makes this project work.[42]

For those concerned about the threat of violence by white nationalists, this community safety model also means training people in practical self-defense skills. The Haymaker Gym on Chicago's South Side was formed to confront this need, responding to the 20 percent increase in hate crimes in the city.

> We believe that fostering material resistance starts with the most intimate of material forces—our bodies. We grow our potential as we learn what our bodies are capable of doing together. Revolutionary movements around the world have made use of the

---

40 Cop Watch is a diverse organizing model where community members observe and record the police in their interactions with the public, and create the specter of accountability to the community outside of the organs provided by the state.
41 Gabriel Holguin, interview with author, July 11, 2017.
42 *Anti-Racist Neighborhood Watch: Quick Start Manual and Resource Packet* (Portland: Portland Assembly, 2017).

solidarity and strength that physical training fosters, but there are few, if any, political gyms across the so called United States.[43]

As a community run, donation-based gym with an anti-oppression focus, they are trying to embed themselves in the neighborhood by offering practical skills that create a space for politicization.[44]

The issue of defense is especially relevant for those active in antifascist organizing, as the growing clash has put them in the crosshairs of the organized white supremacist movement. In March 2017, Trump continued his rallies and events, drumming up broad support while his administration hit policy walls. The "Make America Great Again" (MAGA) rallies energized the furthest reaches of Trump's far-right support base, with events like the one in Huntington Beach, California, on March 25, 2017, where participants displayed signs with anti-Semitic slogans from the *Daily Shoah*. Protesters were targeted for violence at the MAGA rallies, attacked by flag-waving militants and police alike. While Philly Antifa shut down the Philadelphia event, it became open season for those on the left. This targeting of Antifa has become a priority of the Alt Right, petitioning to have Antifa listed as a "terrorist organization."[45] New Jersey law enforcement named Antifa an "extremist organization" in 2017.[46] State repression, vigilante racist violence, and the collusion between the two actors are component parts of this, which necessitates the building of stronger community bonds.

In response to the shutdown of Milo Yiannopoulos at UC Berkeley in January and the cancelation of a talk by Ann Coulter just weeks later, Alt Light mouthpiece Lauren Southern, previously of "Canada's *Breitbart*," *Rebel Media*, led a "free speech" rally in Berkeley. A new class of "American nationalists" rallied around this string of events, dressing in outlandish garb and ready to fight the opposition. New celebrities, like the buffoonish "Based Spartan" who showed up in a metal chest piece, and Kyle "Based Stickman" Chapman, were joined by those dressed in sparring pads and

43 Anonymous founder of Haymaker, interview with author, April 15, 2017.
44 Ibid.
45 "Declare Antifa a Terrorist Organization," Change.org, https://www.change.org/p/president-of-the-united-states-declare-antifa-a-terrorist-organization. (Note: Ironically, this petition is run by a foreign national.)
46 "Anarchist Extremists: Antifa," State of New Jersey Department of Homeland Security and Preparedness, June 12, 2017, https://www.njhomelandsecurity.gov/analysis/anarchist-extremists-antifa.

using "Kek" flags as capes. This confluence, which Spencer Sunshine identifies as "Independent Trumpism" because Trump is their uniting ideological figure and because of their lack of affiliation with any official organs of the GOP, shifted matters toward the language of open warfare.[47] That day, as cameras recorded the chaos, right-wingers drew blood in melees with counter-protesters, many were savagely beaten, and Nathan Damigo was seen punching a young woman in the face.[48]

A culture has formed specifically around fighting what neo-fascists broadly label as Antifa, which could be anything from liberal Democrats to Communist Party members. The "Fraternal Order of the Alt Knights" is the militant wing of the Proud Boys, led partially by Chapman, whose goal is to arm members of the organization to attack the left. The newly formed American Guard, also called the Vinlanders, has drawn from the Patriot aesthetic, yet has recruited explicit neo-Nazi types, including members of gangs like the American Front who can be seen sporting RaHoWa (racial holy war) tattoos.[49] Attracting Alt Right celebrities like Augustus Sol Invictus, the organization likens itself to a nationalist organization against "foreign intervention" and "foreign aid."

> The liberties, rights, and freedoms we seek apply to United States citizens only. They don't extend past our borders. We encourage citizens of all other nations to work for them in their own countries.[50]

These organizations are calling for a militant street force for violent retribution on a left they believe to be a threat. Their structure is similar to the Soldiers of Odin (SOO), who use scare tactics to inspire fear of non-white immigrants, presenting vigilante patrols as the solution. The SOO has grown to dozens of chapters on multiple

47   Spencer Sunshine, "The Growing Alliance Between Neo-Nazis, Right Wing Paramilitaries and Trumpist Republicans," *Colorlines*, June 9, 2017, https://www.colorlines.com/articles/growing-alliance-between-neo-nazis-right-wing-paramilitaries-and-trumpist-republicans.

48   "Video of Woman at Berkeley Protest Sparks Outrage," *CBS News*, April 17, 2017, http://www.cbsnews.com/news/berkeley-protest-video-of-woman-getting-punched-sparks-outrage/.

49   "Behind the American Guard: Hardcore White Supremacists," Anti-Defamation League, March 30, 2017, https://www.adl.org/blog/behind-the-american-guard-hardcore-white-supremacists.

50   "The Four Pillars of Constitutional Nationalism," *The American Guard*, http://www.theamericanguard.com/about-1.html.

continents, proving to be a material threat to refugees, especially as they present themselves as an extralegal retaliatory force.

With these organizations growing, the threat to the well-being of neighborhoods with targeted populations is palpable. This potential for violence is nothing new for communities of color, but the increasingly organized nature of it, and the normalization of extrajudicial racial revenge, is something communities have to grapple with.

Higher Learning

Antifascist organizers have been targeting the areas where fascists are seeing the most growth for their movement. The college campus is one of the largest of these, a space that has been inaccessible for the far-right in recent decades. The Alt Right have defined themselves as uniquely Millennial—white nationalism for an upper-middle-class college crowd—and the campus is a focal point.

In terms of organizations, the Traditionalist Youth Network has maintained itself as a leader among white nationalists, primarily because it has created a bridge between the working-class "insurrectionary" groups and the Alt Right. Started by Matthew Heimbach at Towson University, TradYouth originally focused on traditionalism as defined through strict Christianity, racial nationalism, traditional family and gender roles, and opposition to an international capitalism they see as cosmopolitan and Hebraic. Building his brand of Third Positionism, he focused on recruiting in the South, Midwest, and areas where well-paying blue-collar jobs have become scarce. Heimbach has been traveling and meeting with other white nationalists in recent years, from speaking at the American Freedom Party conference in 2013 to Seig Heiling with the Aryan Terror Brigade. Always smiling and cordial, Heimbach tries to woo those around him by avoiding racial slurs and making himself appear the ever-friendly brand of stormtrooper.[51]

TradYouth became known for their outgoing street activism, finding clever ways to provoke the liberal sentiments of left-leaning city folk so they can scrape the few supporters that rise to the top. They protested campus appearances of antiracist author Tim Wise, calling him "anti-white," often trying to manipulate

51   "Matthew Heimbach," Southern Poverty Law Center, n.d, https://www.splcenter.org/fighting-hate/extremist-files/individual/matthew-heimbach.

sympathy from non-white passersby with well-rehearsed appeals to "fairness." In Bloomington, Indiana, near where Heimbach settled down to be near TradYouth co-founder Matthew Parrot and Heimbach's new wife, they protested a local bookstore with signs saying, "Tradition Is Our Mission." He has also made inroads abroad with organizations like Greece's Golden Dawn and Eastern Orthodox Christian nationalists.[52]

TradYouth and their new political wing, the Traditionalist Worker Party (TradWorker), now boasts some five hundred members, many of which they share with Patriot and skinhead organizations. In June 2016, TradWorker was set to hold a rally on the steps of the California State Capital in Sacramento, along with dual-members the Golden State Skinheads and the SacTown Skinheads. They were met by hundreds of protesters organized by Sacramento Antifa and By Any Means Necessary (BAMN) who interrupted the event before it could even begin, confronting most of the skinheads as one of the largest riots in the city's history ensued.[53] Ten people ended up hospitalized with serious injuries, as skinheads, brandishing large knives, laid into protesters, leaving many bleeding as street medics desperately knelt to save lives.[54]

While TradYouth has drawn from blue-collar neighborhoods and actively recruited union members, Identity Evropa skyrocketed in popularity through 2016 by embedding themselves at colleges and blending in with the pressed collars and "fashy" swoops of the Alt Right. Nathan Damigo, Identity Evropa's founder, is an Iraq War vet who spent several years in prison for attacking a Muslim cab driver after he returned from service. After his parents publicly stated that Nathan's crime should be seen as a symptom of PTSD, Damigo was featured on the HBO series *Wartorn*.[55] He later took over the civic-nationalist organization the National Youth Front, which, after a similarly named evangelical church threatened a lawsuit, Damigo

52   Musonius Rufus and Matthew Heimbach, "Rebel Yell 119: TradYouth, Matt Heimbach," podcast audio, *The Right Stuff*, MP3, 1:42:59, May 27, 2016. https://radio.therightstuff.biz/2016/05/27/rebel-yell-119-trad-youth-matt-heimbach/.

53   BAMN's full name is the Coalition to Defend Affirmative Action, Integration and Immigrant Rights and Fight for Equality By Any Means Necessary.

54   Mike McPhate, "10 Injured During White Nationalist Protest in Sacramento," *New York Times*, June 26, 2016, https://www.nytimes.com/2016/06/27/us/7-injured-during-white-nationalist-protest-in-sacramento.html.

55   "Meet the Damigos: All American White Supremacy," Northern California Anti-Racist Action, December 21, 2016, https://nocara.blackblogs.org/2016/12/21/meet-the-damigos-all-american-white-supremacy/.

rebranded as Identity Evropa, after Identitarian projects in France like Generation Identity.[56]

Structured mainly as a fraternal organization, Identity Evropa invites to its membership people of "European descent," though this precludes biracial, transgender, or openly gay members. Mixing street activism and community building, their numbers soared as they hit dozens of campuses from coast-to-coast with posters featuring bold letters and mottoes like "Let's Become Great Again" with images of classical Greek and Roman statues. Playing into the retro-futurist themes common on the Alt Right, their aesthetic is intended to enhance their appeal, hailing to a unique set of design standards that are hip, ironic, and definitely "white." Their hope is to grow a presence on campuses so they can begin to work on campaigns, such as pressuring the administration to drop "anti-white teachers" and to make it "safe for white people" again.

In May 2016, Identity Evropa teamed up with Richard Spencer from NPI, and Johnny Monoxide from *The Right Stuff* and Red Ice Radio, to create an event called the "Alt Right Safe Space." The plan was simple: announce the event just days in advance to throw off antifascist protesters, and do a speak-out and "soap box" in the historic "Free Speech Plaza" at the University of California at Berkeley. They argued with students for hours, with Spencer trying to mock and confuse young people who challenged him and Damigo declaring any opposition "anti-white."[57]

In October 2016, Damigo led a handful of supporters to an Embarcadero sidewalk near Pier 14 in San Francisco for an "anti-immigration" rally that lasted a mere fifteen minutes. They attempted to divert leftist protesters by publicly announcing that it was to be held at Malcolm X Plaza at San Francisco State University, which left them alone, both from opposition and from any media coverage. They have continued what they call "Operation Seige," a full frontal propaganda assault on campuses around the country, often with support from College Republican organizations. This has created one of the most aggressive contact points between Identity Evropa and antifascist organizations, with posters often acting as a signal to organizers that the Alt Right is now active on a particular campus. Groups like Turning Point USA are looking for a right-wing campus

---

56   Richard Spencer and Nathan Damigo, "Allies of Color," podcast audio, *The Radix Journal*, MP3, 46:59, December 8, 2015, http://www.radixjournal.com/podcast/2015/12/8/allies-of-color.
57   Nathan Damigo, interview with author, 2016.

synthesis, and they are having a huge showing on campuses, with chapters at a reported one thousand colleges.[58] Unity and Security for America is trying to take the Alt Right's focus on immigration to Republican statehouses in the South, using code words like "defending Western Civilization."[59] Neither is definitively Alt Right, but instead a new conservative culture that is more receptive to those ideas than institutions past.

Richard Spencer chooses to focus on state schools since they have a mandate to allow the public meeting and event space and are less cowed by public pressure. This defensive posture has forced Spencer to hold NPI conferences only at publicly owned facilities in recent years, noting that the state will usually protect them while private hotels often fold to pressure from antiracist campaigns.

This was true at Spencer's November 2016 appearance at the Texas A&M campus. As one of the largest public universities in the Texas system, security prepared for Spencer's event in the same way they did for the tens of thousands of "Aggies" that show up to football games. A former student, Preston Wiginton, brought Spencer to speak, and the university obliged after forcing him to pay over $3,000 for security. Spencer, who had been battling increased fame and media scrutiny all year, was harsh and combative with the crowd, often calling his challengers "fat" and laughing hysterically.

For antifascist organizers, the Texas A&M appearance provided insight into options for movement growth. After an uproar from students, Texas A&M chancellor John Sharp created one of the largest diversity rallies in the school's history to coincide with Spencer's appearance. Outside of the venue, hundreds of protesters massed at every entrance, attempting to push their way through security. Inside, more than a third of the audience engaged in disruption, with many dressed as clowns walking in front of the stage holding satirical signs saying things like "White Flour."[60]

Spencer has said he is going to continue these university appearances, prioritizing a "campus tour" in the vein of Milo. This could allow him opportunities to aid regional Alt Right groups

---

58   Heather Sells, "Turning Point: Is the Youth Vote Really All That Liberal?" *CBN News*, April 28, 2016, http://www1.cbn.com/cbnnews/politics/2016/april/turning-point-is-the-youth-vote-really-all-that-liberal.

59   "We Are Unity and Security for America," Unity and Security for America, http://www.unityandsecurity.org/protect-the-west.html.

60   Richard Spencer, "Richard Spencer at Texas A&M," *Radix Journal*, December 7, 2016, http://www.radixjournal.com/blog/2016/12/7/richard-spencer-at-texas-am.

in recruiting but will also be a rallying point for antiracist campus groups. Which side will see the most sustained level of growth and whether Spencer will actually be allowed to speak by many of the universities who have staked their name on building diversity are the real questions. In December 2016, Spencer announced the "Danger Zone Tour," continuing his nostalgic branding of all things Alt Right within the synth-pop 80s aesthetic that Spencer enjoys. He embarked on a $50,000 fundraiser to accommodate the cost of such a tour, including the increasingly prohibitive costs of security that the growing strength of antiracist opposition has necessitated. Along with creating more paid institutional staff for NPI and *Radix Journal*, Spencer intended to foster a financial base and use 2017 for a massive push onto campuses as a way forward and securing a Millennial base—though it failed to materialize as intended.[61] A wrench was thrown in this plan as NPI lost its non-profit status in early 2017, due more to his own financial mismanagement than political pressure. Now that Spencer is a nationwide celebrity, there are people willing to host him, and since he relies mainly on state-funded colleges, he will have a larger chance to maintain dates as he books them. Spencer intends to steadily increase his public conferences and rallies, but though he has seen some growth, the antifascist explosion has quickly out paced it. After his 2016 preconference dinner was disrupted by antifascists from the One People's Project and Smash Racism DC, he has retreated to only having well-vetted private dinners matched by public facilities for conferences.[62] The various *Right Stuff* meet-ups and regional gatherings, their "pool parties," and the New York and Northwest Forums are also private, but though they have created an "extreme vetting" process to dissuade entryism, antifascist groups are breaking through the barriers by doing research, infiltrating private message boards, and eventually revealing the desperately guarded locations.

The campus has a special place of importance for the far-right as they want to alter the "culture," robbing the hegemony of leftist cultural theory in the halls of "the Cathedral." This Gramscian battle for the soul of American meta-politics seems unlikely to succeed for those now in academia, but dramatic shifts can happen once unlikely characters sink their hooks in institutions designed to shape

---

61   Richard Spencer, "2017 Giving," *Radix Journal*, December 21, 2016, http://www.radixjournal.com/giving/.

62   Richard Spencer, "Millenniyule 2016: Richard Spencer," *YouTube*, December 24, 2016, https://www.youtube.com/watch?v=-uQ4wytISGQ.

popular opinion. This new focus on campus postering is prominent across the Alt Right, as people connected with *The Right Stuff* started blanketing the University of Michigan and Iowa State with similar posters asking "euro-Americans" to "BE WHITE" in September 2016. At U of M, President Mark Schlissel and other administrators publically denounced the posters and are now launching a massive Diversity, Equity, and Inclusion plan on their campus. While *The Right Stuff* called their postering campaign a victory, the real result was that campus antiracist activism fostered a climate where Alt Right attempts at recruitment are met with institutional projects that undermine the racist narrative.[63]

When Milo was booked to speak at the University of Wisconsin at Milwaukee, students created an ad hoc organization called the Coalition Against the Ultra-Right, which integrated unaffiliated students with seasoned groups like the IWW and Standing Up for Racial Justice (SURJ). They created a three-staged organizing plan that can serve as a model for how to address the "Alt Right campus circuit." They began by addressing the administration, pressuring them to cancel Milo's appearance. While some administrations are vulnerable to this, in Milwaukee this pressure ended up forcing the university to withhold student funding and to hire private security. An open letter and petition was an incredible outreach tool that synced campus departments and organizations with the anti-Milo effort, and this turned them into a block of opposition. Young Americans for Freedom pulled out of the event, and, with the climate heating up, the administration had to schedule meetings with the organizers, which pushed the larger issues of campus racism and transphobia into the open. Turning Point came to Milo's aid and was forced to spend $4,000 of its own money on security. The Coalition organized a demonstration to coincide with the speech. They created a mass movement push for this event, getting their own space with large enough contingents that they were easily able to push out Milo's media people when they tried to force their way in. Next, disruptions of the event itself were planned, forcing Milo to cancel the "meet and greet" and turning the space into a warzone. On reflection, organizers acknowledged they needed to address the issue of "doxxing" of antiracist protesters as Milo and his supporters

63   Ken Biglin, "Update: Three Types of Racially Charged Posters Found on University of Michigan Campus," *The Michigan Daily*, September 26, 2016, https://www.michigandaily.com/section/campus-life/racially-charged-posters-found-university-michigan-campus.

exposed several people's identities online for ridicule. The issue of "freedom of speech" was also bandied about, both by Milo supporters and the school's administration. This kind of red herring is one that organizers need to come out in front of to shift the conversation to the material threat that Milo and his movement cause to marginalized groups on campus. For the Alt Right, free speech per se has never been an issue of importance, instead it is an easy tool to use to appeal to liberal values and cement their own access to a platform. Coordinated action inside of events, exploiting the ticketing system to overwhelm it, using waves of disruptions that are more difficult to quarantine, and planned actions inside the venue are the kinds of tools that shift control away from the speaker and into the hands of organizers looking to stop it from being able to meaningfully continue. The Coalition is continuing their campaign to shame the administration and are making the campus a "no go" zone for the Alt Right. Making these coalitions permanent fixtures on campus allows them to continue to set campus priorities and create a persistent threat to the Alt Right's targeting of the student body.[64]

Antifascist student groups have grown along with those using an "Antifa" label, with dozens of projects sprouting up throughout 2016. As Identity Evropa and students announced a plan to bring Milo to the University of California at Berkeley, the same place they had their "Alt Right Safe Space" with Richard Spencer and Red Ice TV, Berkeley Antifa put out a call "inviting all allies and the Berkeley community to join us in making UC Berkeley a fascist-free zone." The Berkeley College Republicans forced through a Milo event in February 2017, which was not surprising as many of their members openly associated with Identity Evropa.[65] Instead of asking the College Republicans to pay for the security, Berkeley spent $68,000 to protect Milo's stage, which included over a hundred police officers and a SWAT team on-call. Milo and *Breitbart* promised to release the names of undocumented students, both at the event and online and on posters, an act that would promise violent targeting of undocumented students. While the university knew about the undocumented doxxing plan, it refused to intervene, and white nationalists were focusing on the event for recruitment. Protesters took over the venue, pulled down the metal police barricades, set off fireworks,

64   "Let's Shut Down the Alt-Right College Tour Circuit," *It's Going Down*, n.d., https://itsgoingdown.org/lets-shut-alt-right-college-tour-circuit/.
65   "Everybody Hates the Berkeley College Republicans" *It's Going Down*, n.d., https://itsgoingdown.org/everybody-hates-berkeley-college-republicans/.

and forced its cancelation. The protests continued through the 2000 block of Center Street with fires set both at the venue and surrounding banks, causing an estimated $100,000 in damage. Trump, allegedly under pressure from Bannon, tweeted the following day that "If U.C. Berkeley does not allow free speech and practices violence on innocent people with a different point of view - NO FEDERAL FUNDS?" While few organizations were obvious coordinators of the action—except for BAMN and Berkeley Antifa—large parts of the crowd were autonomously identifying with "Antifa" as a general idea rather than a formal organization.[66]

Many undocumented students came out to the protests once the event was canceled as there was a general culture of fear about what was going to happen to undocumented students of color if the event went on, presumably ramping up scapegoating that would use the crowd's anger to target them. With the event's cancelation, the issue that "many undocumented students lives might have been saved" has been erased from the conversation, and instead the focus is on whether Milo's freedom of speech had been taken away.[67]

At both DePaul and the University of California, Davis, protesters managed to not just create counter-messaging, but to end the appearance altogether. After protests swelled so large at UC Davis on January 13, 2017, the College Republicans chapter that sponsored the event canceled it thirty minutes before start time. The event had paired Milo with Martin Shkreli, nicknamed the "Pharma Bro" after his company dramatically increased the cost of a critical AIDS treatment drug. Since then Shkreli has become an internet "shitlord," even being banned on Twitter for making unwanted advances on a female journalist. The event could only have been shut down through a massive action, with broad-based outreach rather than small affinity group efforts. It was the numbers that forced its cancelation, and the anger that was simmering in the crowd exploded when they pushed their way into the venue and Shkreli was struck with dog feces.[68] Days afterward, Milo's planned appearance at the University of Washington had Red Square packed with protesters

---

66   Josh Harkinson, "All Hell Breaks Loose At Campus Event For Alt-Right Leader Milo Yiannopoulos," *Mother Jones*, February 1, 2017, http://www.motherjones.com/politics/2017/02/uc-berkeley-riot-milo-yiannopoulos.

67   Juan Prieto, "Militant Tactics Against the Right," *Against the Grain*, February 14, 2017, https://kpfa.org/episode/against-the-grain-february-14-2017/.

68   Paul Dalila-Johari, "Protesters Shut Down Milo Yiannopoulos Event at UC Davis," *CNN*, January 14, 2017, http://www.cnn.com/2017/01/14/us/milo-yiannopoulos-uc-davis-speech-canceled/.

clashing with police. The hall holding the talk ended up only half full as Milo's supporters had difficulty accessing the building. As the crowds swelled, a Milo supporter opened fire on protesters, sending one IWW member to the hospital with a critical stomach wound.[69]

These events reveal the willingness of the Alt Right to escalate as their profile expands, as well as what the normalization of bigotry means. The threat of opposition was so large that few wanted to touch Milo even though he drew crowds, and insuring and securing his events became next to impossible. After Milo got a $250,000 advance for a book from a Simon & Schuster imprint, *Chicago Review of Books* and some booksellers announced boycotts. It wasn't until a video was released of Milo defending child sexual abuse that the book was finally canceled.[70] Milo now was financially toxic, because of both his opposition and his own comportment. Increased opposition forced outlets, whether for publishing or for event hosting, to weigh whether or not it was really worth the firestorm they would surely endure.[71]

This campus model is semi-universal, especially given the Alt Right's collegiate priorities. Instead of relying on insular groups that focus on private campaign planning, the coalitions that shut down Milo operated in plain sight. The groups planning disruptions may have a certain amount of privacy in coordination, but they relied on the growth of a mass movement behind them to raise the profile of the issue, pressure the administration, and create the public protests that were effective. The same structure could be easily applied to public facilities hosting conferences, neo-Nazi rallies where mass opposition is necessary, and to replicate this anytime white nationalists head onto a stage. The growth of the Alt Right relies on the ability to shift from their private associations and build a public presence, and this move to the mainstream is where they are seeing mass opposition. This has also signaled the growth of larger mass campus antifascist projects, such as the Campus Antifascist Network, which has been coordinating students with faculty unions to confront these organizations as they enter campus.[72]

---

69   Mike Carter and Steve Miletich, "Couple Charged with Assault in Shooting, Melee During UW Speech by Milo Yiannopoulos," http://www.seattletimes.com/seattle-news/crime/couple-charged-with-assault-in-shooting-melee-during-uw-speech-by-milo-yiannopoulos/.

70   The book was eventually picked up by another publisher.

71   Claire Fallon, "Reminder: Boycotting Milo Yiannopoulos' Publisher Is Not Censorship," *The Huffington Post*, January 6, 2017, http://www.huffingtonpost.com/entry/milo-yiannopoulos-censorship_us_586fbbc0e4b099cdb0fcc4fe.

72   Nell Gluckman, "Faculty Members Organize to Fight 'Fascist' Interlopers on

Charlottesville

The conflict between the Alt Right and Alt Light hit a fever pitch at the same time as a renewed controversy of Confederate monument removal emerged. In a move to regroup, to reinvigorate, and to simply remain in the headlines, various strands called for a "Unite the Right" rally for August 12, 2017 in Charlottesville, VA. It was a way of coagulating the disparate elements of the dissident right—it was to be a show of force for Alt Right true believers. After the Alt Right's upsurge it had begun to falter, and without its more moderate counterparts it needed to see if it could stand on its own.

Hoping to get in on the action, Jeff Schoep of the neo-Nazi National Socialist Movement (NSM) announced they would join, something that even Spencer had hoped to avoid, testing the bounds of unity.[73] The NSM's call to show support for "White History and Heritage" was Alt Right opportunism at its very finest. The Alt Right's primary celebrities were slated to attend: Mike Enoch of the *Daily Shoah*, Michael Hill of The League of the South, Matthew Heimbach of the Traditionalist Workers Party, Baked Alaska of his own myopic YouTube stream, and others would join Spencer. This would be a time to squash the beefs of the past and reclaim the "Big Tent" of the Alt Right. However, by returning to their explicit white nationalist roots and jettisoning the populist wave they rode into the American consciousness on, they shrank their own tent.

In advance of the rally, Airbnb announced that it would cancel reservations for attendees, the result of the same wave that pushed PayPal and Patreon from supporting Alt Right donation wrangling.[74] After Mike Enoch called on air for guns, Redneck Revolt announced that they would enter Emancipation Park in Charlottesville bearing firearms as a protective agent, walling against a potential slaughterhouse.[75] The Appalachian Redneck Revolt branches

Campuses," *The Chronicle of Higher Education*, August 31, 2017, http://www.chronicle.com/article/Faculty-Members-Organize-to/241081.

73   Sarah Viets, "Neo-Nazi Misfits Join Unite the Right," Southern Poverty Law Center, July 26, 2017, https://www.splcenter.org/hatewatch/2017/07/26/neo-nazi-misfits-join-unite-right.

74   Kyle Swenson, "Airbnb Boots White Nationalists Headed to 'Unite the Right' Rally in Charlottesville," *The Washington Post*, August 8, 2017, https://www.washingtonpost.com/news/morning-mix/wp/2017/08/08/airbnb-boots-white-nationalists-headed-to-unite-the-right-rally-in-charlottesville/?utm_term=.53fd023b98a7.

75   Appalachian Redneck Revolt Chapter, "Call to Arms for Charlottesville," Redneck Revolt, August 10, 2017, https://www.redneckrevolt.org/single-post/CALL-TO-ARMS-FOR-CHARLOTTESVILLE.

were there two days in advance when hundreds of white nationalists led a torch-lit march toward the multiracial St. Paul's Memorial
Church where Cornel West was speaking, surrounding the historic
building and refusing the congregation exit.[76] This march, which
ended with a shockingly savage racist mob attack on Black Lives
Matter protesters, used Tiki torches for light and chanted slogans
like "blood and soil" and "Jews will not replace us." Leading the
charge was Christopher Cantwell, the anarcho-capitalist turned violent racialist fond of saying "[L]et's fucking gas the kikes and have
a race war."[77] Earlier that day he allegedly pulled a gun on someone
in a Wal-Mart parking lot.[78] The morning of the rally, Cantwell
tucked multiple handguns on his person and brought along two
semi-automatic rifles. "We're not nonviolent, we'll fucking kill
these people if we have to," Cantwell told *Vice*, "I'm carrying a
pistol, I go to the gym all the time, I'm trying to make myself more
capable of violence."

    Solidarity C'Ville, a coalition of churches, antiracist groups, and
Black Lives Matter organizations did weeks of work to build up
the base that would challenge the visitors. The morning of the rally,
counter-protesters were dwarfed by a thousand nationalists, though
antifascists were able to block access to their rallying point. Confrontations with the protesters erupted into aggressive street fights,
with a protester of color singled out and beaten with metal poles by
four white nationalists after the rally.[79] With dozens of arrests and
injuries, the Alt Right event was canceled by law enforcement in a
chaotic dispersal of forces. The counter-protesters continued their
actions, heading down side streets. A Dodge Challenger driven by
Vanguard America associate James Alex Fields plowed headfirst into
the crowd, sending bodies flying over the hood as screams bounced
off the walls. As people were pulled from the wreckage, and long
after Fields shifted into reverse and fled at drag-race speeds away
from the attack, nineteen were found to be seriously injured and one

---

76   Redneck Revolt, Facebook Post, August 11, 2017, https://www.facebook.com/
        RedneckRevolt/posts/613118022410170.

77   Quoted at: https://www.splcenter.org/fighting-hate/extremist-files/individual/
        christopher-cantwell.

78   "Charlottesville, VA: Unite the Right Plans on Friday Surprise Torchlit Ral-
        ly at UVA," *It's Going Down*, August 11, 2017, https://itsgoingdown.org/
        charlottesville-va-unite-right-plans-friday-surprise-torchlit-rally-uva/.

79   Yesha Callahan, "White Supremacists Beat Black Man With Poles in Charlot-
        tesville, Va., Parking Garage," *The Root*, August 12, 2017, http://www.theroot
        .com/white-supremacists-beat-black-man-with-poles-in-charlot-1797790092.

woman, local activist Heather Heyer, was dead.[80] Shortly after authorities released her information, *The Daily Stormer* founder Andrew Anglin said: "The real tragedy is what happened to the car. It was a very nice car, worth much more than the life of whoever died," saying that he was glad Fields "killed the fat slut."[81]

Within hours the entire country erupted with candlelight vigils in the name of Charlottesville in every major city. As Heather Heyer's family desperately tried to pull together an impromptu memorial, they were forced to cancel after the threats from white supremacists became so severe they feared another act of terrorism on their family.[82] The next day, Alt Right organizer Jason Kessler tried to hold a press conference to respond to the attacks, but the protesters overwhelmed him, sending him running down the street under police protection.[83] As the roar in response to the tragedy hit the airwaves, U.S. politicians rushed to waiting cameras to decisively, if disingenuously, denounce the white nationalist violence. Trump issued a tepid statement naming the KKK and neo-Nazis, but refused to identify the Alt Right and later accused what he coined the "Alt Left" of instigating the racists to violence.[84]

Participants in the torchlight march and rally were doxxed in record numbers, some even fired from their jobs and denounced by their families in the days after. In the sleepy upstate New York village of Honeoye Falls, a snapshot of local man and alleged *Daily Stormer* affiliate Jarrod Kuhn led the local group Eastside Antifascists to

---

80 "Alleged Charlottesville Driver Who Killed One Rallied with Alt-Right Vanguard America," Southern Poverty Law Center, August 12, 2017, https://www .splcenter.org/hatewatch/2017/08/12/alleged-charlottesville-driver-who-killed-one-rallied-alt-right-vanguard-america-group.

81 "After Praising Trump's Statement on Charlottesville, a Neo-Nazi Website Celebrates Murder of Counterprotester Heather Heyer," *Media Matters for America*, August 13, 2017, https://www.mediamatters.org/blog/2017/08/13/ after-praising-trumps-statement-charlottesville-neo-nazi-website-celebrates -murder-counterprotester/217610; As of the writing of this, the quotes are taken from articles no longer available on aboveground websites and instead simply in archive on articles through the Tor browser only.

82 "Vigil for Heather Heyer Cancelled After 'Credible Threat,'" *WDBJ7*, August 13, 2017, http://www.wdbj7.com/content/news/Vigil-for-Heather-Heyer-cancelled-after-credible-threat-440207223.html.

83 Daniel Politi, "Organizer of White Supremacist Rally Gets Chased out of His Own Press Conference," *Slate*, August 13, 2017, http://www.slate.com/blogs/ the_slatest/2017/08/13/jason_kessler_organizer_of_white_supremacist_rally_ gets_chased_out_of_his.html.

84 "Full Text: Trump's Comments on White Supremacists, 'Alt-left' in Charlottesville," *Politico*, August 15, 2017, http://www.politico.com/story/2017/08/15/ full-text-trump-comments-white-supremacists-alt-left-transcript-241662.

begin a flyering campaign to out him to his neighbors. Once the media descended on Kuhn he desperately tried to disassociate himself from the Nazi contingent, announcing that his "life is over" and saying he will have to move out of his hometown to start over.[85] For Eastside Antifascists, and for many in antifascist circles, these tactics show there are consequences for affiliating with genocidal racialism. "You don't get to be a weekend Nazi," points out Eastside Antifascists organizer Peter Berkman. "You don't get to participate in deadly neo-nazi riots and then quietly return to your community like nothing happened."[86]

GoDaddy refused to host websites like the *Daily Stormer*, and Richard Spencer could not find a venue for his own press conference, forcing him to stuff a bevy of angry reporters into his Arlington loft in Charlottesville's wake. Social media had its largest mass shuttening to date as Twitter suspended Alt Right logins, Facebook took down pages, Mail Chimp canceled accounts, SoundCloud dropped white nationalist podcasts, and the dating apps Tindr and OKCupid banned Christopher Cantwell after he made a buffoonish spectacle of himself at the rally. His behavior led to criminal charges for "illegal use of gases and injury by caustic agent or explosive."[87]

Cloudflare refused to service the *Daily Stormer* in its first ever act of individual website removal, a move that, while making its CEO Matthew Prince uncomfortable, was necessary after the community asserted that the company was responsible for the content Anglin was publishing. "I'm sick of this, fuck them, they're off the Internet," said Prince about Anglin after looking at exactly what the *Stormer* had been disseminating. The ability of these tech companies to unilaterally pull the plug on objectionable content has ominous overtones for the radical left as well, but it shows, more than anything, the power of collective action to sway giant institutions.[88]

85 Lucy Pasha-Robinson, "'My Life is Over': Man Who Attended Charlottesville Neo-Nazi Rally Forced to Move Away after Being Identified," *The Independent*, August 18, 2017, http://www.independent.co.uk/news/world/americas/neo-nazi-charlottesville-identified-move-white-supremacy-rally-unite-right-life-over-jarrod-kuhn-a7899596.html.

86 Peter Berkman, interview with author August 22, 2017.

87 Matt Stevens, "Christopher Cantwell, White Nationalist in Vice Video, Braces for Charges," *New York Times*, August 21, 2017, https://www.nytimes.com/2017/08/21/us/christopher-cantwell-charlottesville.html.

88 "Meet the CEO Who Kicked Neo-Nazis Off the Internet," *Vice News*, August 23, 2017, https://news.vice.com/story/meet-the-ceo-who-kicked-neo-nazis-off-the-internet.

While people like Mike Enoch insisted that Charlottesville was a victory, and that Fields was not an aggressor, the social mood so completely turned on them that it was hard to see how they could bounce back.[89] Enoch himself was sent reeling after he was named, along with twenty-three other white nationalists, including David Duke, in a lawsuit from a survivor of the car attack.[90] Spencer's upcoming Texas "White Lives Matter" rally was quickly canceled, and while AltRight.com declared Charlottesville the "beginning of the white civil rights movement," it could rightly be seen as the beginning of the public's realization that insurrectionary white supremacy is a material threat.[91]

The following weekend an Alt Right rally was planned in Boston, but its fifty participants were met by an estimated 40,000 antifascists that flooded the city's streets and crushed the event before it started. The Alt Right did create unity out of Charlottesville—it just wasn't for their side. The last weeks of August were filled with Alt Right attempts at public celebrations, which were met by an increasing cadre of organizers. It was more than this, though. It was direct action trainings, art showings, coalition meetings, long-term planning. Organized resistance and the construction of radical left meta-politics was everywhere.

It wasn't just that the tide had turned on the Alt Right—they had always been unpopular—or that a fascist movement was shown to have consequences—they have time and time again—it was that all the pieces came together, the reality of the situation was obvious, and the growth of a mass movement against it was exploding.

Mass Action

Many of these fascist organizations saw community support in the populist climate of the 2016 presidential election, but antifascist mass movements rather than only small, tight-knit groups, have developed in the elections' wake. The use of mass mobilizations is crucial because of the public nature of many white nationalists, who

89   Mike Peinovich, "TDS#181: Dot Wang," *The Right Stuff*, August 15, 2017, https://therightstuff.biz/2017/08/15/the-daily-shoah-181-dot-wang/.

90   Alan Feuer, "2 Sisters in Charlottesville Sue Far-Right Leaders Over Car Attack," *New York Times*, August 16, 2017, https://www.nytimes.com/2017/08/16/us/2-sisters-in-charlottesville-sue-far-right-leaders-over-car-attack.html.

91   Vincent Law, "Charlottesville Was a Turning Point for White People in America (Updated)," AltRight.com, August 13, 2017, https://altright.com/2017/08/13/charlottesville-was-a-turning-point-for-white-people-in-america/.

are feeling emboldened to recruit openly. The growth of Black Lives Matter as a nationwide movement provides an additional example of mass mobilizations as the response to racial disparity, especially in terms of aggressive policing, which has become obvious to a new generation of young people. While BLM developed in response to a wave of police killings, it provides an infrastructural benefit for organizers going after white supremacists.

For a mass antifascist movement, this means developing campaigns that focus on specific targets and have material outcomes. This model has been proposed by groups like the IWW's General Defense Committee (GDC), a project that many IWW locals have taken on as a community organizing and self-defense project that goes beyond the workplace organizing the union is notorious for.

The IWW GDC 14 in the Twin Cities is a leader, confronting fascist organizations by mobilizing mass community support. They began in 2009 with protest actions against the National Socialist Movement, which was headquartered just south in Austin, Minnesota. The NSM was protesting a YWCA workshop on racism, yet the three Nazis who arrived were met with hundreds of counter-protesters. Besides supporting the growing movement against police violence that would evolve into Black Lives Matter and the prisoner support that inspired the Incarcerated Workers Organizing Committee, they took antifascist work head-on, including disruptions of Holocaust denier David Irving's events and the targeting of a local German restaurant where a Nazi-themed private party took place (complete with theatrical SA uniforms).

The GDC focuses on a "mass approach," creating a campaign strategy that is open, public, and reaches out to the broad community that could be threatened by racist violence. These extensive campaigns draw on the tactics seen both in organized labor and antiracist organizing. Twin Cities GDC organizer Travis Elise thinks that the mass movement approach is what can interrupt the growth of far-right movements while they are in utero. "If we had a mass movement several years ago, maybe the Alt Right wouldn't exist."[92]

In November 2016, the GDC took on the neofolk band Blood and Sun and its frontman, Luke Tromiczak. The band is one of the more well-known American neofolk acts associated with the "folkish" impulses of bands like Changes. Robert Taylor of Changes is a former member of the white nationalist Minutemen and

92   Travis Elise, interview with author, December 21, 2016.

American Front, and is friendly with Tromiczak. The GDC asked
Tromiczak to make a public break with the fascist sector of neofolk, and for venues to drop Blood and Sun from their scheduled
dates. Tromiczak responded by publicly relenting on his band's
Facebook page and denied he ever had these relationships. This ignores his collaboration with the National Socialist black metal outfit
Anti-Theist Disseminations, his questionable Valkut chest tattoo,
and his Brown-Shirt concert outfit.[93] The Cactus Club in Milwaukee, the Marble Bar in Detroit, and other venues dropped Blood and
Sun from their bills after the public campaign from the GDC began, and the campaign continued to get former partnering venues to
deny Tromiczak their stage.[94] The "Operation Equinox Tour" that
Blood and Sun was traveling with, which was organized by nationalist website *Heathen Harvest*, saw similar opposition in 2015, when
antifascist organizers confronted them at the Philadelphia show and
participating bands had gear damaged.[95]

This mass approach makes it possible to sync certain constituencies with broad approaches to antifascism without reinventing
the structures that are in place. In certain parts of the country, the
Midwest in particular, the IWW is central in a variety of struggles.
The base is then able to bring in community self-defense, increased
security, antifascist confrontation, and strategies from ARA and
Antifa. These tactics and strategies could easily be adapted for new
organizations or other activist brands, but with the GDC they are
tying into the legitimacy that the IWW has gained in organizing circles in their regions.[96]

White nationalists need some way to broadcast their message
to new audiences. One attempt is to host public conferences, which
antiracists have increasingly worked to shut down. *American Renaissance* has been a focal point for counter-organizing, despite pleas
from organizers that they are simply a moderate political gathering
concerned with "European Americans." The One People's Project has been confronting these organizations for years, as well as a

---

93   "Twin Cities Antifascists Kick Out Neo-Fascist Luke Tromiczak," Twin Cit-
     ies General Defense Committee, December 16, 2016, https://twincitiesgdc.org
     /2016/12/16/tcantifa-v-luketromiczak1/.
94   "Steps You Can Take to Cancel Nazi Blood & Sun Shows," Twin Cities General
     Defense Committee, December 16, 2016, https://twincitiesgdc.org/2016/12/16/
     antifa-v-tromiczak-action/.
95   "Fascist Bands' Van Wrecked in Philly," *It's Going Down*, n.d, https://itsgoingdown
     .org/fascist-bands-van-wrecked-philly/.
96   Erik Foreman, interview with author, December 1, 2016.

range of white nationalist projects from neo-Nazi political parties to anti-immigration radicals. Founded by Daryle Lamont Jenkins, OPP mixes organized confrontations and campaigns with extensive research, working to both expose the white nationalist community to public scorn and to pull together tangible results from campaigns looking to stop their message from spreading.[97]

The OPP has prioritized confronting conferences for the "suit-and-tie" fascist intelligentsia, making the National Policy Institute a primary target. At NPI's November 2016 conference—the same one where Spencer caused sweeping controversies and called out "Hail victory"—the OPP and Smash Racism DC confronted members of *Red Ice Media* shooting video out front and sent them running back into the venue. The night before, they led an action into the pre-event dinner, as participants indoors were taking cheeky photos of themselves doing Roman salutes.[98] The contingent entered the restaurant and forced Spencer out. Maggiano's canceled the dinner and donated the $10,000 made during the evening to the Anti-Defamation League.[99] Before the conference, a pressure campaign from the OPP and Smash Racism DC forced one venue to pull their contract.

For these actions to be successful you need to be able to mobilize bodies. Whether through boycotts, bad press, or community rejection of commercial institutions, the proof that an organization has weight in numbers adds consequences to ignored demands. These institutions, though maybe sympathetic to the aims of antiracist organizers, make economic decisions, not moral ones. The threat then is that organizers will extend the toxic shadow of the white nationalists to the business, a cost far too high for whatever they are being paid.

For years the *AmRen* conference was graciously held at the Dulles Airport Hyatt hotel in Washington D.C. After years of pressure led by OPP, the Hyatt finally refused the rental. In 2008, the conference had to move to a more expensive location, the Dulles Crown Plaza, who rolled out the red carpet until they realized the crowd it brought and then they blocked *AmRen* from returning

97   Daryle Lamont Jenkins, interview with author, September 1, 2016.
98   John Zangas, "Antifascists Storm National Policy Institute Dinner," *DC Media Group*, November 20, 2016, http://www.dcmediagroup.us/2016/11/20/antifascists-storm-national-policy-institute-dinner/.
99   Benjamin Freed, "DC Restaurant Apologizes for Hosting White Nationalist Dinner and Donates Proceeds to Charity," *Washingtonian*, November 21, 2016, https://www.washingtonian.com/2016/11/21/dc-restaurant-hosted-white-nationalist-dinner-donates-proceeds-anti-defamation-league/.

the following year. In 2010 *AmRen* was on the run, denied at each D.C.-area hotel after organizers created a campaign that targeted hotel management with mass community outreach, letting them know the conference's content. Not only was their hosting hotel receiving a string of angry complaints, so was every hotel in town. When Jared Taylor tried to pivot the conference location he found a corridor full of closed doors, no one willing to stand with *AmRen* against an army of opposition.[100]

The following year, OPP continued this pressure when *AmRen* tried to hold its 2011 conference in Charlotte, North Carolina. Taylor tried to keep its Airport Sheraton location a secret until it was absolutely necessary, yet once information went public the Sheraton was notified and pulled the *AmRen* contract. No other hotel would have them after local politicians and activists became aware of the conference's line-up, forcing them to cancel the event for the second year in a row.[101] Since then they have relied on a government-run facility deep in the Montgomery Bell State Park, a rural area outside of Nashville, Tennessee. As conference goers enter, OPP and other antifascist organizations are there to greet them, hoping that pressure will reach critical mass so that hotel management will follow the trend of severing *AmRen*'s contracts.

A mass movement is required to undo the gains of a large race realist and anti-Semitic movement by shifting the discourse away from their talking points, and making spaces—both digital and physical—unwelcoming to ideas that manipulate facts and victimize minorities. Traditional antifascist organizing now includes race realist and anti-Semitic targets, though many of these institutions have larger budgets than traditional neo-Nazi projects and attempt to insulate themselves with their dollars. People like Jared Taylor have been invited to college campuses, and it is imperative that mass movements halt these sorts of events altogether.

Mass movement antifascism is neither new nor separate from other approaches. Even the most insular groups will join coalitions and large marches when it is effective. The model taken from Anti-Fascist Action starting in the 1970s in the U.K. was to amass huge community walls to meet fascist parties in the streets, with

100 Alexander Hart, "The Saga of American Renaissance's 2010 Conference: 'Anarcho-Tyranny' In Action," *VDare*, February 16, 2010, http://www .vdare.com/articles/the-saga-of-american-renaissances-2010-conference-anarcho-tyranny-in-action.
101 Jenkins, interview with author, September 1, 2016.

some participants willing to directly engage with them while others provide weight to the action through mass participation. Developing a mass antifascist movement in the U.S. is obviously necessary, and gathering thousands in the streets is now viable.

The confrontation against fascists requires great participation if it is to go beyond fleeting victories. Seeing beyond the entry of Nazis into a punk music venue, or the creeping anti-Semitism into an anti-war organization requires an analysis of how these groups function, where they come from, and the conditions under which they are created. This cannot happen with only a micro-cadre, limited by narrowly defined militancy. Instead, we need a network of projects with broad opportunities for participation and a range of options for how to tackle each individual effort and weave them into a larger patchwork of antifascism. "If you have militancy without the mass politics, the masses aren't going to support the militancy," points out Lisa Roth of JBAKC.[102] The point is to connect with those outside of the ideological core, not just to expand the scope of possible work, but also to simultaneously shift the culture, connecting various issues and developing an ethos that reflects an ideological commitment to equality. These lessons are learned by most militant antifascist organizations as they find ways to connect with different cultural constituencies, from maintaining a presence in music subcultures to building mass coalitions for public actions.

Antifascism must also be part of an emerging working-class consciousness, to be of and for the working class, and to develop structures that maintain the struggle in relevance to the community. Kevin Van Meter notes that this needs to be embedded in the lived experience of the public, allowing for a connection between the organizations and the surrounding populace that will enable it to keep doing the work.

> These antifascist groups are going to have to address their own self-reproduction and their own survival. If that is slush funds for legal counsel, if that is safe houses, if that's creating infrastructure… Because you want the larger community to come to the defense of antifascist forces when they're under attack.[103]

Antifascist work is a piece of the larger mass working-class struggle for survival and progress, and it should come out of the

102   Lisa Roth, interview with author, July 2, 2017.
103   Kevin Van Meter, interview with author, June 8, 2017.

experiences and needs of the class rather than the ideological impo-sition of experienced organizers.

Restating the Obvious

While education is key to mass movements, it is especially crucial when dealing with a political menace that is ephemeral and diffi-cult to pin down. Even the most politically astute corners of the left will be stretching to find a universal definition of fascism, es-pecially given fascism's break from the uniform interests of capi-tal. Broad-based community education should be integrated with existing antifascist organizing, educating people about how fascist movements work, what they look like, and exactly where they will be coming from. Fascism feeds on weak points in the left, espe-cially in areas of conflicting identity politics, and so ongoing dis-cussions about those crossover points is critical to sealing up left movements from entryism.

Faced with false "race and IQ" arguments, as well as the entire set of ideas making up Human Biological Diversity, most people do not have the talking points ready and accessible to refute them. The idea that racial groups are intellectually stratified is common-ly known to be pseudoscience, yet educational and social institu-tions have not made the mountains of evidence for racial equality readily accessible. Arguments about the effect of environment on sub-population cognitive development from people like J. Philippe Rushton can appear as scientifically sound, but only when the scientific consensus about the intellectual development and evo-lutionary geography is unknown.[104] We need to reclaim access to science in a fashion that is understandable, as part of the ongoing process to understand the historic role of racism. Grassroots proj-ects must educate new members on a range of issues relevant to their work. Anti-Racist Action used an eighty-five-page resource packet for membership to understand gender and sexuality, the his-tory of the extreme right, and stories, report backs, and analyses of actual engagements with fascists.[105]

What we need is to develop long-standing educational institu-tions to develop the scientific understanding of human populations

104   Ashley Montagu, "The IQ Mythology," *Race and IQ*, Expanded Edition (New York: Oxford University Press, 2017), 36–39.
105   *ARA Education Packet* (Toronto: Anti-Racist Action, 1994).

and the history of inequality in shaping existing social relations. These types of educational programs have always been a part of successful antiracist organizing. In 1989, the Louisiana Coalition Against Racism and Nazism formed to confront the electoral victory of David Duke, who had won a state legislative seat in Louisiana. Duke had spent ten years tempering his rhetoric, attempting to use a well-crafted dog whistle and rising populist anger to mainstream his ideas. When he ran for senate in 1990, and governor in 1991, the coalition mobilized a large campaign to keep the focus of the election on Duke's racism and the consequences it would have for the state.

After the campaign, those who had worked on the coalition formed the Southern Institute for Education and Research. The goal was to create programs to teach children the history of the Southern civil rights movement, the Holocaust, and American white supremacy. The institute focused on rural areas of the Deep South, hoping that this work could unseat a Duke-like figure in the future by eliminating support for him ahead of time. When Duke returned in 2016 to run for state senate on the heels of Donald Trump's success, he barely received a few percentage points, largely because of the education work that was done by the coalition and, later, the educational institute.[106]

SURJ was formed after Barack Obama's election in 2008 and the racist backlash that followed and has made education of white antiracists a key part of their program. They focus on the lived experiences of both people of color and white people who retain a certain amount of privilege, drawing together these experiences into an organizing framework that shows white accomplices the material benefit of confronting racism in white communities. SURJ attempts to center all educational programs on an organizing component, making action the natural result of increased consciousness. Since its founding, SURJ has coordinated with dozens of organizations around the country, often using a "white ally" model to work on intercommunity racism that passes between well-intentioned neighbors and the rising tide of reactionary violence that feeds on the fears and anger of the white working class.[107]

---

106   Lawrence Powell, phone interview with author, November, 2016.
107   Carla Wallace, phone interview with author, November 14, 2016.

Rural Struggle

Broad-based community organizations with a range of tools play an especially critical role in the rural areas that dominate the U.S. As the militia movement grows across rural America, so does its opposition. Through the 2015 Sugar Pine Mine and 2016 Malheur Wildlife Refuge occupations, Oregon's Rural Organizing Project (ROP) defined itself as a leader by creating regional resistance networks as a community counter-base to the Patriot recruiting efforts. Formed in response to the anti-LGBT Abnormal Behaviors Initiative from the Oregon Citizens Alliance in 1992, which would have blocked government money to organizations "promoting homosexuality," ROP has gone on to bring progressive campaigns to the more conservative areas outside of Oregon's bigger cities.

When the Oath Keepers of Josephine County began their month-long occupation of the Sugar Pine Mine, frightened county residents began assessing the situation with ROP. They set a meeting time and began researching the Oath Keepers with the help of the antifascist publishing institution, Political Research Associates. Josephine County was experiencing a budget shortfall at the time, and that had depleted almost all public services. At the same time, the hard libertarianism of the Patriot groups was pushing a "No New Taxes" campaign that would further deepen the financial crisis. The Oath Keepers' answer, as is often the case, was to create Community Preparedness Teams, a non-governmental institution, controlled by militia members, to take up the role of state services.[108] By meeting community needs from their own ideological perspective, the militia presents itself as the answer to the current crisis, further embedding their own explanations and outcomes for the calamity the communities are in. Community engagement is then offered within their institutions, and people who want to be better stewards of their regions are often ushered into militia projects since they have already "proved their worth."

The day after the Oath Keepers rallied in Medford in front of the Bureau of Land Management office, ROP and community supporters held a press conference where community leaders spoke about the fear of, and intimidation by, militias. The Oath Keepers tried to disrupt the press conference, shoving cell phones in organizers' faces and revealing their behavior to a waiting army of media. Among the militia members to arrive was former sheriff Gil Gilbertson, who

---

108   Spencer, *Up in Arms*, 106–14.

had become a nationwide militia celebrity through his role in the Patriot-affiliated Constitutional Sheriffs and Peace Officers Association. ROP created a signature campaign with a local paper, which received more than a hundred public petition signatures in the rural county within twenty-four hours. By bringing together those frightened by militia intimidation, it was enough to get things started, and if the Patriots were going to try and dominate the public discourse, then organizers would create counter-narratives to show that the militias do not speak for the community.[109]

In advance of the Malheur occupation, locals in Harney County held public meetings to tell the militias to drop their mobilizations. When ROP got the message that the militias were heading to Bend on their way to the wildlife refuge, they organized a demonstration that "greeted" the group in front of local media. As the occupation was in full swing, ROP organized solidarity demonstrations in towns all around Oregon, bringing thousands into the streets to undermine militia talking points about local support, of which there was little. On the January 20 Day of Action, the voice of the public was made clear: the militias needed to leave. Shortly after, on February 1, Harney County residents came out in force to the county courthouse, more than doubling the number sent by the Patriots. At this rally "some people with the paramilitaries began harassing, threatening, and intimidating locals, including shouting in their faces and sticking yellow shooting targets on them."[110] The protests raised the profile of the opposition to the militias, shrinking the Patriot morale. For those residents feeling isolated, ROP's strategy was effective in giving them back their voice, providing a network of support, and showing the militia that they were not welcome. In nearby Grant County, seventy people showed up to protest a Patriot meeting the Bundys arranged. While the militia tried to block the entrance, the group found a way in and staged a silent protest. With the support of ROP, they formed Grant County Positive Action, and went on to join Harney County protests and arrange community education events, letters to the editor and ad campaigns and to pressure the county to pass a resolution condemning the militia occupation.[111]

ROP's commitment to confronting the militias did not come without its blowback as organizers faced threats of violence, so

---

109   Ibid.
110   Ibid., 112
111   Ibid.

much so that staff members needed security at their homes and all ROP events. Their experiences led them to create the *Up in Arms* guidebook that, besides giving detailed information about the militia movement, provides outlines for how to counter militia propaganda and protocols for organizing in response to the militias, including how to hold events, install security, and do research.[112]

Reporting from Montana

Montana Human Rights Network (MHRN) is similarly structured to the ROP, with a network of local organizations across the state building on progressive values such as "pluralism, equality and justice." As well as putting forward policy initiatives and doing local education, they support victims of hate crimes, often through legal channels. MHRN also monitors and challenges extremist groups throughout the state. They have six affiliated local groups that meet individually, receiving support from the larger network, including funding and staff time.[113]

In 1995, at a time when as many as 20 percent of the state's population was in support of the radical fringe, the MHRN started a landmark campaign against the growing militia movement in the area. Their plan was to narrow the range of support for the militias by continuing to highlight the long trail of violence and white supremacist ideas that floated inside the Patriot camp. They worked with groups like Prairie Fire and the Northwest Coalition Against Malicious Harassment to address the rise of hate groups out of the "farm crisis." This strategy of exposure helped to shift media representation and then public perception of the militia movement, giving the voice back to the people who felt terrorized.[114]

Oregon Action

Seeing rampant Islamophobia as one of the sharpest edges of the Patriot movement, a perspective tacitly encouraged by the Trump administration, Oregon Action (now part of Unite Oregon) challenges Islamophobia in rural regions. They have focused on the southern

---

112 Joanne Zuhl, "Oregon's Radical Rural Right," *Street Roots*, October 11, 2016, http://news.streetroots.org/2016/10/11/oregon-s-radical-rural-right.
113 "About Montana Human Rights Network," Montana Human Rights Network, n.d, http://www.mhrn.org/.
114 Levitas, *The Terrorist Next Door*, 312.

Rogue Valley to address racial injustice in the same way they have addressed issues like contemporary racial "redlining" and gentrification in Portland. In semi-rural and conservative cities like Medford, Oregon, they organized "Not in Our Town" actions against Islamophobia after anti-Muslim posters and threats blanketed the city and nearby Jackson County.[115]

A mass movement approach is central to all of this work. While the militias have been loud, the use of mass-based solidarity has shown their relative weakness in comparison to united communities where neighbors are looking out for each other. Since the militias respond to crisis with violence, often patrolling the streets with firearms, the answer from these organizations was not to match the firepower, but instead to overwhelm them with numbers and strategic reframing of the narrative. This has undermined the main recruitment tool the militias had: the reliable support of the community.

The absence of a left narrative and structures of solidarity are what has allowed Patriot groups to create such a deep foothold throughout rural America. It need not be this way as the continuing farm crisis, the environmental catastrophe of "fracking," and the lack of new industries is something that left ideas of class-consciousness and action can provide tangible answers for. This will only happen if rural areas are actively addressed, and elitist liberal notions of urban intellectual superiority are suppressed in favor of a deeper understanding of the shared economic conditions between working-class people struggling both in the plains and the urban core.

In the Valley

In the Flathead Valley of Montana, Love Lives Here (LLH) has been organizing regionally as an affiliate of the MHRN. With hundreds of members across the small and medium-sized townships between the mountains, LLH began a high-profile set of campaigns addressing Richard Spencer, who called the Flathead Valley resort-town of Whitefish home. Spencer was living in a $3 million home owned by his parents for part of the year, the rest of the time renting an apartment in Arlington, Virginia, to be closer to Washington D.C. In 2014, shortly after Spencer was deported from the European Union for organizing a "pan-European" conference in Hungary, LLH began

---

115 "Not in Our Town! Action Against Islamophobia," Facebook Events, December 7, 2017, https://www.facebook.com/events/556221017835820/.

notifying residents that one of the most prolific white nationalists in the U.S. was sharing the ski lifts with them. After Spencer found himself in a fight with Republican strategist Randy Scheunemann at the Whitefish Mountain Resort, LLH started a campaign to pass a regional piece of legislation preventing Spencer's organizations from holding conferences in their area. Business owners had already started telling Spencer not to return to their establishments, including an incident where a barista refused to serve him and his pregnant wife.[116] City Councilman Frank Sweeney had contacted the Southern Poverty Law Center for advice on how to develop a "no hate" ordinance, yet they ended up passing a weaker resolution in favor of diversity.[117]

After Spencer became a household name in 2016, it came to light that Sherry Spencer, his mother, owned commercial property in the valley. While Sherry presented herself as simply the doting parent to a "political thought criminal," her own track record of fundraising for fringe right-wing candidates, her appearance at the white nationalist H.L. Mencken Club, and the fact that Richard used her address as the IRS-registered headquarters for the National Policy Institute, made her suspect. A local activist began campaigning to have Sherry publicly disassociate with her son's fascism and to sell the property that she was profiting from, with a suggestion that a small donation to the MHRN would be a sign of good faith. This incensed Richard Spencer who, in an act of ironic verbal gymnastics, identified MHRN as a "hate group" that was "extorting" his family.[118] The *Daily Stormer* began a harassment and doxxing campaign against MHRN organizers and supporters, specifically targeting Jewish members of the Montana community who never thought they would see images of the Holocaust used to elicit fear at their synagogue.[119]

Yellow stars with the word "Jude," German for Jew, were placed over images of a local real estate agent and her twelve-year-old son.

116   Richard Spencer, phone interview by the author, September 14, 2016.
117   Spencer, Richard, "Frank Sweeney: An Enemy of Freedom," *Radix Journal*. N.p., December 23, 2016, http://www.radixjournal.com/blog/2016/12/23/frank -sweeney-an-enemy-of-freedom.
118   Richard Spencer, "The Attacks on My Mother," *Radix Journal*, December 21, 2016, http://www.radixjournal.com/blog/2016/12/21/the-attacks-on-my-mother?rq=whitefish.
119   Lois Beckett, "How Richard Spencer's Home Town Weathered a Neo-Nazi 'Troll Storm,'" *The Guardian*, February 5, 2017, https://www.theguardian.com /us-news/2017/feb/05/richard-spencer-whitefish-neo-nazi-march.

The harassment hit such a fever pitch that the Montana governor canceled a scheduled trip to Whitefish.[120] As Alt Right and anti-Semitic literature began showing up in downtown Whitefish, neighbors became hardened in their alliance with LLH. Supporters of the *Daily Stormer*, which labeled LLH a "Jewish paramilitary organization," called in threats to local businesses, like the boutique Buffalo Café, also submitting low reviews on Yelp to besmirch the commercial appeal of the town. Councilman Sweeney spoke out to the climate of fear that Alt Right trolls instituted during the 2016 Christmas season in Whitefish, saying "Why anybody would think it's OK to treat another human being like that is beyond me."[121]

In response to the anti-Semitic attacks, LLH started a holiday campaign by handing out "Montana Menorah" cards that could easily be slid into windows, peacefully rallying the Menorah's spirit as a memory of perseverance amid surrounding armies of persecution. Escalating, Anglin called for an Alt Right march in Whitefish for January 2017 against what he called the "Jewish" campaign of hate against Sherry Spencer.[122] He promised to ship in two hundred skinheads from the Bay Area, including from the Traditionalist Worker Party and Golden State Skinheads—both of which have been mired in violent controversy—as well as an alleged member of Hamas. Anglin went on David Duke's internet radio show to rally for an attack on the "Jewish power structure" in an act of pogromatic terror reminiscent of Kristallnacht.[123]

Despite arctic winds, LLH rallied the Flathead Valley on January 8, bringing together hundreds with speakers and musicians. The strategy was twofold: to bring the community together, and to reframe the larger conversation to one of a determined confederation of locals against the forces of organized racism. To do this they used softened

---

120   Shane Burley, "The Alt Right's War on Whitefish, and the Growth of an Opposition," *Gods & Radicals*, February 13, 2017, https://godsandradicals.org/2017/02/13/the-alt-rights-war-on-whitefish-and-the-growth-of-an-opposition/.

121   Vince Devlin, "Whitefish Dealing With Backlash from White Supremacist Website," *Missoulian*, December 22, 2016, http://missoulian.com/news/state-and-regional/whitefish-dealing-with-backlash-from-white-supremacist-website/article_ea5e7c61-ffdc-5044-8bca-79cda3a6ef9b.html.

122   James King, "Alt-Right Plans Armed March Through Montana Town To Scare Jews," *Vocativ*, December 23, 2016, http://www.vocativ.com/386984/alt-right-armed-march/.

123   "White Nationalist Announces Plans to Bus White Power Skinheads to Whitefish," Institute for Research & Education on Human Rights, December 29, 2016, http://www.irehr.org/2016/12/29/white-nationalist-announces-plans-bus-white-power-skinheads-whitefish/.

messaging about compassion and diversity, creating a "Wall of Empathy" with notes of encouragement from around the country.[124]

The Missoula IWW GDC and the Alliance of Intersectional Power organized the public action to confront the Nazis, which LLH shied away from.[125] While some antifascist organizers were critical of the approach LLH took, including the questionable decision to forego physical opposition, their choices had utility. As with the rest of the MHRN, the regional organizations had done the long-term community building that is needed for creating an impenetrable wall to Alt Right recruitment. This lacked the final component, however, of the public action in opposition, but direct action groups could then build on the foundation laid by LLH so the "no platform" strategy had more potential. When combined, both approaches become syncretic and help build a mass movement.

Anglin was only able to get a sidewalk permit for the neo-Nazi's planned Martin Luther King Jr. Day march, which they were calling the "James Earl Ray Day Extravaganza," after the man who assassinated King. Their permit was eventually revoked entirely, and Anglin promised to hold the march a month later, yet it never came to fruition. Antifascist organizers held their counter-demonstration anyway, shifting the focus to a broad-based community action against the Alt Right and the climate of fear that white nationalists had created in Montana. As one Montana organizer pointed out, the results were successful because of the role that each organization played, an approach that would not have existed without the integration of the multitude.

> It may not have been a coalition in name, but it essentially acted as one: unity in purpose, diversity in tactics. By the end of the discussions, no one questioned the need for a public show of opposition and no one was using the language of outsider/insider… People have been won over to the idea that we actually need to talk about tactics, that we need to be in the same room, or at least on the same call if we're spread out across the state, in order to debate.[126]

---

124 Vince Devlin, "Hundreds Rally in Sub-Zero Temps to Show Love, Not Hate, Defines Whitefish," *Missoulian*, January 7, 2017, http://missoulian.com/news/local/hundreds-rally-in-sub-zero-temps-to-put-a-different/article_78e7a29d-142e-55c1-a8eb-6d68386fd62e.html.

125 Montana Antifa, "Facebook Profile," Facebook, accessed, February 18, 2017, https://www.facebook.com/MontanaAntifa/?fref=ts.

126 Eric Ruder, "How We Made Montana Nazis Back Down," *The Socialist Worker*, January 17, 2017, https://socialistworker.org/2017/01/17/how-we-made-montana-nazis-back-down.

Montana continues to be "contested ground." Just a few months later an Alt Right politician, former Youth for Western Civilization (YWC) vice president Taylor Rose, ran for Montana House District 3. He amassed a following while writing for the far-right website *WorldNetDaily*, which also employed YWC founder and Wolves of Vinland member Kevin DeAnna. While Rose was certainly a fringe candidate, he received support from Montana Republicans like Senator Dee Brown. Richard Spencer himself has suggested he may run for a congressional seat in Montana, yet his infamy makes that unlikely.[127]

Reform?

So-called re-entry programs have always left a bad taste in the mouths of antifascist organizers because it reframes the issue of white supremacy from one of political ideology to one of mental illness, or simply "bad choices." But these programs can be an important component of a mass-based antifascist movement. While re-entry programs can erase the conscious fascist politic from individuals, the tradition of youth recruitment, which seeks to draw poor white kids into the most violent neo-Nazi projects in the country, needs to be countered.

In October 2016, Derek Black, son of *Stormfront* founder Don Black, went public about living the double-life of a white nationalist and a college student. Black's campus peers engaged with him over time, having a series of dinners with him. When challenged in this trusting environment, his ideas were shattered. Black's story, while inspirational, may be an exception rather than a rule, but it presents a unique scenario for people with cracks forming in their ideology and looking for a way out.[128]

Former white supremacist gang members who left that life behind, and embraced a new way of thinking in a broad multicultural community, created Life After Hate in 2011. They have created a program for research and education, using many of the methods for transitioning people between life paths similar to prison re-entry

127   Ben Collins, "Another Knockout in Richard Spencer's Backyard," *The Daily Beast*, January 24, 2017, http://www.thedailybeast.com/articles/2017/01/24/another-knockout-in-richard-spencer-s-backyard.html.

128   Eli Saslow, "The White Flight of Derek Black," *Washington Post*, October 15, 2016, https://www.washingtonpost.com/national/the-white-flight-of-derek-black/2016/10/15/ed5f906a-8f3b-11e6-a6a3-d50061aa9fae_story.html.

programs that provide access to a stable life. Their programs, like the Strong Cities Network, are focusing on long-term community building as a solution to the growth of inner-city racialist organizations, and ExitUSA is for members of groups like the Hammerskins who need intense support while getting out. These institutions have always been a favorite of liberal politicians, which is why the Obama administration took a special shine to them and offered them a grant through the Department of Homeland Security's "Countering Violent Extremism" program. When Trump came into office, he argued for changing the name of the program to "Countering Radical Islamic Extremism," keeping in line with his Islamophobic rhetoric, and then rescinded Life After Hate's grant. If organizations like this are going to have a stable role in undermining white supremacist formations, it's best to fund them through the supportive hands of the surrounding community and not to rely on the state.[129]

Labor First

On the hot night of August 10, 2016, nineteen-year-old African American Larnell Bruch was walking out of a Gresham, Oregon, 7-11 when Russell Courtier brutally ran him down with his car. Courtier was a member of European Kindred (EK), a white supremacist gang recruiting en masse in Oregon prisons and flooding drugs into poor Portland suburbs. While most violent white supremacist formations are typically small, rarely more than a handful of members, EK has been growing rapidly as members radicalized inside prison are looking for support upon release.

In response to EK's growth, a group of organizers, some who had been working with prisoners through the IWW's Incarcerated Workers Organizing Committee (IWOC), began to use those connections and knowledge of prison conditions to develop an antifascist strategy that would incorporate those on the inside as leaders. Coordinating with prison activists like former white supremacist Joshua Cartrette, IWOC and the Anarchist Black Cross help prisoners to create political reading groups, which is difficult given the hostility from prison gangs and officials blocking political material from entering cells. For those coming out, the Pacific

---

129   Josh Harkinson, "The Trump Administration Is Pulling a Grant From a Group That Combats Neo-Nazis," *Mother Jones*, June 23, 2017, http://www.motherjones.com/politics/2017/06/the-trump-administration-is-pulling-a-grant-from-a-group-that-combats-neo-nazis/.

Northwest Antifascist Workers Collective was formed to help ex-cons get jobs in trade-union apprenticeship programs or from a list of felon-friendly employers.[130] The collective created a strategy that pressures trade unions to take a strong antiracist stance and to cre-ate barriers for white supremacist workers who have been insulated from employment consequences. The International Union of Paint-ers and Allied Trades Local 10 and the Carpenters Local 1503 passed anti-hate group resolutions, something that will be happening in other locals. By creating antifascist collectives internal to building trades, they can push the hand of stewards and union leadership to fire employees with open neo-Nazi affiliations.[131]

For the labor movement, Trump's presidency, supported by a radical GOP Congress, Senate, and majority statehouses and gov-ernorships is a major concern, as nationwide Right to Work, attacks on Medicaid, and the erosion of collective bargaining rights are im-minent. Fascism has always put unions in its sights, viewing the most successful social movement in history as one of the most effective blows against systematized inequality. Trump's history in business exemplifies this approach, and while he invited some building-trades leaders to the White House, there is little future for organized labor in this Trumpian proposal. As Erik Foreman articulates, "Trump's fascism seeks to finish off the legal framework of labor relations un-der postwar liberalism, dealing the coup de grace to an institutional labor movement that has long been hemorrhaging members."[132]

These attacks on the labor movement are not new, however, and the liberal order that came before Trump has allowed for the power of capital to weaken these organs of resistance. If the tools of collec-tive workplace action are going to confront a reactionary ground-swell, then they also need to be available to go after the underlying neoliberal social relationships that create the crack Trump inhabits.

The resistance is therefore in the "other" workers' movement—among those who never were included in the legal mechanisms of the compact of postwar liberalism in the first place, such as immi-grant workers, the unwaged labor of women, and students. They are joined by a new "other" workers' movement: the rebel rank-and-file of the institutional unions, such as teachers and public

---

130   Tyler Bridges, phone interview with author, December 22, 2016.
131   Tom, interview with author, December 22, 2016.
132   Erik Foreman, "Fight to Win!," *ROAR Magazine* 5 (Spring 2017): 24.

sector workers, and increasingly, self-organized groups of workers who have never belonged to a union. As the state falls under the sway of fascist control, the weapons of this resistance are increasingly extralegal: from protests to strikes, highway blockades and physical confrontations. While increasingly bold in tactics, resistance to fascism is so far largely conservative, in the true sense of the word: it seeks to conserve the liberal order. Until now, its battles have been mostly defensive, and if they are won, will merely put liberals back in power. The real destruction of fascism can only be accomplished by a new workers' movement, unencumbered by the sacred cows of the bureaucracies that grew up under corporate liberalism.[133]

Mass participatory unionism, which focuses its power on the ability to withhold labor and solidarity, is a major tool in this fight. The ability of the working class to organize is what robs dominant institutions of their ability to exploit.

The unions themselves offer one of the largest working-class institutional spaces, whose shift toward "social unionism" marks a public acknowledgment of the role of oppression in collective struggle. The pressure of the rank and file on large unions shows an incredible potential to bring institutional weight behind antifascist projects. From the use of large community spaces to financial commitments, labor unions can become foundations for intersecting resistance. The force of Trumpism and the ascendency of right populism have allowed organized white supremacy and the anti-worker forces to link up, and this creates common cause on the left. Labor can find alliance in this community connection, and they will need it as traditional institutions of labor power erode. Union halls can then become busy spaces for social movements, both inside and outside of the worksite, a place where all of the barriers to working-class survival can be confronted.

The Community, United

The organizational issues that people choose to confront, from creeping fascism to labor or environmental work, is often set by precedent, what they have seen work before, rather than the uniqueness of a new context. All antifascist work has been labeled "Antifa"

---

133   Ibid.

recently, yet not all projects are centered on the direct action and confrontational, close-knit organization that Antifa and Anti-Racist Action were built on. Getting back to basics is important when considering how an organizing approach can solve a particular problem, thinking about the component parts of radical organizing and how they will achieve distinct ends. Solidarity networks can be considered "organizing stripped down to its bare essentials," the core of community organizing work seen as people with a common interest coming together to put pressure on a target for a desired effect.[134] The strategy that the Seattle Solidarity Network (SeaSol) developed and that has become popular around the country was to confront incidents of wage theft and tenant exploitation, from stolen security deposits to inflated move-out costs. When looking at the experiences of those involved, the larger issues of class conflict were often experienced in very simple and basic ways: the boss stealing a barista's tips, a landlord refusing to return a security deposit, or a missing final paycheck. "If it is just the basic tools of organizing isolated, then they can be ported wherever a united community in pressure can result in changing the circumstances in the neighborhood."[135] This requires a large sphere of support in the surrounding community, people who voluntarily come out to support a particular campaign because they share affinity with the person in turmoil. The hope is that networking and victories expand that periphery, as well as the willingness to take action in that community sphere. This can evolve into meeting direct community needs, such as defending those under racist attack or pushing back at white nationalist projects.

Antifascist organizing can adopt a similar approach when confronting businesses that are collaborating with fascists, from venues that host acts like DiJ or powerlifting gyms that rent space to male tribalists like Jack Donovan. After a base is built in the community, the demand can be made on the business to drop those affiliations, and if they refuse, then community boycotts, protests, and other actions can proceed, including publicizing the business owner's behavior. This serves to educate the community, which is necessary if organizers are going to connect the often-confusing world of countercultural fascism and the Alt Right with white supremacist terrorism.

---

134 Shane Burley, "Solidarity Networks as the Future of Housing Justice," *ROAR Magazine*, February 28, 2016, https://roarmag.org/essays/us-housing-solidarity-networks/.
135 Cold B and T Barnacle, *Solidarity Networks: Examples and Ideas of Direct Action* (Edmonton, Alberta: ThoughtCrimeInk, 2012), 6–17.

As the Alt Right stoked a response from the left with its provocations around the country, antifascist organizations exploded, with many groups composed of organizers new to this type of work. The Chelsea East Boston Antifascist Coalition (CEBAC) popped up directly after Trump was voted in, yet the organizers came from the broad world of social movements rather than explicit antifascism. This is an opportunity to use the lessons of those movements, from LGBT organizing to the battle for reproductive rights, mixing winning strategies with antifascist objectives.[136]

These strategies and new organizations confront fascism by approaching it exactly where the material threat is evident. By not just reinventing the wheel, their approach will be inventive and fluid as the situation changes in the U.S. As organizations develop and grow over time they must maintain an adaptive nature, creating praxis inspired by experienced struggle rather than by picking a model from past successes and endlessly replicating it. Each situation is unique and changing. Skinhead gangs and the KKK could shrink; increasingly abstract New Right and Alt Right players could replace traditional fascist projects in the U.S. Antifascist organizations are adapting to these new realities, but the real shift will be in how they actualize long-term goals that are not just reactive to the appearance of neo-Nazis in a particular social space but proactive in halting nationalist expansion altogether.

Fascism has always fed on weaknesses in the left, the ideological inconsistencies, the internal clashes, and the inability to live up to its own radical promises. The alternative to this is consistency, the ability to build a left opposition that sees through its contradictions and knows how to address the ongoing struggle against racism, sexism, queerphobia, and intersecting forms of oppression. For people to give up privilege they need to see solidarity as the exchange, and the material benefits and promise of that need to be shown clearly. This means focusing on results rather than abstractions, seeking material gains to chart a pathway forward for all oppressed people. Opposition to fascism is, more than anything, a strong intersectional movement that counters the arguments fascism uses to fuel its base, a proposition that requires a change in the culture and priorities of organizations. The absence of a strong understanding of issues of

---

136 Spencer Sunshine, "The Changing Face of Antifascism," *Truthout*, January 18, 2017, http://www.truth-out.org/news/item/39128-the-changing-face-of -antifascism.

race and racism and a politic that answers the discontent exploited by fascists has created this space, and it is up to antifascists to close that up and dig deeper.

According to Political Research Associates, there are some key things to keep in mind if organizers are going to stem the right's influence. The first is to "do your homework," understanding there are complexities on the right that you must differentiate. This also means understanding the variance of opinions on the left, in contrast to how the right wants to address issues like abortion, immigration, or affirmative action. The second point is for organizers to stay calm and collected, focusing primarily on getting documentation, addressing the issues, critiquing the outcomes of far-right policies, and avoiding sloganeering, insults, and ideological banter. The final point, which may be the most central, is that organizing, now and permanently, is the answer for those who want to confront fascism. Keep supporters—the circle around an organization that gives weight to the work of the key organizers—informed about what is happening with the far-right. Success in this organizing means expanding the circle beyond organizers, including the clergy, community leaders, and others that contribute to a united front. Patience may be the most pertinent and difficult aspect of this work, since it takes time to reach critical mass—especially when the right finds an advocate in the country's highest political office.[137]

Think It Over

Movements for equality and liberation must do a better job clarifying their key strategic concerns and their motivating politics. Entryism, or simply the adaptation of far-right politics into social movements pushing the boundaries of the radical left, is a dynamic vessel for fascist growth and comes largely from the uncritical application of problematic ideas. Political objectives must be consistent, and organizations need internal reflection. We must pick our allies carefully, understand why we maintain those relationships, and question whether our aims could be co-opted by constituents that would do our cause harm. Political projects need to be seen in a larger ideological context and give proper scrutiny to new ideas as they

---

137 "Ground Rules and Tips For Challenging the Right," Political Research Associates, November 8, 2016, http://www.politicalresearch.org/2016/11/08/ground-rules-and-tips-for-challenging-the-right/#sthash.

are integrated, considering where they come from before embedding them into the patchwork of "critical analysis." This does not mean compromising openness to new ways of thinking, quite the opposite, but it demands we trace ideas back to their origin and see how they connect with our larger vision. If you are confronting the stifling loneliness of mass production in the consumer assembly line, alienated from your labor and feeling the effects of wage inequality, do you critique capitalism and its maintenance of hierarchy, or does your language and talking points originate from a desire to return to a mythic premodern form of life? Often times, in an attempt to venerate the indigenous and find enemies in the current crisis, we find allies in the nightmares of the past, whether real or fetishized. Instead, we must engage in an ongoing project of challenging the "creeping fascism" as it makes its way into left spaces, especially when unassuming people carry it in, unaware of its roots.

Implicitly problematic behaviors need to be decoded and challenged. Many new skinhead and National Anarchist groups actually draw on racial nationalists from other parts of the world, including Japan and Latin America, in a false multiracial "brotherhood," sharing a vision of ethnic separatism on which they find common cause. Inside of Palestinian solidarity circles, many activists have spouted conspiracy-laden anti-Semitic venom, all the while engaging in the hard work of ending Israeli apartheid. Inside of the moody world of neofolk, identitarianism, and Third Positionist politics, queer people (usually gay men who are male tribalists) are sometimes welcome.

The issue remains the politics and not the identity of the individual espousing them. Pushing Third Positionist synthesis ideas—whether from people of color, queer people, gender nonconforming people, or Neo-Nazis—is never acceptable. The same is true of people of color who have sided with nationalist movements that push racial separatism, artists who uncritically appropriate fascist tropes, and conspiracy theorists reviving images that vilify Jews. Having consistent ideas that minimize contradiction about what is acceptable and what is not can protect these spaces and projects against even the most well-disguised Trojan Horse. Clear positions on multiracial inclusion, anti-Semitism, immigration, and gender identity can help to set the standards for what is acceptable, even if those standards remain broad enough to include a diversity of opinion.[138]

---

138   Spencer Sunshine, "Drawing Lines Against Racism and Fascism," Political Research Associates, March 5, 2015, http://www.politicalresearch.org/2015/03/05/

It also means practicing open dialogue, and not using labels like "fascism" carelessly.

The left is further challenged by how to account for the levels of anti-Semitism that have become commonplace in certain areas of discourse. The desire to liberate can include an impulse to dominate and repress, an effect of authoritarian conditioning. The willingness to capitulate to bigotry in the name of liberation is the defining quality of fascism's slow leftist entry, and traditional anti-Semitic attitudes have made this so. The inability to completely deal with conspiracy theorists on the left, Israeli nationalists' manipulation of very real anti-Semitism, and the populist caricatures used when discussing the violence of international capitalism, has widened the break between growing anti-Semitism and the left's commitment to antiracism. These political issues must be unpacked to see their component parts, how they play on bigotries, and exactly how attitudes toward Jews remain largely unchanged, even while the concept of anti-Semitism is rejected. The glue that binds anti-Semitism and allows it to fester is our unwillingness to look at the behaviors critically, our unwillingness to stand against its proliferation.

For international solidarity movements, it means adding a critical lens to revolutionary leadership that strays heavily from the politics that inspires radicals to support liberation movements in the first place. The Three-Way Fight analysis—that in a conflict there is often the working class, the bourgeois class, and a reactionary revolutionary movement that represents the interests of neither—offers a framework for this. This provides an additional bulwark against the tendencies of movements to side with ethnic nationalist or authoritarian leaders in anti-imperialist organizing, allowing organizers to create a more complex picture of political situations that then allow the liberation of oppressed people to be separated from manipulative nationalist leadership. This is the clarification of politics rather than the abandoning of movements.

This analysis also helps address reactionary politics that do not have a direct connection to far-right movements, such as Trans Exclusionary Radical Feminism or Deep Green Resistance (DGR). DGR saw fast growth in the early 2000s, building locals across the country to confront the environmental crisis by proposing radical direct action as the solution. Including a mix of Deep Ecology, radical feminism, and primitivism, Lierre Keith pushed the notion that

drawing-lines-against-racism-and-fascism/#sthash.

transwomen were simply men accessing women's spaces and power.[139] It was DGR's treatment of trans and gender-nonconforming people that halted their growth, providing reason to throw them out of spaces like Portland's Law & Disorder Conference. These controversies, as well as the fatalistic and elitist beliefs in their political program, ended their wing of the radical ecology movement, broke their connection with Earth First!, and helped push the ecological movement further in the direction of egalitarianism by virtue of a failed example of reactionary synthesis.

Entryism is a serious concern, especially as its signifiers are not typically understood. This requires that movements committed to anti-oppression politics see their ideas through to their logical conclusions, as well as providing boundaries on alliance.

---

139   Crescenzo Scipione, "Hateful Sophistry: The Misguided Transphobia of Deep Green Resistance - Black Rose Anarchist Federation," Black Rose Anarchist Federation, May 29, 2013, http://www.blackrosefed.org/locations/portland/.

The Heart of Resistance

Gramscians of the Left

Fascists claim that the left has won the battle over meta-politics, and they are correct. New Left organizers in the 1960s, despite their flaws, set the tone for the values, ideas, and underlying passions that have fueled broad sections of America's conscience ever since. Though the Reagan administration and the Moral Majority began to take a swing at the culture starting in the early 1980s, left-influenced social ideas are the standard for young people and considered intelligent, artistic, and freethinking, even if they do not always translate to practical politics downstream.

It is this cultural hegemony that the far-right has begun to target and these meta-politics that they want to reshape, creating a cultural base on which to build a political superstructure. By focusing on cultural ideas instead of political ones, it is easier to claim "apolitical" status, which allows them to influence the cultural attitudes that turn into politics down the line.

An organized antifascist mass movement must take meta-politics seriously, looking to undermine the Alt Right's narratives on identity, science, and art. While this has begun in social media culture through the undermining of their memes and talking points, there needs to be an ongoing process of celebrating and expanding multicultural society, equality, and freedom. In the world of radical politics, these foundational ideas are too often discussed with apprehension, as though they are too obvious or passé. These aspirations must be reinforced and made relevant, returning them to aesthetics and cultural spaces. It requires internal consistency, clarity of the left's values, and a revolutionary vision. Through its capitulation, the creation of institutional "left" forces that are always moderated and invited into systems of existing power, the left has lost its ability to challenge the "status quo" and prevent a truly alternative vision to the misery of neoliberalism. The right gains ground when the left cannot prove its purpose, and a culture of left ideas that are clear, effective, and prophetic sets the meta-political framework that robs that right of its only claim.

One facet of changing the culture is to "increase the social cost of oppressive behavior to the point that those who promote it see no option but to hide."[1] Trump's ascension has given a pass to more casual forms of bigotry and violence that social standards had previously held tenuously in check. Fascism, both institutional and as an insurgent movement, requires passive support by the populace, an approval through actions rather than words. The ideas of "no platform" used in antifascist organizing must be applied throughout the culture. This concept, which Mark Bray labels "everyday antifascism," takes the tactics of antifascist organizing and expands it to interactions that have often been deemed non-political,

> An antifascist outlook applies this logic to any kind of interaction with fascists. It refuses to accept the dangerous notion that homophobia is just someone's "opinion" to which they are entitled. It refuses to accept opposition to the basic proposal that "Black Lives Matter" is a simple political disagreement. An antifascist outlook has no tolerance for "intolerance." It will not "agree to disagree."… If the goal of normal antifascist politics is to make it so that Nazis cannot appear uncontested in public, then the goal of everyday antifascism is to increase the social cost of oppressive behavior to such a point that those who promote it see no option but for their views to recede into hiding.[2]

The antifascist project must be centered in communities determining social standards themselves and creating a culture that disallows the viciousness of bigotry.

---

1   Mark Bray, "Trump and Everyday Antifascism Beyond Punching Nazis," *ROAR Magazine*, January 23, 2017, https://roarmag.org/essays/trump-everyday-antifascism/.
2   Ibid.

Just as with the development of an effective left, if this movement it going to be centered in the community then there needs to be cohesion. Fascism builds from a sense of alienation, so we need "high trust" communities where people can count on one another. Not just as an act of insulation, but to build effective resistance on the basis of trust, understanding, and kindness. The movement itself will then feed on the lived experiences of those inside the community, on the actual needs that the public has rather than those politically imposed by a radical class externally. Where this organizing will be most influential is the critical point of rupture, since "fascism is most effectively fought in the areas of its influence." Sometimes these are in "contested spaces," and other times they are simply inside the community's dominant institutions: the church, the union hall, the locker room.[3]

Blurred Lines

People often blur the lines between different approaches to the problem of fascism. Many draw a distinction between "militant" and "liberal" approaches to fascism, with militants being those that meet neo-Nazis in the community and liberals the ones that do more traditional "activist" work. This is a false distinction that is built largely on a subtext of moral indignation rather than strategic judgment. Saying that one is willing to directly engage with white nationalists is, by and large, a statement about their commitment to challenging the threat posed by fascism, but it doesn't answer whether direct conflict is always the correct strategic choice. The flip side to this is to assume that those labeled as "liberal," meaning those dedicated to building a mass movement, are less committed and unwilling to make sacrifices in order to pose a significant threat to the forces of white supremacy. Instead of making this determination before the critical moment, organizations should find a bridge between these views and to look at what advantages large masses of supporters give to a movement.

A paradox is often created with small groups that are based on close affinity and a commitment to violent intervention. To be successful, these organizations must have a tight security culture and membership restrictions, ensuring member commitment to the project. This closed nature can limit the ability to grow beyond

---

3   "The Antifascist Militia," *Antifa Forum* (2017), 20.

the confines of those already doing the work. That is fine since the approach relies on people with a certain level of training and commitment, something that cannot be easily extended to hundreds or thousands, where varying participation levels threaten the tight-knit culture. Therefore, groups with a closed format require coalition partners when participating in protest actions that are not simply situations for direct conflict. The actual tactics and strategy should be dictated by the situation, reading the community environment, seeing what organizational options and partners are available, and at what level the willingness for confrontation may be compromised when dozens turn into thousands. Today many organizations using the Antifa label do this seamlessly, yet the militant tradition still creates some divisions.

After Jeremy Christian took the life of two Portland, Oregon, residents on May 26, 2017, the organizers of the "Free Speech" rallies he participated in, which operated as a cover for the Alt Right, pushed ahead with a downtown rally sheltered in a federal park. Rose City Antifa and the Pacific Northwest Antifascist Workers Collective collaboratively put together a counter-action for June 4, 2017, drawing thousands from across the radical and left spectrum, who amassed in the park across the street. Knowing who would likely be in attendance, they sent out lists of known neo-Nazis and fascist organizers, doxxing them before they were able to stroll with the impunity offered by the "Guardians" security. The International Socialist Organization organized a more tepid rally to the north of the park at City Hall, splitting the crowd but still drawing almost a thousand people from local progressive groups. The south side saw a labor block of largely building-trade unionists, making the connection between workplace struggle and the historic legacy of fascism as enemies of worker self-activity. While the socialist party created their own action for fear of being associated with "Antifa," the history of militancy proved less of a problem since the vast majority of the crowd joined the more militant wing of the protest. The three actions dwarfed the "Free Speech" rally that had drawn Alt Light celebrities like Kyle "Based Stickman" Chapman and recent Alt Right converts like Baked Alaska. Though the police did attack the antifascist crowd with "riot control" projectiles, the far-right assortment was outnumbered so dramatically that it was a clear victory for the left. While it took several types of messaging to get the numbers up, the result was mass opposition, and could have been even larger if a greater degree of trust was put in those organizations that had been fighting the threat of insurrectionary white supremacy for years.[4]

The distinction for radical antifascist action can then be made between advocates of community solutions and proponents of state ones instead of between traditional community organizing and direct engagement. Hate speech and hate crime laws have been put in place across Europe as a solution to nationalist upswings that bring regular violence against marginalized communities. These laws are interpreted through a liberal parliamentary state system, which reflects the inherent class and hierarchical dynamics of the society, and therefore do not act as a neutral protector of "human rights." At any point and time, the infrastructure of hate speech laws can be turned against the left or other factions, especially if those movements present a real challenge to state hegemony. Likewise, hate crime laws are disproportionately used against those on the lowest end of the social ladder, as is true of most tools of law enforcement. For a radical left antifascist movement, the community must be able to deal with the violence of white supremacy without relying solely on the arbiters of the state. Such reliance is at odds with the long-term vision of a truly equal society.

No Platform

The battle over space has dominated recent media coverage of the struggle between formal antifascist organizations and nationalists. This clash, like all of the hundred years of antifascist struggle, is not new, but dates back to communist organizers entering Chicago German-American Bund meetings and disrupting the podium before speakers could start riling the crowd up. The goal is not to debate the fascists but to shut down their capacity to organize.

This often bewilders liberals as it violates the conception that the "solution to hate speech is more speech." The issue of fascist speech is less one of ideas; it's secondary to the problem of fascist organizing. Public speeches are, by their nature, attempts at recruitment for the perpetuation of ideas and organizations. The successful event, whether in a formal meeting hall, a musical performance, or a rant on a street corner, is the opportunity to take these ideas and transmit them, reproducing participation and expanding the mission. Remembering that violence is a key tenet of fascism, it follows

---

4   Dan Vincent, interview with the author, June 5, 2016.

that the ability of their movement to grow correlates to their capacity for violence. The use of "no platform," the refusal to grant access to public space, is an issue of organizing, not speech.

Free speech is instead a conflict over state intervention. Free speech as a political concept was birthed in response to state institutions that threatened violence because of some form of speech, whether in traditional Western nations or in authoritarian "left" regimes. Free speech, and the leftist defense of it, is a response to the state's imposition on speech, not the practical ability of speech to be upheld in any and all situations. While there are hate speech laws in effect in many European nations—which can and do imprison people for things like public Holocaust Denial—this is generally not the line that most antiracist organizations use as praxis. The antifascist approach to speech is through direct democracy; the community revolt not against words but against the promise of action. If fascist public speech is organizing, then the refusal of the platform is the community responding in kind. Free speech is not an abstract right guaranteed by the state, but instead a belief that people should be free of state strictures—not that they should be without community accountability. As Anti-Racist Action founder and Industrial Workers of the World member Kieran Knutson points out, "we are not opposing the free speech of fascists...what we are opposing is the organizing of fascists."[5]

Direct confrontation remains an important component for organizations that push a "no platform" strategy. The Antifa project directly matches fascists in the streets, to shut down events, to interrupt marches, and to push them out of bars and social spaces. Sometimes Antifa's confrontational approach wins without any confrontation. In March 2013, white nationalists in Oregon were planning for a "White Man's March" to mobilize supporters from the downtown Portland Waterfront Park, a social center adjacent to a string of trendy bars and commercial locations. Rose City Antifa organized over three hundred supporters to overwhelm the event, holding a concert and public march. In December 2015, they again mobilized a massive contingent to meet the Hammerskin Nation's public event in honor of deceased member of The Order, Bob Matthews. In both cases, the white nationalists failed to show up to their own event, opting for private gatherings.

---

5   Kieran Knutson, "Militant Tactics in Antifascist Organizing – Interview Transcript," Three Way Fight, April 26, 2017, http://threewayfight.blogspot.com /2017/04/militant-tactics-in-antifascist.html.

Thinking Internationally[6]

Fascism developed as a unique political movement in industrializing Europe, and antifascism developed along with it. These resistance movements evolved globally adapting to local conditions. Since that struggle is across national borders, connecting those movements is not just a show of strength, but a necessity if antifascists are going to defeat the populist upsurge.

Antifa International was a media collective focused on sharing news and information from antifascist projects around the world. Seeing the increased need to support organizers facing state repression, they created an ongoing fundraising campaign that would distribute money to activists facing criminal proceedings or in medical need after fascist attacks. Starting in 2015, the International Antifascist Defence Fund began using a "Decisions Crew" that fields requests and comes to consensus on how the funds should be distributed.[7] The Decisions Crew has about four hundred members from organizations across seventeen countries, all of which are donors. "We believe that antifascism does not recognize borders and in times like these international solidarity with other antifascists is one of our best weapons," says one of the prime organizers of the fund. "Being able to demonstrate genuine solidarity with antifascists and antiracists around the globe is one of the most effective ways we know of to further antifascism."[8]

Destroying the Narrative

As Identitarian and Traditionalist movements create their own meta-politics, undermining these narratives harms fascist political aspirations. This may seem obvious, but Traditionalist ideas both feed on left-wing tropes and attempt to provide answers for the discontent felt in modern consumer capitalism. It requires us to present clear left counter-narratives that critique capitalism and its alienation from a multiracial perspective and presents the universal "quest for identity" as one decoupled from exclusionary tribalism. The romanticism for

---

6   This book focuses almost entirely on the U.S. This decision comes only from the need to shrink the subject down to a manageable size and to provide extended focus into the uniqueness that fascism has in the U.S. This should not be taken as a statement of importance, but instead that fascism's context in other countries requires its own unique perspective.

7   The fund can be found at https://intlantifadefence.wordpress.com.

8   Walter Tull of The International Antifascist Defence Fund, interview with the author, July 4, 2017.

pre-Christian folkways, which is heavily exploited by neo-fascists, often comes from the desire for indigenous religions and customs seen as an alternative to the destructive machine of industrial capitalism. This impulse must be shifted to a focus on the egalitarian, democratic, and liberatory elements of indigenous cultures as an alternative to the far-right's focus on "traditional" hierarchical social ordering. The far-right does not own the right to reclaim ancestral religions or organic communities, thus it requires an active reframing by the left so they are not the only purveyor of ancestral memory.

Counter narratives are effective in undoing problematic leftist dialogues that allow fascists to gain entry. Cultural appropriation, a concept discussed on the left, critiques the colonial attitudes by which white people use the cultural and religious items of a non-white culture in profane ways. During periods like the Great Awakening or the "hippie" revival of the 1960s, the turn toward Eastern and indigenous spirituality created a mind-set of entitlement that picked from sacred items acquired through colonialism, such as elements of Hindu spiritual practice, refusing the reverence they were owed.

While this is a valid critique, when it is broadened beyond these confines it can create an essentializing narrative about race and culture. If all items that are specific to the culture of one ethnic group are only accessible by that ethnic group, then it creates a strong ethnic divide. Identitarians utilize this narrative: that culture is the property of ethnicity because it is bound to a people in *essential* ways. Instead, the left wants to see cultural exchange and spiritual movements that are considerate and adaptable, even if we abhor the innapropriate use of sacred cultural artifacts and traditions. The reality of cultural appropriation, from the naming of sports mascots to the now-iconic image of white Millennials dancing with headdresses on at music festivals, is obscured by the blanket assumption that all cultural exchange is appropriation, which instead solidifies borders between cultures.

Consistency is crucial, and racial nationalism should be resisted in all its forms, whether from the left or the right. Ethnic nationalism has a long history in the battle to undo colonialism and support national liberation struggles. Non-white ethnic nationalism, especially movements like Black Nationalism and Chicano Nationalism in the U.S., are fundamentally different than the racial nationalism proposed by the right. At the same time, they present limitations and maintain a narrative around racial exclusivity and often rely on racial essentialism, palingenic mythologies, and reactionary social policies. Oppressed people have the right to self-determination, and having open conversations against racial nationalism as an endgame and about the importance of multiracial organizing is crucial. Antifascist movements fighting for consistency need to reclaim cosmopolitanism as a concept, one that sees ethnically exclusive societies as antithetical to liberated ones.

Gender is also a critical concept in the greater meta-politics. Second Wave Radical Feminism has provided unintentional avenues of contact for the Identitarian right, which sees stark divides between genders and looks toward figures like Simone de Beauvoir as a sort of gender identitarian.[9] While Trans-Exclusionary Radical Feminism is largely rejected on the left, expanding the critique of gender roles and binaries further develops a framework for undoing gender essentialism. The far-right attempts to appeal to men by triggering nostalgia for a period of unchecked patriarchal power. They attempt to draw women by presenting a "traditional" vision of domesticity as the alternative to the alienating world of contemporary work, reifying their vision of gender roles. The left can counter this by looking at the real elements the right draws on, like the discontent with modern life under consumer capitalism.

Unseating the appeal of these trends is critical, accepting the parts of their critique that are useful and developing a more complete analysis that does not cede ground to those offering reactionary avenues for critique. The crisis of male violence can be confronted without resorting to blaming sex-workers and marginalizing trans people, and the issues of imperialism and ongoing colonialism should be given a revolutionary edge by a truly egalitarian, anti-capitalist vision that sees the necessity of multiracial community. This cannot be a side note, a rearguard defense, but instead must be embedded deeply in the way that ideas are developed so that motivations like alienation and displaced identity are never ignored during the creation of coalitions and practical political tools, therefore ceding them to the right.

Normalization

Various types of organizations, from the member-heavy non-profits to the decentralized movements that confront skinhead

---

9   Alain de Benoist, interviewed by Bryan Sylvain, "Interview with Alain de Benoist," translated by Greg Johnson, *North American New Right*, Volume One (2012): 92.

gangs terrorizing local music venues, are seeing their numbers sky-rocket. A new sense of urgency has ignited a left afraid fascism will be normalized. This has already begun as many campaigns meant to target fascist entryism have had diminishing returns because fascist ideas are now mainstream. In May 2016, several skinhead bands were set to play the annual Oi!Fest concert, which brings together gangs and subcultural nationalists even across some racial lines. Bands like OxBlood have a multiracial line-up, but, as their lyrics and associations reveal, they are hardline on racial nationalism no matter what the ethnicity is, and reserve particular venom for Muslim immigration. Organizers were not surprised to find that an Islamophobic band was playing down the street when Islamophobia was being spewed at well-funded rallies performed by the GOP nominee for president. The concert eventually had to hop between venues until it finally had a booking at the now defunct Santos Party House in Brooklyn. At the concert, photos were taken of neo-Nazi patches and stickers and crowd members Seig Heiling (or "waving to Kyle").[10]

Open Islamophobia has proved a popular recruiting tool internationally with groups like the European Defence League and PEGIDA, which are fronts for explicitly fascist movements who see combating the "Islamization of the West" as a top priority, since these groups use the popular appeal of Islamophobia to normalize xenophobia. In America, Islamophobia is so rampant in mainstream conservatism it seems like white nationalist talking points have become mainstream. To counter that, many organizations are doubling down on the vision they want to see, understanding the ways that various forms of oppression intersect and reinforce each other, and that can accurately explain the fascist roots of politics that are as common as tax breaks and Bible quotes. Existing projects, in many cases, must pivot and reconsider how their organizing structure can be reconfigured for a new racist context.

With Their Violence

The violence of the right is a defining quality, not just ideologically, but in their historical behavior. Even in moments of self-defense the

---

10 "Black Bear Apologizes For Oi!Fest, Santos Party House Closes Down," *Antifascist News*, May 31, 2016, https://antifascistnews.net/2016/05/31/black-bear-apologizes-for-oifest-santos-party-house-closes-down/.

left is absent the systemic brutality that defines the far-right. It is just one degree of separation from the most button-down fascist ideologues to the haunting ultra-violent media spectacles created by white supremacist murders, like the Oklahoma City bombing in 1995. While people like Jared Taylor say that they abhor violence, they then speak, without a shred of irony, about "peaceful ethnic cleansing."[11] Their work has influenced Alt Right murderers and created cover for members of some of the most violent racialist groups in the country. The violence of the Alt Right has continued to escalate, influencing disaffected adherents of the right and giving permission to unleash racially motivated rage. This led directly to a string of Alt Right murders in 2017, including the stabbing of a black homeless man by James Harris Jackson, the killing of Bowie State University student Richard Collins III by Alt Right enthusiast Sean Urbanski, and the Islamophobic attack by Jeremy Christian on a Portland train that left two dead and one in the hospital. As the public "free speech" events led to coordinated violence, and the race riot and eventual murder that took place at the Charlottesville "Unite the Right" rally, the Alt Right's strategic language of nonviolence has been revealed as a smokescreen. As the mass shutdown of Alt Right social media took place after the violence, AltRight.com went open in their support of Lone Wolf violent terrorism. "The Alt-Right is finished debating, negotiating, surrendering," wrote white nationalist Vincent Law. "We're ready to close ranks and fight for what is ours. Post-Charlottesville our fleet lies at the bottom of a deep and troubled sea and we can only march on forward like Cortez once did."[12] A "soft target" approach has become evident as groups like Identity Evropa began disrupting left events in Florida, the neo-Nazi Rise Above Movement tried to break up antiracist events in Santa Monica, and Vanguard America members publicly harass protesters. This happens at the same time as synagogues and black businesses are vandalized, meaning that both aboveground and clandestine attacks are on the rise.[13]

As the Alt Right's violence is made evident, the opposition has to destroy their façade and reveal their viciousness. Organizations

11   Daniel Lombroso and Yoni Applebaum, "'Hail Trump!': White Nationalists Salute the President Elect," *The Atlantic*, November 21, 2017, https://www.theatlantic.com/politics/archive/2016/11/richard-spencer-speech-npi/508379/.

12   Vincent Law, "The Alt-Right is Finished Debating," AltRight.com, August 22, 2017, https://altright.com/2017/08/22/the-alt-right-is-finished-debating/.

13   "Spencer's Website Endorses 'Leaderless Resistance' of KKK," *It's Going Down*, September 1, 2017, https://itsgoingdown.org/richard-spencers-website-calls-leaderless-resistance-kkk/.

like the National Policy Institute exist only as a vessel for cleaning up the image of white nationalism, which has been rightly tarnished with the violence of the 1980s and 1990s. When proof of their violence is blasted onto headlines, we can't let it be forgotten. The violence of both the past and the present should be made obvious, and their moments of cruelty should constantly be thrown back in their face to inform the community and turn public opinion against them. A lesson can be taken from the battle against Golden Dawn in Greece, where their murders of leftist opponents were legendary, but the killing of antifascist rapper Pavlos Fyssas turned the social mood:

> The only positive thing to have emerged from this outrageous situation is the fact that Golden Dawn was almost completely delegitimized in the eyes of the Greek people. This delegitimation was itself mostly a result of the rapid response of the Antifa movement in the wake of the assassination, not of the snail-paced trial or the government's opportunistic response.[14]

After the murder, Golden Dawn's support dropped to less than 7 percent in the 2015 election, down from the 15–18 percent they polled in 2013. Forty percent of its offices have been shut down, the readership of its paper *Embros* is now below a thousand, and Golden Dawn leader Nikolaos Michaloliakos is the least popular politician in Greece. Their own behavior turned the tide, but only because the militant antifascist movement, bolstered by years of movement, made it so.[15]

Contested Spaces

The fascist neofolk, black metal, and post-industrial music scene has seen a stream of controversial confrontations and venue cancelations. DiJ, as the highest profile of this scene, has had events shut down so regularly that they often put up venue information just hours before the show begins. In Portland, Rose City Antifa organized confrontations and protests at venues hosting DiJ, leading to flurried engagements between antiracists and concert attendants.

---

14   Leonidas Oikonomakis, "The Night that Changed Everything," *ROAR Magazine*, #5 (Spring 2017): 68.
15   Ibid.

Venues have gone as far as to ban Nazi imagery from concert attendees, yet Nazi skinheads and well-known racist organizers are seen in attendance, and nationalist ideas are generally accepted.[16] After the string of protests, DiJ did not return to Portland, and Rose City Antifa's strategy has been replicated as cities and venues become "no go zones" for the band.

Bands like Blood and Sun have been exposed by NYC Antifa and other antifascist groups that have gotten venues to pull their contracts, a strategy that has also been used against tours planned by Heathen Harvest and an array of fascist-leaning musicians. Events like Stella Natura, a California-based music festival organized by the folkish Asatru Folk Assembly and its founder Stephan McNallen, hosted many of these bands, which treated it like a summer music festival rather than a white nationalist meetup.[17] Bands including Changes and Upward Path have even provided music for the white nationalist NPI conference, performing at the same event where conference goers were recorded rising up with "Seig Heil" salutes to chants of "Hail Trump, hail our people, hail victory!"[18]

While many of these bands are up front about their beliefs, many are less ideological. Current 93, for example, seems to have no racialist content to their music, yet they to do extensive collaborations with bands like DiJ (as well as doing collaborations with members of the anarcho-punk band Crass). These groups need to be confronted and expectations of them made clear: they must put up barriers against the neo-Nazi wing of the scene. This can be where internal agitation from the music culture itself is key, and a rift can form that further alienates the problematic elements.

These cultural spaces should be considered the same as the explicitly political ones, as they fuel the cultural evolution that is essential for the identitarian tribalist movement. The Alt Right's attempts at developing an arts-centric meta-politics is how they take a foothold in the social dialogue, which is why the principle of "no platform," where communities refuse to let neo-fascists have

---

16   "Neofolk Or Neovolk? One's Personal Take on the Death in June Concert in Baltimore, MD," One People's Project, September 25, 2013, http://www.onepeoplesproject.com/index.php/en/archive/86-archive/1257-neofolk-or-neovolk-ones-personal-take-on-the-death-in-june-concert-in-baltimore-md.

17   "Neofascist: Heathen Harvest, Neofolk, and Fascist Subcultural Entryism," *Antifascist News*, February 13, 2016, https://antifascistnews.net/2016/02/13/neofascist-heathen-harvest-neofolk-and-fascist-subcultural-entryism/.

18   "About," NPI Events. n.d, http://npievents.com/.

an opportunity to publicly speak or perform, has been extended to jackbooted punk musicians and ironic Brown-Shirted hipsters just as it has to KKK recruitment.

Swaying Popular Institutions

There's no denying that religious institutions, both organized and decentralized, are hugely influential in the U.S. Leftists often reject them out of hand because of the (largely) reactionary role they play, from evangelicals to the Catholic Church. To dismiss them, while focusing on other working-class institutions, is to misunderstand a critical component of American life: while there are 1.4 million workers in labor unions, there are a 120 million who attend church. Revolutions often rise and fall in relationship to the churches, and so avenues to shift the dynamic and confront the churches' role in accepting oppressive state power can have results.[19]

While the church's status as the defining arbiter of morality has declined, spiritual institutions still dramatically sway perspective and determine the non-economic ways that people interact with their community. Churches define "justice," the "common good," and how "outsiders" are understood. The GOP built its success on church power, defining itself in the '50s and using evangelical coalitions beginning in the '80s, and the left largely abandoned them as it found solace in urban liberalism. These are platforms of potential resistance, organizations with the largest working-class constituency and public moral declarations in our favor. From their earliest conceptions, churches have been centers of struggle, which is why governments and institutions of coercion capture them to extend the reach of those mechanisms of moral control deep into the psyche of the populace. To avoid them, to ignore their potential, is to cede powerful ground to the right when they provide potent opportunities.

The Southern Baptist Convention, which confederates hundreds of white congregations with historically black ones, made headlines when it hosted its 2017 convergence in Phoenix. A well-known black preacher in Texas, Dwight McKissic, proposed formal repudiation of the toxic white supremacy of the Alt Right. The proposal explicitly denounced the "totalitarian impulses, xenophobic

---

19   Nathan Schneider, "No Revolution Without Religion," in *We Are Many*, edited by Kate Khatib, Margaret Killjoy, and Mike McGuire (Oakland: AK Press, 2012), 256–58.

biases, and bigoted ideologies that infect the minds and actions of its violent disciples."[20] Acknowledging the role the church has in racial stratification, the "curse of Ham" doctrine that many Christians used to suggest that dark skin was a curse bestowed on lower peoples, he argued the church needed to act as a bulwark against these "retrograde ideologies." Some congregations found this divisive, and the resolutions committee refused to hear the proposal.[21] In the 2016 presidential election, when the GOP candidate was known for what could be mildly termed "un-Christian" behavior, white evangelicals voted for him at a higher margin than they did George W. Bush, one of their own. While Bush offered them moral absolution, Trump offered them power, and they voted with white interests as the key, not Christianity.[22]

The public backlash shifted things quickly and the five thousand delegates at the convention voted in favor of the resolution, calling the Alt Right "Satanic." With the convention representing 15 million people, one of the largest religious contingents in the country, this resolution creates a huge barrier to far-right entry into the heartland.[23] James Edwards, who hosts the *Political Cesspool* radio show and is involved in white nationalist projects from the Council of Conservative Citizens to the American Freedom Party, is a vocal Southern Baptist. He declared that the forces of "Soros" ensured this type of "pathological altruism,"[24] and said it proves that "just as all of our institutions have been perverted and subverted, so has the church."[25]

The need to influence the church is pragmatic, not a declaration of the church's progressive nature—and we need not convert to their faith to do mass movement work with them. By influencing its decision making, as well as institutions like the Catholic Church, the

---

20 Jacey Fortin, "In Quick Reversal, Southern Baptists Denounce White Nationalists," *New York Times*, June 15, 2017, https://www.nytimes.com/2017/06/15/us/southern-baptist-convention-alt-right-resolution.html.

21 Ibid.

22 Reza Aslan, "The End of Values Voters," Slate's Trumpcast, *Slate*, April 28, 2017, http://www.slate.com/articles/podcasts/trumpcast/2017/05/white_evangelicals_and_donald_trump_on_trumpcast.html.

23 Jacey Fortin, "In Quick Reversal, Southern Baptists Denounce White Nationalism."

24 The idea of "pathological altruism" was created by Kevin MacDonald to describe the pseudoscientific belief that white people have an innate kindness that allows them to be taken advantage of by other groups.

25 James Edwards, "The Satanic Verses," AltRight.com, June 23, 2017, https://altright.com/2017/06/23/the-satanic-verses/.

moral standard used by many communities can be shifted toward antiracism. It is also strategic for people of faith, who can take up the responsibility of inter-community organizing to shift the culture of these spiritual institutions. Religion is a hugely influential factor in people's lives so antifascists need to link up, organizing with members of those congregations to develop mass resistance to fascism. For those affected by the outcome of the convention, a decree from the pulpit denouncing the Alt Right as an enemy and limiting its influence creates an argument for ongoing work against white supremacy. The churches provide numbers, money, and real estate, the institutional support that projects need to grow, as well as a structure based on community relationships.

Black Resistance

Community self-defense has been essential in black communities facing generational terror both from the state and its insurrectionary street soldiers. Subcultural antifascist projects associated with music scenes have often been monoracial, stemming from the argument for whites to "police their community." While there is logic to this, it can make movements insular, lacking the long-term political vision that multiracial organizations possess.[26] The history of American antifascism is actually multiracial, with communities of color often taking a vanguard role in creating strategy from lived experience and broadening what antifascism means. As Mike Bento, organizer with NYC Shut It Down, said, "From the anti-lynching campaigns in the early part of the last century up through the Civil Rights Movement and to the Black Panthers: These are all antifascist movements."[27] With the growth of Black Lives Matter, movements led by people of color on their own terms have changed the way that issues like police brutality are discussed, but those issues overlap so completely with the ongoing legacy of organized white supremacy that it would be negligent to see those projects as outside antifascism.

---

26   To suggest that ARA, Antifa, AFA, and other militant antifascist organizations were only white, is far from the truth. This is only to cite those movements that were largely monoracial, with white antifascists confronting white violence in white areas.

27   Mike Bento quoted in Ashoka Jegroo, "Fighting Cops And The Klan: The History And Future Of Black Antifascism," *Truthout*, February 21, 2017, http://www.truth-out.org/news/item/39539-fighting-cops-and-the-klan-the-history-and-future-of-black-antifascism.

Even in the earliest resistance to fascism, black-specific organizations provided leadership in a movement where they rarely were recognized for their instrumental role. The white supremacy employed to suppress white workers' opposition to slavery built the foundation for fascism in the U.S. The "facts" of racial inequality propositioned to white workers were disseminated consciously by a ruling class set on slave labor for the building of the trans-Atlantic agricultural and manufacturing economy, and the suppressed wages for the white working class would never have been accepted if they were not offered something in exchange. That was an emotional appeal, the feeling that if they could not have warm food on the table and a sturdy roof over their head, at least they were not those biologically inferior non-whites.

In the years of the Spanish Revolution, between 1936 and 1939, the vast majority of cultural figures in places like Harlem were members of the Communist Party. The party's focus on building a Popular Front against fascism relied on connecting black radicals with liberals, and on an internationalist vision that sought to move beyond just confronting racism in urban areas and the South.[28] As fascist Italy tightened its iron grip on Ethiopia in 1935, black communists in Chicago organized a rally of ten thousand people in solidarity—in direct violation of the protest ban enacted by then-mayor Edward J. Kelly. This drew on the years of support that the black community had given to Ethiopia as it was facing colonial expansion, and organizers like W.E.B. Du Bois linked U.S. racism with the treatment of Ethiopia in his speech to the Harlem League Against War and Fascism. During an era of mass persecution, there were still ninety African American volunteers in the Abraham Lincoln Brigades, the volunteer force that fought Franco in Spain.[29]

In the U.S., the KKK was a paramilitary formation spreading violent terror across the country. For some organizers in the Southern civil rights movement, armed community defense was a necessary component of defying the volcano of extrajudicial killings erupting from the psyche of a white working class maintaining Jim Crow. When Robert Williams, a black military veteran, took over the Monroe, North Carolina, chapter of the NAACP, he took the almost

---

28   Mark Naison, *Communists in Harlem During the Depression* (Urbana, Illinois, University of Illinois Press, 1983), 193–94.
29   William Loren Katz, "The Forgotten Fight Against Fascism," *The Huffington Post*, June 11, 2014, http://www.huffingtonpost.com/the-zinn-education-project /the-forgotten-fight-again_b_5483988.html.

defunct organization in a direction that was relevant to a community under the very real threat of violence. Chartering with the National Rifle Association, they formed the "Black Guard" to place militant defenders against the Klan in black neighborhoods and utilized Williams's military experience to give weapons training. That year, when a white man was acquitted for the brutal sexual assault of a black woman, Williams took to the courthouse to declare that people of color could not depend on the legalities of the state to protect them. "There is no law here, there is no need to take the white attackers to the courts because they will go free and that the federal government is not coming to the aid of people who are oppressed, and it is time for Negro men to stand up and be men and if it is necessary for us to die we must be willing to die," he said in an impassioned press conference. After being rejected by the mainstream civil rights movement, charged with kidnapping after defending a white couple from Klan attacks, and with his family under siege by Klan leaders, Williams sought political asylum in Cuba.[30]

For many black liberation organizations that grew through the 1950s and '60s, fascism was a frame to understand white populism, from the development of agrarian identities in the South to the role of white workers in neoliberalism. The Black Panther Party for Self Defense (BPP) was founded in Oakland, California, in 1966 by black communists seeking to create a project that ran counter to the state, arguing that the government's role was to enforce white supremacist class rule. They built structures of support and "decided to stop asking for integration," taking control of the community by creating stable institutions. Through the radicalization of neighbors they sought to become a revolutionary force against both the police and reactionaries.[31]

The BPP adopted the United Front Against Fascism concept from Georgi Dimitrov's address at the Seventh World Congress of the Communist International in July–August 1935.[32] It argued for

30   "Negroes with Guns: Rob Williams and Black Power," *Oregon Public Broadcasting*, http://www.pbs.org/independentlens/negroeswithguns/rob.html.

31   John Hulett, "How the Black Panther Party Was Organized," in *The Eyes on the Prize Civil Rights Reader: Documents, Speeches, and Firsthand Accounts from the Black Freedom Struggle, 1954–1990*, ed. Clayborne Carson, David J. Garrow, Gerald Gill, Vincent Harding, Darlene Clark Hine (New York: Penguin Books, 1991), 278.

32   Robyn C. Spencer, "The Black Panther Party and Black Antifascism in the United States," *News from Duke University Press*, January 26, 2017, https://dukeupress.wordpress.com/2017/01/26/the-black-panther-party

a broad-based coalition, a "popular front," of forces across the political spectrum in opposition to fascism. Calling fascism "the open terrorist dictatorship of the most reactionary, most chauvinistic, and most imperialist elements of finance capital," Dimitrov set forth an analysis that would be used by Marxists and the BPP for decades.[33] The "power of finance capital," as they continued to call it, centered fascism into the shifting sands of capitalism, and they placed themselves in the decades-old struggle against fascism.[34] The modern order of white supremacy has peaks of fascism, which can reconstruct the nature of that status quo, furthering the existing violence of social relationships.

The BPP brought together almost five thousand people in 1969 for the United Front Against Fascism conference, organized with the Young Patriots and Students for a Democratic Society to create a "national force" against fascism and the institutional racism of capitalism in America.[35] The conference exposed tensions as theoretical positions were hashed out, especially when women from the Panthers confronted a culture of "male supremacy" and asserted, "there cannot be a successful struggle against Fascism unless there is a broad front and women are drawn into it." The confrontation with state repression was central, emanating from the repression pushing back at the black liberation movement that would later be identified as COINTELPRO. They organized the National Committee to Combat Fascism (NCCF) for community control over policing, and within a year the FBI listed 18–22 chapters in cities around the country.[36] In Berkeley, where the conference was held, the Intercommunal Committee to Combat Fascism started as an NCCF chapter and continued primarily as a BPP chapter, with white members continuing BPP community programs.[37]

The historical white supremacy of American society was a cause of today's new fascism, allowing movements to confront racism, like

---

-and-black-antifascism-in-the-united-states/.

33 Georgi Dimitrov, *Selected Works*, volume 2 (Sofia Press 1972), 86–117.

34 This is not a theoretical position that I share, though the point about the capitulation of finance to fascist movements is well taken.

35 Robyn C. Spencer, *The Revolution Has Come: Black Power, Gender, and the Black Panther Party in Oakland*, Reprint Edition (Durham, N.C., Duke University Press, 2016), 116.

36 Robyn C. Spencer, "The Black Panther Party and Black Antifascism in the United States."

37 "The Intercommuncal Committee to Combat Fascism (ICCF)," It's About Time: Black Panther Legacy & Alumni, http://www.itsabouttimebpp.com/our_stories/Chapter1/The_iccf.html.

Black Lives Matter to redefine what antifascist resistance looks like. Why Accountability, a female led project challenging police-on-black violence in New York, confronted Gavin McInnis, the founder of *Vice*, whose own "civic nationalism" has made him an Alt Light leader with his Proud Boys. Following a "no platform" strategy, they shut down his NYU appearance, and McInnis hid in the back and left without showing his face. As white nationalism grows into an amalgamated mess, and clear lines between fascism and implicit American racism are blurred, there are opportunities for connecting broad antiracist movements with explicitly antifascist ones. Black Lives Matter changed the face of the American left completely, and an antifascist mass movement must draw from that well if it intends to remain relevant to the lived suffering of white racial revenge.[38]

Modern projects like the Huey P. Newton Gun Club, named for the Black Panther Party co-founder, were formed along the same community defense model. After the 2013 killing of an unarmed man by Dallas police, Yafeuh Balogun and Babu Omowale created the coalition of regional clubs to teach communities under siege how to create a defense structure outside the vestiges of the state. When the upswing of Islamophobic action happened in 2016, they were prepared to defend those communities, counter-protesting right-wing actions at a Nation of Islam mosque in South Dallas.[39]

All of this builds on existing forms of resistance, both in long-term sectoral organizing, such as labor or environmental organizing, and the growth of consciousness during Trump's ascent. There are tools in place, unions continuing to organize, antiracist projects working one township at a time, water protesters blocking the commercial exploitation of indigenous land. If the fascist movement is making a play for the dominant organs of people power, then every component part of the left has a role. Shifting existing projects to reflect the new reality is crucial, and they can then support antifascist-specific organizations that are going head-to-head with white nationalists. The support of undocumented workers by labor organizations is an example, understanding that ICE raids and

38 Ashoka Jegroo, "Fighting Cops and The Klan: The History and Future of Black Antifascism," *Truthout*, February 21, 2017, http://www.truth-out.org/news/item/39539-fighting-cops-and-the-klan-the-history-and-future-of-black-antifascism.

39 Madison Polly, "A New Wave of Left-Wing Militants is Ready to Rumble in Portland – and Beyond," *Mother Jones*, May/June 2017, http://www.motherjones.com/politics/2017/06/antifa-movement-anti-trump-politics-nazi/.

racist street attacks increase vulnerability for immigrant workers. This commitment of resources and support can then be tapped by organizers' whose prime project is confronting the growth of the far-right, creating a copacetic relationship that maintains long-term projects while making them relevant to impending threats. This means pivoting, not restarting.

Zoé Samudzi and William C. Anderson dig into the conception of blackness as the social "outsider" in their seminal essay, "The Anarchism of Blackness." Black liberation has always been conceived of outside of the state and the dominant liberal institutions since, no matter their stated intent, they act as extensions of white supremacy. Without institutions of liberal reform to fully realize the vision, "Black America can be understood as an extra-state entity because of Black exclusion from the liberal social contract."[40] The reality of black exclusion then creates the impetus for counter-power, eradicating the power of white supremacy through sovereignty from state control, and in direct contest to it. Antifascism, then, is not conceived in a way that simply protects the liberal state from nationalist subversion, or sees the state as adequate protectors of marginalized communities, but instead as a revolutionary project that extends beyond its role as a reaction to reactionaries. According to Samudzi and Anderson:

> Antifascist organizing must be bold. The mechanisms working against us do not entertain our humanity: they are hyper-violent. They deal death and destruction in countless numbers across the non-Western world while turning domestic Black and Brown neighborhoods into proxies for how to treat sub-citizen "others." The militarization of police, border regimes, stop-and-frisk and ICE are clear examples of how the state regards the communities it targets and brutalizes. At the very least, a conversation on self-defense that does not mistreat our survival as a form of violence is deeply needed. And it would be even better if such a conversation normalized antifascist organizing that prepared people for the possibility of a fight, instead of simply hoping that that day never comes and respectably clutching proverbial pearls at those currently fighting in the streets. Everyone has a stake in the fight against fascism.[41]

---

40   Zoé Samudzi and William Anderson, "The Anarchism of Blackness," *ROAR Magazine* #5 (Spring 2017): 77.
41   Ibid., 80.

Fascism is the hyper-realization of the promise created by institutionalized white supremacy and hierarchy, and the struggle against it will be just that: struggle. This does not prioritize one form of organization over another, but instead puts victimized communities at the front of strategic vision.

It is for this reason that the black antifascist struggle was founded in revolution, not due to periods of increased assault on black communities, but because the persecution of people of African descent is constant and unending, with moments of fascism stemming from the persistence of white supremacy. The BPP maintained this vision, not only as black liberationists but also as communist cadre, determined to change society systemically. Chicago member Fred Hampton said:

> Revolution is nothing but like having a sore on your body and then you put something on that sore to cure that infection…We're gonna organize and dedicate ourselves to revolutionary political power and teach ourselves the specific needs of resisting the power structure, arm ourselves, and we're gonna fight reactionary pigs with international proletarian revolution. That's what it has to be. The people have to have the power—it belongs to the people.[42]

Antifascist principles may differ from the Maoist-inspired politics that Chicago BPP leader Fred Hampton spoke of, but the antifascist approach is rooted in undoing the conditions that formed fascism rather than just a return the world to its pre-crisis state.

A Revolutionary Feminism

DC's Metro cars were overflowing on the morning of January 21, 2017, people were waiting hours to shuffle into packed cars just to make it inside the city limits. The crowd shifted like waves, moving where circumstances allowed them. In the sea of women, signs like "Refugees Welcome" and "Keep Your Laws Off My Vagina," were displayed above heads. Washington saw almost half a million flood the streets for the Women's March, while an estimated 5 million participated worldwide.[43] A massive 408 actions occurred

---

42   Fred Hampton, "Fred Speaks," in *The Eyes on the Prize Civil Rights Reader*, ed. Clayborne Carson, et al., 504.

43   Daniel Politi, "Women's March on Washington Was Three Times Larger than Inauguration," *Slate*, January 22, 2017, http://www.slate.com/blogs/the_slatest

across the U.S., with at least 2.6 million people (many estimates put it over 3 million), making it the largest protest action in the history of the U.S.[44] Just hours after the votes were in on November 8, Teresa Shook, an attorney in Hawaii, started planning a mass action of women in the capital. Building on Trump's blatant misogyny, and its reverberations in the culture, the themes of sexual assault and women's healthcare were prime in the popular imagination, and the idea of the march was on the tip of everyone's tongue as it gathered steam. The images of women fighting back colored the growing "resistance," and in the airport actions less than two weeks later against the travel ban you could still see the pink "pussy hats"—an icon in contrast to Trump's claims of "grabbing women by the pussy." There was a tacit unity in the numbers, however brief, and despite the problematic nature of the white and middle-income blind spots behind the march, the actions showed the ability to organize as feminists against gendered violence in the wake of increasingly hostile nationalist forces.

The liberalism of the Women's March is partly due to its association with Hillary Clinton, a "bad avatar of feminism" who had let women down for years. In the time between Clinton's challenge to Obama and her 2016 run, pop feminism became fashionable. The consumerist aspirations of much of this culture, focusing on self-help diatribes and in selling back sloganeering, were crippled by a Clinton loss. The inability of "white feminism" to confront issues of anti-blackness, transphobia, and poverty had to be confronted, yet there was still a mass willing to take action against misogyny.[45]

It would be wrong to say that antiracist movements have always been kind to feminism, but the partisan nature of antifascist movements requires an analysis of patriarchy. In Britain, the Women's Committee Against War and Fascism (WCAWF), part of a worldwide growth of antifascist committees, formed to fight the growing threat of fascist organizations in the U.K. With direct participation from the Communist Party, the WCAWF created a mass propaganda

/2017/01/22/women_s_march_on_washington_was_three_times_larger_than_inauguration.html.

44 Heidi M. Przybyla and Fredreka Schouten, "At 2.6 Million Strong, Women's Marches Crush Excpectations," *USA Today*, January 22, 2017, https://www.usatoday.com/story/news/politics/2017/01/21/womens-march-aims-start-movement-trump-inauguration/96864158/.

45 Amanda Hess, "How a Fractious Women's Movement Came to Lead the Left," *New York Times*, February 7, 2017, https://www.nytimes.com/2017/02/07/magazine/how-a-fractious-womens-movement-came-to-lead-the-left.html.

campaign to connect with women who were being recruited by fascist formations. They organized large marches against fascist street action, but also against militarism and in favor of women's rights. Their fundraising in support of the revolutionary side of the Spanish Civil War, and the battle against the Falange, unified the opposition to fascism as an international struggle.[46]

In 1992, the Jewish Feminist Antifascist League (JFAFL) formed at an evening Rosh Hashanah party after the Heritage Front grew in Toronto. They created a horizontal organizational structure that eschewed hierarchy, using consensus and a focus on the lived needs of the women in the group and the surrounding community. Since they often had to contend with a "good intentioned liberalism that can be quite dangerous,"[47] they brought the issues back to the real violence perpetrated by fascist groups. Their first action came after a professor at the University of Toronto invited the Heritage Front to his classroom to discuss race, a decision made from the liberal effort to "get both sides" of the argument. JFAFL put out a pamphlet about the Heritage Front and organized a demonstration at the university with the support of Anti-Racist Action. The Heritage Front amassed across the street, taunting the women with megaphones from behind a police line. The JFAFL used seemingly benign strategies like letter writing campaigns to confront massive issues, hoping to convey to those in positions of authority that their constituency was large.

YouthLink were shelters for young women, often survivors of sexual violence, and after the Heritage Front began threatening staff, a petrol bomb was placed in their building. Management's response was to just close the operation down rather than stand up to fascist terrorism. JFAFL organized a letter writing campaign for the community to show opposition, but they also supported the young women in the shelter to stand up publicly and denounce the Heritage Front's violence. The JFAFL created a strong feminist culture that saw fascism from an anti-oppression viewpoint. To commemorate the anniversary of the Warsaw Ghetto Uprising, where Jewish internees rose up against their Nazi captors, they did an informational rally focusing on the women resistance fighters who are often left out of narratives about the war.[48]

46   David Hann, *Physical Resistance*, 52.
47   Les Tager, "From the Archives: Jewish Feminist Antifascist League (Jewish Digest 1993)," *Treyf Podcast*, April 20, 2017, https://soundcloud.com/treyfpodcast/from-the-archives-jewish-feminist-antifascist-league-jewish-digest-1993.
48   Ibid.

Anti-capitalist groups like Feminist Fightback in London have created an ideological base whose anti-oppression politics are a foundation for the hyper-oppression pushed by fascist movements.

> We're inspired by the politics of a range of anti-capitalist feminist struggles, and believe that no single oppression can be challenged in isolation from all other forms of exploitation that intersect with it. We are also committed to fighting for a feminist perspective and awareness of gender issues everywhere in our movement—not marginalising 'women's rights' as a separate issue.[49]

In response to a planned march by the English Defence League (EDL), a fascist formation that has made Muslim immigration their prime target, Feminist Fightback came together with United Against Fascism and Global Women's Strike in a fierce feminist counter action. The EDL likens themselves as the protector of white womanhood from the sexual violence they argue is perpetrated by Islamic refugees and immigrants, so Feminist Fightback found it important to rupture that narrative by having a strong block of feminist activists that would blow away their crude caricatures of Islam and show that their mission of "protecting women" is a lie. Their belief is that the EDL should never make a public show without a public opposition, and that opposition can be built along feminist lines to highlight the revolutionary potential of femme consciousness.[50]

Many established feminist organizations have been dealing with threats from far-right organizations that link anti-abortion frenzies, homophobia, and white nationalist themes. The Bay Area Coalition for Our Reproductive Rights (BACORR), started by members of Radical Women, was forced to become monitors of far-right groups given the threat of clinic bombings. As a coalition, they organized actions counter to far-right projects like Operation Rescue, which violently confronted abortion providers on the anniversary of *Roe v. Wade*. BACORR is not the type of project that usually gets linked with antifascist organizing, but that is largely from a lack of correlation and communication. The threat on abortion providers has been coming out of the fringes of the Patriot and white power movement for decades, and this has where they have found some of the deepest

49   "About Us," Feminist Fightback, http://www.feministfightback.org.uk/about/.
50   "Feminist Antifascism: A Report Back," Feminist Fightback, November 3, 2011, http://www.feministfightback.org.uk/feminist-antifascism-report-back/.

analogues in the GOP's continued assault on women. Reproductive rights organizations then see this on two fronts: the threat of vio lence on clinics and the systemic erosion of care access, and those are brought together in extremist events that BACORR had determined to make the focal point of organizing. It was no longer just advocacy for increased access, it was about naming names and identifying and challenging the forces that were on the attack.[51]

The Trumpian landscape facilitates the syncing up of women's issues with larger antifascism by the pressure of circumstance. While Trump's racialist policies are giving the green light for ICE and state agencies to ramp up attacks on immigrants and people of color, while also emboldening the renegade fascist movement, he is also promising a full assault on reproductive rights, women's healthcare, institutions in support of sexual assault survivors, and the economic stability of working-class women. These attacks form a material threat to women and can help unify struggle, as long as that struggle does not continue to center white women's experiences or exclude transwomen and gender-nonconforming people.

White Working Class

What popular rhetoric of white privilege ignores is the material ways that white workers are robbed by the promise of class collaboration through "whiteness." From the wage suppression of white workers through antebellum chattel slavery to the use of racial tensions to bust industrial unions, whiteness is a failed promise to white work ers even if it provides nominal benefits. Working-class white anti-racism is the bridge that will traverse American post-manufacturing angst and the failure of rural economies, back toward a common struggle for equality. The white working class has been the well that fascism drinks from, offering feelings of superiority at the cost of material benefit. In years past, rural states that now lean "red" were actually bases for left organizing, from Kansas's centrality in ear-ly socialist organizing and abolition to the striking miners of West Virginia who gave us the term "redneck" for the red bandanas they wore. The issue, from the factory floor to the tractor, is a choice between perceived privilege and cross-racial unity. Either the right

---

51   Marit Knutson, "Bay Area Action for Abortion Rights on Jan. 24: Come Out to Protest the Right-Wing "Walk for Life," *Freedom Socialist*, December 2008, http://www.socialism.com/drupal-6.8/articles/bay-area-action-abortion -rights-jan-24-come-out-protest-rightwing-walk-life.

or the left will increase in size and effectiveness. As the old union maxim went, "if we don't talk to them, someone else will," so it's crucial to find a shared language of struggle that will undermine the effectiveness of the far-right message that desperately wants to turn the experience of working-class oppression into divisions along the lines of essentialized identity.

In different eras of struggle, the "reactionary white worker" has been the center of insurrectionary white supremacy in ways that disregard the material interest white workers have in antiracism. As Ahmed Shawki writes, the language of white identity critically hinders the white working class as it limits their material interests, fosters class collaboration, and erases all other experiential identities:

> Acceptance of racist ideas by white workers should not be confused with their having a material interest in perpetuating racial oppression. The history of racism in the United States is not only a history of Black oppression, but also of the ability of the ruling class to use racism to maintain its power and wealth. From the poor whites of the South under slavery to the racist workers of today, adherence to racism ensures *their own* subordination.[52]

Capitalist competition requires that white workers enforce privilege as an avenue to advantage. In a civilization marked by brutal rivalry, division can be stratified for the advantage of one particular group. This logic, baked into the social fabric, pits white workers against their own interests, battling for meager advantages instead of uniting with workers of color and marginalized communities to confront those at the top of the socio-economic pyramid.[53] When white workers forego privilege, they get solidarity in response, a tool that extends far deeper than the advantages they believe they get through institutionalized white supremacy. White nationalists promise a return of privilege if we accept class collaboration, and the only answer the left must provide is a revolutionary vision that can take white workers far beyond the tokens of white supremacy. This cannot just come in vague affirmations and moral appeals, but in very concrete proposals, a pathway that is carved out of victories.

---

52 Ahmed Shawki, *Black Liberation and Socialism* (Chicago: Haymarket Books, 2006), 241–42.
53 Ibid., 245.

The Bastards Motorcycle Club has challenged the image of biker gangs affiliating with white supremacist street organizations by coming out as an antiracist organization. Started in North Carolina by Steven "Chavez" Parker and Joseph Guinn, the idea was to take advantage of the tight-knit organization that keeps bike clubs together, but to be open in their vision of an LGBT, multiracial, feminist-positive collaboration. Across the South, the Bastards have met the KKK and neo-Nazi organizations having public rallies, using language that speaks to the same base the rural white nationalist organizations use as their feeding ground.[54]

With the idea that the white working class was responsible not just for the ascendancy of Trump, but also for the rejection of left radicalism in favor of right populism, Redneck Revolt completely refused to abandon or ignore white workers. Redneck Revolt was built out of the experiences of Kansas Mutual Aid, which, after seeing infiltration from state police investigators, began doing firearms trainings in a very public way. They named their project the John Brown Gun Club after the abolitionist who targeted slavery through armed struggle, and tabled gun shows in rural states, side-by-side with KKK and racialist militia organizations. By speaking some of the same language, first being opposed to gun restriction laws and, second, rejecting the political establishment entirely, they were finding common ground with the same pool of potential recruits that Patriot organizations turn to. This praxis was turned into Redneck Revolt, where a "big tent" organization was formed that refused to abandon the white working class or simply resort to alliance. In a world where black-and-white partisan issues often define identities and geographic enclaves, guns have proven to be an effective point of commoning, and the group can build on the same aspirations of community self-defense that the Patriot militias often brand themselves with. In the same way that militias provide community services, Redneck Revolt has built mutual aid projects, avoiding leftist subcultures by going for direct community bonds united along common classed experiences. In Silver Valley, North Carolina, the local chapter does large food dispersals at cattle shows, often coming with crops they grew themselves. People are invited to join in, share what they have, and a network grows out of a collective self-interest rather than an NGO-managed charity. Harm reduction, especially

---

54   Madison Polly, "A New Wave of Left-Wing Militants Is Ready to Rumble in Portland – and Beyond."

needle exchange in areas marked by opioid overdose, is a part of this, and they find that the bonds of direct experience speak louder than the color of the flag.

All the while, Redneck Revolt has provided an armed community solution to the growth of fascist organizing. Publicly, they are often found wielding firearms at events, providing security, but they also conduct trainings on gun safety. Weapons are brandished without covering their faces, identities are not hidden—instead they are open members of the neighborhood, ready to have conversations with people who may act with the inverse of their politics. Standing up at town halls, getting interviewed in small-town papers, and being dependable has made them a visible part of the communities they are in, and when they are willing to engage people where they are at, they have had the ability to put a wrench in recruitment to many far-right organizations. This has meant having open lines of dialogue with militias, being open and honest about their intent, and also challenging groups like the Oath Keepers to live up to their public denouncements of racism, and actively driving a wedge between neo-Nazis and the Patriot organizations. In places like Southern Michigan, when Kalkaska town president Jeff Sieteng made public comments supporting the murder of Muslims, a slew of neo-Nazi groups descended on the town in support. With the police force unprepared for this kind of arrival, Redneck Revolt members came armed to simply act as a barrier between the townspeople and the racists, a sight that left them celebrated nearly as heroes. By avoiding leftist jargon, and instead outlining a platform that explains their ideas in plain language, they end up appealing to people in working class Southern, Midwestern, and mountain towns in a way that the vast majority of the fragmented left would be unable to. This has meant recruiting former 3%ers and libertarians, committing to work out some of the political ideas internally.[55]

Beyond the Fascist Vanguard

What pulls many to organize, beyond the seasonal losses and victories, is the hope of fundamental societal transformation. People stick with radical struggle because those particular issues are a gateway to a more structural reconfiguring of society. Unionists saw the point of rupture in the workplace—where workers realize their own power

---

55   Beth Payne of Redneck Revolt, interview with author, August 6, 2017.

and collectively challenge the point of production—as a window to a new world. Housing, ecology, abolition of white supremacy, queer liberation, and feminism are similar pieces in the larger puzzle of undoing the complex web of social hierarchy. The struggle against fascism provides the same opportunity, if the roots of its violence can be grounded in the fertile soil of intersecting oppressions.

The practical tools used to challenge white nationalism can function in a larger revolutionary project, which sees a future for non-hierarchical, cosmopolitan societies. Strong communities, based on personal and supportive relationships, ongoing challenges to white supremacy, patriarchy, and heteronormativity, and the fundamental opposition to inequality are what underlies the rejection of fascism. It is not enough to just stave off momentary violence, or even to restore the pre-revolutionary order, but instead we must win a "three-way fight" against the reactionaries and the systems of power that birthed them.

These battles against fascism and institutional oppression are not separate struggles—one against capitalists and another against the mixed consciousness of the white working class. Instead, they interact, even if they have different interests, and strong movements founded on a radical vision confronts both manifestations. The revolt against the "barbarism" of late-capitalist crisis is not limited just by the terms set by the opposition, but also by the dreams of those that reject the assumptions of identities. A perfect blueprint would be nice, an infographic for antifascist organizing brought to scale in Trump's America, but our reality is more hopeful. The answer was always here, embedded in the structures and spirit found in successful relationships built on the power of kindness and solidarity.

"Antifa" is used as a boogeyman by the right in the cartoonish way that they construct archetypes to signal to their base. Today "Antifa" is a term with dual meaning: it evokes fear in the right—of a militant left—while functioning as a practical solution to the growth of fascist insurrectionary violence. Antifascism rose as a wave in the U.S. in 2016, and its manifestations were more broad and numerous than those that can properly be called Antifa, yet the right was too blind to see it. While many newcomers flocked to the ideal of militant antifascism, the truth is that Antifa was only one channel for this resistance—albeit a particularly strategic one. Antifa was essential for the expanding movement to directly impede the threat, and adherents risked themselves to halt the growth of these fascist groups.

An antifascist resistance was growing and it wasn't beholden to one model, it was experimenting with options, ideas, approaches, and, most importantly, drawing in people. While the right had been quick to label the opposition as "Antifa"—militants they saw dressed in balaclavas and black clothes—the new reality was so much more frightening for them: *the culture had become antifascist.*

Antifascism, historically and in the present, is a sea of possibilities, defying simple characterization. The approaches themselves, building on community and labor organizing, social intervention and mutual aid, counter-institutions and community fortification, antiracist struggle and economic revolt, exposure and education, all create an interconnected quilt. In this way antifascism itself is characteristic of the unified faces standing together. Fascism is hopelessly dystopian, expecting to enter history through incidental insurrections and promoting identitarian inequality. Its undoing is hastened by the nightmarish threat of a right populist wave contrasted with the promise of class-conscious, multi-ethnic liberation. The people involved in antifascist resistance define its character, instructed by their own experiences and uniqueness, creating an entire library of strategies to employ on many fronts. Fascism today is then defined by its inverse: the antifascism that is overtaking it.

Fascism has shown the world its grotesque dreams. Now it's time for antifascists to be visionaries and increase our ranks. Through mass engagement we can undo rising fascist movements while providing the experiential transformation of consciousness necessary to take bigger steps. Antifascism today has the potential to reach millions who can then build on their own experiences and cultivate a collective, liberatory vision based on freedom and equality. By refusing to learn from the militants who have defined the struggle for decades we risk returning to hollow—and always temporary—reformism. The left that wants to defeat fascism has to offer something. It has to be dangerous again. It has to be willing to win.

The face of government has changed, as has the role of the ideological far-right. The shifting sands have not destroyed the resistance, it has shown the results of inaction. The failure of the liberal establishment has left only the tools of organizing that come from the outside, those modes of resistance that have never left. Today we have what we have always had, each other, and this time that is what we have to count on.

Resource List

Websites

Anti-Defamation League | www.adl.org
The ADL is an almost hundred-year-old organization out of the anti-racist Jewish tradition, and has been a leader in exposing anti-Semitism, racism, and discrimination.

Anti-Fascist News | www.antifascistnews.org
AFN does articles and commentary on fascist politics, most specifically the Alt Right, from an organizing mind-set.

Institute for Research & Education on Human Rights | https://www.irehr.org/
A far-right monitoring project headed by anti-fascist author Leonard Zeskind, often looking at underreported areas of the far-right.

It's Going Down | www.itsgoingdown.org
IGD is a massive informational and reporting project that brings together dozens of organizations to publish a large stream of activist news from the radical left. They have become a central hub for anti-fascist reporting, all in the trenches of organizing projects and with some of the most up-to-date information on fascist formations.

Journal of Fascism Studies | http://www.brill.com/fascism
This academic journal is an incredible resource for research and analysis on the historical development of fascism and brings together some of the critical work of people like Robert Paxton, Roger Griffin, and the New Consensus.

The One People's Project | www.onepeoplesproject.com/

As both an organizing and reporting group, the One People's Project has been a defining feature of anti-fascist organizing in the U.S. Their research and reports on the far-right names the names, and they have different segments like the Rogue's Gallery, Idavox, and the main site that share up-to-date information on the far-right.

Political Research Associates | www.politicalresearch.org/

PRA does deep research and reports on the far-right, ranging from the militia movement to the Alt Right. This includes long-form research stories and projects done in conjunction with community organizations like the Rural Organizing Project.

The Southern Poverty Law Center | www.splcenter.org

The SPLC is the largest anti-fascist organization in the country and mixes workshops, reportage and publishing, training for government officials, legal support and organizing. They are a deep resource for profiles on the far-right and have a history of lawsuits that have taken down organizations like the United Klans of America, White Aryan Resistance, and the Aryan Nations.

Three-Way Fight | Threewayfight.blogspot.com

This is the blog of anti-fascist author Matt Lyons and built on the "Three-Way Fight" concept of fascism. This includes some of the best articles and blogs about third positionist trends in twenty-first century fascism, all within an anti-capitalist perspective.

The Torch Network | www.torchantifa.org

Bringing together different anti-fascist groups into a common network, Torch Network's website acts as a feed for the research and reports that each member organization is doing in its area.

We Hunted the Mammoth | www.wehuntedthemammoth.com/

Building on how the far-right approaches gender, WHTM has chronicled the Men's Rights and new misogynist movements, especially as they interact with the Alt Right and white nationalism.

Who Makes the Nazis | http://www.whomakesthenazis.com/

An archive of articles, reports and research on fascist influence in music, countercultural, and occultist circles. This is the most extensive resource on the fascist neofolk and related music scenes and ties together many of the more syncretic trends on the far-right.

Books

Alexander Reid Ross, *Against the Fascist Creep* (AK Press, 2017)

Robert O. Paxton, *The Anatomy of Fascism* (Vintage, 2005)

Mark Bray, *Antifa: The Anti-Fascist Handbook* (Melville House, 2017)

Sean Birchall, *Beating the Fascists: The Untold Story of Anti-Fascist Action* (Freedom Press, 2013)

Leonard Zeskind, *Blood and Politics: The History of the White Nationalist Movement from Margins to Mainstream* (Farrar, Straus and Giroux, 2017)

James Ridgeway, *Blood in the Face: The Ku Klux Klan, Aryan Nations, Nazi Skinheads, and the Rise of the New White Culture* (Thunder's Mouth Press, 2nd Edition: 1995)

Constantin Iordachi, ed., *Comparative Fascist Studies: New Perspectives* (Routlege, 2009)

Don Hammerquist and J. Sakai, ed., *Confronting Fascism* (Kersblebedeb, 2nd Edition 2017)

Matthew N. Lyons and others, *CTL-Alt-Delete: An Anti-Fascist Report on the Alternative Right* (Kersblebedeb, 2017)

Deborah Lipstadt, *Denying the Holocaust: The Growing Assault on Truth and Memory* (Plume, Reprint Edition: 1994)

Janet Biehl and Peter Staudenmaier, *Eco-Fascism Revisited: Lessons from the German Experience* (New Compass Press, 2011)

Matthias Gardell, *Gods of the Blood: White Separatism and the Pagan Revival* (Duke University Press Books, 2003)

Elinor Langer, *A Hundred Little Hitlers: The Death of a Black Man, the Trial of a White Racist, and the Rise of the Neo-Nazi Movement in America* (Picador, Reprint Edition: 2004)

Angela Nagle, *Kill All Normies: Online Culture Wars from 4Chan and Tumblr to Trump and the Alt Right* (Zero Books, 2017)

George Michael, *Lone-Wolf Terror and the Rise of Leaderless Resistance* (Vanderbilt University Press, 2012)

George Hawley, *Making Sense of the Alt-Right* (Columbia University Press, 2017)

M. Testa, *Militant Anti-Fascism: A Hundred Years of Resistance* (AK Press, 2015)

Stephen Jay Gould, *The Mismeasure of Man* (W.W. Norton & Company, Revised & Expanded Edition: 1996)

Robert Walt Sussman, *The Myth of Race: The Troubling Persistence of an Unscientific Idea* (Harvard University Press, 2016)

Roger Griffin, *The Nature of Fascism* (Routledge, 1993)

Dave Hann, *Physical Resistance: A Hundred Years of Anti-Fascism* (Zero Books, 2015)

Ashley Montague, ed., *Race and IQ* (Oxford University Press, Expanded Edition: 1999)

Tamir Bar-On, *Rethinking the French New Right: Alternatives to Modernity* (Routledge, 2013)

George Hawley, *Right-Wing Critics of American Conservatism* (University Press of Kansas, 2016)

Matthew N. Lyons and Chip Berlet, *Right-Wing Populism in America: Too Close for Comfort* (The Guilford Press, 2000)

Daniel Levitas, *The Terrorist Next Door: The Militia Movement and the Radical Right* (St. Martin's Griffin, 2004)

George Michael, *Theology of Hate: A History of the World Church of the Creator* (University Press of Florida, 2009)

Spencer Sunshine and others, *Up in Arms: A Guide to Oregon's Patriot Movement* (Political Research Associates and the Rural Organizing Project, 2016)

Martin Durham, *White Rage: The Extreme Right and American Politics* (Routledge, 2007)

George Michael, *Willis Carto and the American Far Right* (University Press of Florida, 2008)

Index